Awakening Your Sexuality

Also by Stephanie S. Covington, Ph.D.

Leaving the Enchanted Forest (with Liana Beckett)

AWAKENING YOUR SEXUALITY

A Guide for Recovering Women

Stephanie S. Covington

HarperSanFrancisco
A Division of HarperCollins*Publishers*

The first-person stories and case examples in this book accurately reflect the feelings, experiences, and circumstances expressed by patients, their families, and friends, but all names, locales, and identifying details have been changed.

This book is not intended to be used in place of therapy or professional support.

Credits and acknowledgments appear on pages 295–96.

AWAKENING YOUR SEXUALITY: *A Guide for Recovering Women.* Copyright © 1991 by Stephanie S. Covington, Ph.D. Printed in the United States of America. No part of this book may be used or reproduced in any manner whatsoever without written permission except in the case of brief quotations embodied in critical articles or reviews. For information address HarperCollins Publishers, 10 East 53rd Street, New York, NY 10022.

FIRST EDITION

Library of Congress Cataloging-in-Publication Data

Covington, Stephanie.
    Awakening your sexuality : a guide for recovering women / Stephanie
    Covington — 1st ed.
        p.   cm.
    Includes bibliographic references and index.
    ISBN 0–06–250190–9
    ISBN 0–06–250222–0 (pbk.)
        1. Women—Sexual behavior. 2. Hygiene, Sexual. 3. Sexual
disorders. 4. Self-respect. I. Title.
HQ29.C68   1991
613.9'54—dc20   90–56442
                                                                          CIP

91   92   93   94   95   RRD(H)   10   9   8   7   6   5   4   3   2   1

This edition is printed on acid-free paper that meets the American National Standards Institute Z39.48 Standard.

*To my daughter Kimberley, whose journey toward
womanhood has been a joy to me*

Contents

Acknowledgments

Without certain people, this book could not have been written. I particularly want to thank the women whose names do not appear on this page, but whose life experiences appear throughout the book. These are the anonymous women—participants in my original research, psychotherapy clients, and women in recovery. They shared their experience, strength, and hope, allowing me to participate in their growth process. They also shared with me the most intimate part of their lives, their sexuality.

A number of friends, companions, and professional colleagues have explored with me the various issues in this book: Liana Beckett, Maria Bowen, Alice Clawson, Anne Dosher, Molly Gierasch, Dee Grayson, Lisa Hirschman, Rokelle Lerner, Ken MacDonald, Peter McDade, Pam Miller, and Sharon Young. Their insight, humor, and willingness to pursue the mysteries of life have provided me with many hours of stimulating conversation and thought.

The many versions and revisions of this book were created with the help of Coletta Reid and Naomi Lucks. Their individual expertise and style are evident throughout. Mary Phillips provided insightful suggestions. I appreciate all of your assistance.

My editorial consultant, agent, and special friend, Roy M. Carlisle of Mills House, provided creative genius, support, and encouragement. I can't imagine writing a book without him.

Barbara Moulton, editor at Harper San Francisco, managed to remain enthusiastic and committed to the project throughout its many lives.

Susan Bennett, my assistant, manages the office and the many details of my life with patience, consistency, and gentleness. Her presence is a gift.

I am grateful to you all.

Awakening Your Sexuality

Introduction:
An Awakening

The awakening to the mystery of life is a revolutionary
event; in it an old world is destroyed so that a new and better one may take its place, and all things are affected by the
change. We ourselves have become mysterious strangers in
our own eyes and tremblingly we ask ourselves who we are,
whence we came, whither we are bound. Are we the being
who is called by our name, whom we thought we knew so
well in the past? Are we the form we see in the mirror, our
body, offspring of our parents? Who, then, is it that feels
and thinks within us, that wills and struggles, plans and
dreams, that can oppose and control this physical body
which we thought to be ourselves? We wake up to realize
that we have never known ourselves, that we have lived as
in a blind dream of ceaseless activity in which there was
never a moment of self-recollection.

—J. J. van der Leeuw

This is a book for women in recovery. Many women have used alcohol
and drugs to numb the emotional pain of their childhoods and to live in
a world that discourages the qualities that are essential for female existence.

But you do not have to be alcoholic or chemically dependent to
recognize the issues discussed in this book. They are common to most

women in our society and are likely to strike a chord deep within you. As women, we find innumerable ways to distract our attention from the truth of our inner selves; compulsive attention to food, relationships, family, work, and even shopping can distract us and provide a temporary fix to counter our pain.

This book may serve as validation for what you have already come to know and feel, and as you read you may feel affirmed and more empowered. Or you may find that you need to read slowly and digest the material slowly because it stirs up painful memories and challenges your beliefs. I hope this book will suggest connections for you, highlighting aspects of your own life and opening up entirely new levels of understanding.

Awakening to your sexuality does not mean that you are Sleeping Beauty waiting for the Prince's kiss. That is society's dream: it is a fairy tale, and it will never happen. The process of becoming aware is something you choose to begin because you are ready to experience the fullness of life. It happens to you when you decide you are ready. That time can be now.

Coming to understand yourself is a gradual process that requires love, patience, and nurturing. Like a bulb that must germinate underground in warmth and solitude, the awakening of your sexuality begins deep inside of you. As you nurture yourself, your sexuality will grow stronger, gaining vitality, until it breaks through and reaches toward the light. There it can grow to enrich not only your life but the lives of those you choose to love.

If you have been frightened, confused, ashamed, or disconnected from your sexual self for a long time, this flowering may seem impossible. Yet it is within the reach of all women. Remember: the first step toward change is awareness. We can change only those things in our lives that we are aware of—this is as true of our sexual selves as it is of our addicted selves. By beginning to read this book, you are choosing to become conscious about and connected to your authentic sexuality. As you become aware of your sexuality, which includes your body's feelings and your emotional needs, you are also renewing the personal power of conscious choice that emanates from the center of your inner being and will transform all of your relationships.

Sobriety is about living life fully and completely, and your sexual recovery is integral to the fullness of your life. In addiction you felt isolated and abandoned, but in choosing to acknowledge and awaken your sexuality you are embarking on an inner journey to reconnect with your best friend, your true self. On the way you will learn to trust yourself, to know who you are—alone and with others—and to feel joy in the knowledge that you are alive and aware in a world filled with wonder and mystery.

PART ONE

FEELINGS:
THE INNER JOURNEY

Being together sexually is a way for people to get close, to bond, to connect, to end isolation, to have fun, to play, to enjoy . . . it's about many things. But when our sexuality is defined or influenced by guilt, shame, or addiction, expressions of sexuality are actually quite distanced from our emotional selves and from others.

Each of us has an inner life and an outer life. Our inner life is who we are and how we feel inside; our outer life is how we interact with others. In addiction our inner and outer lives are out of balance. We don't always act on our feelings, and often we don't even know what our feelings are. Part of recovery is getting our inner lives and our outer lives to match.

How well do you know your sexual self? Have you ever really stopped and honestly examined your beliefs or assumptions about what you need and what you want? How does your body really look? What do you know about how your genitals look and feel? What is your range of sexual response? Many women, especially women who have been chemically dependent, have not explored their beliefs and assumptions about their bodies, their sexual activities, their erotic urges, and their capacity for pleasure. Certainly it is tempting to remain in the seemingly safe state of "blissful" ignorance. But is it really safe?

As a child, do you remember playing on the monkey bars? In order to swing and move ahead you had to let go of the bar behind so that you could reach out to the bar ahead. There was a moment when you were holding on to nothing. The momentum of moving forward kept you from falling.

As children, we learn to trust in this movement. But some adults hold on, fear more, and become immobilized. When we stop moving ahead on the monkey bars, we get stuck or we fall. Some children begin again; other children, frustrated by their lack of progress, may choose to avoid and not return to the activity. Opportunities for change and growth cease.

Like that child, you are in motion now. You have to let go of the bar behind as you move forward. There is a moment when you are holding on to nothing. And you don't fall. Your momentum, your forward motion, holds you as you move. This is the almost magical process and experience of transition and change.

Your interest in knowing more about your sexual self, however tentative, is the surest sign that you are ready to let go of the past and move on to an honest exploration of your feelings. Trust in your forward motion to carry you through, and savor that moment of transition.

In the next few chapters we will be exploring the tasks of early recovery. These include the following:

1. Looking at the effects of socialization on your life. What is its impact? What does it teach you to feel about yourself as a woman?

2. Learning to accept your body, just as it is. Part of being sexual is what you do with your body. If you are uncomfortable or unfamiliar with your body, your sexuality cannot help but be affected.

3. Learning about and accepting your genitals. In order to feel sexual pleasure, it is necessary to accept your genitals and to discern and know how they respond to touch.

4. Learning to accept sexual self-pleasuring. When you are able to give loving touch to yourself, you are more able to accept it from a partner and to know what you want from a partner.

5. Learning to become aware of your sexual feelings, which exist separately from your partner or from anyone else. Your sexual needs and desires—your erotic life and sexual energy—exist in their own right.

Try to connect with the feelings these goals stir up in you. You may feel afraid of exploring your feelings about sexuality, especially if you have been disconnected from them over time. Identifying and connecting with your feelings requires a great deal of courage. The fear you may be feeling about being honest with yourself—especially about sexuality—is normal and understandable. Despite our familiarity with sexual images and messages, Americans in general are extremely fearful about sexual issues.

You do not have to eliminate your fear in order to be honest about your sexual feelings. Courage is acting honestly in spite of fear, knowing that the rewards of authentic self-knowledge will carry you forward on your journey of change. These rewards have a rhythm and momentum all their own—all your own.

So take courage. Please treat yourself with gentleness and patience, and allow yourself to absorb this material at your own pace.

Chapter 1

The Past in the Present

The first problem for all of us, men and women,
is not to learn but to unlearn.

—Gloria Steinem

What does it mean to become a sexual woman in our society? What does it mean to have this complex thing called sexuality integrated into our lives in a meaningful way? These are hard questions. They are made even more difficult because we almost never ask them, let alone find answers for them or have answers freely offered to us. My intention in this book is to help you learn how to answer these questions for yourself.

In my work I have been touched by the depth of pain that many women feel about their sexuality. But instead of feeling overwhelmed and angry, I am hopeful. My hope comes from having watched hundreds of women grow in self-understanding and self-love—in recovery groups, in treatment programs, and in individual therapy. However difficult or unattainable this may seem to someone about to embark on this path of recovery, experience has taught me that it is possible for you to change, grow, and find a self to love.

Our Sexual Self-Image

The subject of sexuality usually produces a paradoxical reaction: we're eager to know, but we're afraid of what we're going to find out. How did we come to such a confused state about something that's so basic to human existence?

Our present sexual feelings and actions do not exist in a vacuum. They are molded and influenced by everything that has happened to us in the past. By working with our past and honestly naming all that has happened to us—our sexual training within our families, our childhood experiences, our adolescent sexual experiences, our choice of partners, our sexual behavior while drinking or using drugs—we can move into a new level of sexual freedom and expansion. When this happens, our sexual feelings and actions will have to do with today, not with some unknown carryover from yesterday.

Our sexual self-image begins to be formed by the messages we receive as children about maleness and femaleness. These include what society tells us we should be and the spoken and unspoken messages we receive within our family. If your parents seemed confused, ashamed, or embarrassed to discuss sex or even to think about it, your chances of developing a healthy sexual identity were probably limited. In this you are not alone. Most people in our society have no consistent model for or firsthand experience of healthy female sexuality.

Historically, male expectations of female sexuality, which society reinforces, have been virtually impossible to meet. The old saying, "What a man really wants is a whore in bed and a virgin at the breakfast table," is considered by many to describe the epitome of a "good woman." And heaven help you if you ever got those two confused!

Many people, despite personal experience to the contrary, think that the new openness about sex has solved sexual problems. We certainly seem to have come a long way. After all, at the turn of the century a woman was only supposed to engage in sex for procreation or for a man's pleasure. She certainly wasn't supposed to enjoy it. Of course we're *much* smarter now, at the end of the century: not only are we supposed to engage in sex, we're supposed to like it and to effortlessly achieve multiple orgasms. Quite an evolutionary leap!

We've gone through a so-called sexual revolution, but what has it left us with? "Sex" is found in the images, suggestions, perversions, and devices that are all around us, yet lovers don't know how to communicate with one another about it. The "revolution" has allowed us to be more open about the discussion of sex, and it has dispelled some of the old myths. But in return we're often left with technically "correct" sex that remains very detached and perfunctory. We've lost—or maybe we never had—the ability to be spontaneous and adventurous and to feel sexually gratified as well.

Everybody is expected to be good at sex, though ironically it's the one activity we're not supposed to have seen anyone do. We have no model to help us assimilate the signals we receive from our feelings and experiences in the world. Instead, these physical and emotional messages get all mixed up with images from the external world: our families and society. As a result, most of us are convinced that we're not doing it "right"; that others know a secret we don't possess; that we're doing it too much or too little; that we're "good" at it or "bad" at it; that we know how or don't know how to please the other. We're supposed to be competent and to like sex, but we're not supposed to know anything about it. It's a dirty thing we are not supposed to talk about, yet we're supposed to save it for the one we love. No wonder we're confused!

The truth is that though we are born with genitalia and a sex drive, we have to learn how to identify and express our own sexuality. For most of us, especially women who have used chemicals or alcohol to anesthetize themselves—including their sexual selves—this means starting by unlearning much of what we've learned about sexuality.

We can begin to untangle our mixed messages by sharing our experiences. We're a nation of stutterers and stammerers when it comes to talking about sex, what really happens, and how it feels. Increasing our ability to talk about sex in an authentic way is vital to our sexual recovery. When we can't talk about sex, when we have to keep our sexual feelings, thoughts, and experiences secret, then we will feel ashamed of them. As long as we feel ashamed we will feel that there's something wrong with us and we will be blocked. Our growth will necessarily be limited. It is only when we take our fragmented sexual selves out of that hidden, silent, secret place and sift through the pieces that we begin to realize the possibility of integration and expansion. This, too, is a potential we are born with, one we can all truly possess.

Authentic Sex Talk

When we share our sexual experiences with other women, something wonderful happens: what we previously thought of as individual pathology—that is, what was wrong with only us or our own family—gets put into a universally female context. We see that we are doing and feeling what most women are raised to do and feel. We begin to see the limitations of the provisions that society offers women. We come to have compassion for ourselves as having had few choices and living in a far less than optimum climate for feeling okay or good about ourselves.

In my experience, the most effective way to move through a process of sexual recovery is in a women's group. But it is certainly not the only way. You may choose to share your feelings with a female friend or in individual therapy with a professional counselor. This book will give you the opportunity to hear a variety of women discuss their sexual history and recovery. In this chapter the stories of four women represent four different threads in a common fabric of sexual experience. Perhaps you will find that one of their threads interweaves with yours.

Sarah: Adult Child of an Alcoholic

Sarah* is thirty-eight and identifies as an adult child of an alcoholic. She has viewed herself this way for three years, though she was shocked when she first saw her father, Doug, as an alcoholic. She was surprised and upset when she realized the extent of her own and her family's denial of Doug's problem. Her therapist suggested she attend Al-Anon meetings, a Twelve-Step program for family and friends of alcoholics, where she would find support.

In Al-Anon, she identified her own problems with codependence and relationship addiction, and she joined a women's group focused on those issues. Sharing her thoughts and feelings with other women has

---

*Both Sarah and Paula, who we meet later, were introduced in *Leaving the Enchanted Forest: The Path from Relationship Addiction to Intimacy* by Stephanie Covington and Liana Beckett (San Francisco: Harper & Row, 1988).

helped Sarah to become much more conscious of how she interacts with her husband, Scott.

Sarah feels hopeful and upbeat about her progress in ACA (Adult Children of Alcoholics) recovery, but she is currently in denial about her dependence on prescription pills, which she began using in adolescence.

Paradoxically, it is precisely her awareness of her father's alcoholism that has allowed her to hide this from herself. Since her model for addiction is derived from her father's drinking—and limited to alcohol—she's not yet able to see that her prescription drug use is also an addiction—her own addiction.

Sarah's women's group recently decided to discuss sexuality. They found it very difficult to begin. Few of them had ever talked about sex—not to their partners, to their friends, or even to their therapists. They agreed that it might help to begin by sharing their earliest sexual memories.

"I learned early that touching myself 'down there' was off-limits," Sarah told the group. As she talked she had a striking mental image of her imposing, strong-willed mother, Laura, giving her a bath with her typically detached style. "There was a right way to do everything, and my mother would always start at the top. She'd scrub hard behind my ears, making a comment about how vegetables would start growing there if I didn't keep them clean. Then she'd scrub away on my neck, my tummy, and my elbows, which were always filthy. And then without a word she would magically fly over that part 'down there'—as far as I knew it had no actual name—and pick up her running commentary when she arrived at my dirty knees." Several women in the group laughed, remembering similar experiences. Sarah, buoyed by the empathic response, continued as long-buried memories came rushing to the surface.

"My mother was definitely not comfortable with her own sexuality. Her relationship with my dad was not openly affectionate. I don't remember them ever spontaneously hugging or kissing, even when they thought my brother and I weren't looking. So I just sort of learned to not know about anything.

"In my family we received no information about sex. None. In the fifth grade my mother signed the permission slip for me to see the movie *Growing Up and Liking It*—" Sarah paused as the women chimed in with their favorite parts of that film—they all agreed that the meeting of sperm and egg was the dramatic moment. "Anyway," Sarah continued, "I came home and told her I'd seen this movie, and I was all excited, and my mother just said, 'Oh,' in a really cold voice. I don't know how I got up the nerve, but I asked her, 'What happens to the egg if it's not fertilized?' She had the most tortured look on her face! Finally she forced out her answer. She said, 'Well, how would *I* know?'

"And that was my sex education."

Sarah told the group how frightened she had been when she started menstruating. The memory still made her angry, and her face was flushed beneath her even tan. "I didn't know what was happening to me. And you can imagine how much help my mother was! I came home from school crying, my mother took me in the bathroom and gave me a Kotex and sent me to bed. I just cried for a long time.

"When I told this story to my therapist she said, 'What did you tell yourself? What did you think was happening to you?' I told her that I wasn't sure. I didn't connect what I'd seen in the movie with what I was experiencing, although I had some vague idea of a connection. And I thought the blood was coming from the place where I peed. As I told these things to my therapist, I thought, 'Oh my God, that part of my body was just cut off from me.' And that realization hit me like a bolt of lightning."

When these memories first came back to her, Sarah felt betrayed by her mother. She blamed Laura for the fact that she had been taught to be a stranger in her own body and to grow up disconnected from herself.

Later Sarah came to realize that just as Laura had impressed the stamp of her own personality and its fragments on her daughter, her mother was also every bit the product of her own rigid, formal upbringing. Laura didn't have any opportunity to alter her own misgivings and terror about herself as a mature and sexual woman; she couldn't offer Sarah anything other than her own incomplete concept of what this entailed. Concepts about our bodies and how we treat them come from our families and may extend over generations. Our ideas about sexuality and its meaning and power come from our families too, often from our mothers. These ideas are also influenced by societal messages, which have been reinforced over time.

Laura concentrated on her home, her family, and looking "good"—typical of most women coming of age in the 1950s, who were socialized to believe that home and family should be the focus of every woman's attention. Cultural images were unambiguous and abundant in those days. These images were epitomized by the happy television family: the housewife who dressed in high heels and pearls to do her housework; the housewife who had more than enough time to make a wonderful dinner for her athletic son, her pretty daughter, and her handsome, upwardly mobile or gainfully employed husband who dutifully returned home at the same time every evening. Magazines told women how their houses should look and what meals would make their husbands love them and their neighbors envy them.

All these direct instructions led to the popular assumption that every woman was capable of creating the "perfect life" and that the woman—as wife and mother—was solely responsible for this enormous, endless challenge. Like Laura, many women of her generation still strive in vain to meet these standards, and they cover up or try to ignore what doesn't fit into the picture. Recognizing and incorporating healthy expressions of female sexuality into this life were not part of the idea, so they were not mentioned or encouraged.

Laura viewed her family as an extension of herself. If there was something wrong with them, it could only mean that there was something wrong with her. Thus it was not possible for Laura to admit that her husband, Doug, was an alcoholic. Because she could not acknowledge that she had an actively drinking husband, she could not begin to understand his effect on her view of the world and her place in it. Instead, as the family's most controlling and powerful figure, she existed by relating in a hostile, dependent way to Doug: in doing so she rendered herself powerless to effect change, or even to admit change was necessary. She repressed her impotence and bitterness, stuffing her feelings and looking for external fixes for herself and her children.

Laura—strong-willed, sarcastic, and imposing—was always twenty pounds overweight. Yet she never addressed her weight problem directly. Instead, she projected it onto Sarah, who was actually never overweight. Nevertheless, Sarah remembers being called "fat" or "heavy." Her mother was continually taking her to doctors for diet pills. Feeling unable to live up to the ideal, and convinced that she would need a perfect body to attract and keep a husband, Sarah continued to rely on chemicals. She had no clue about the connection between chemicals, body image, and sexual expression as an adult woman.

It was this early connection between body image and chemical fixes—a connection that was powerfully communicated to her, but in an ambiguous and anxiety-provoking way—that led Sarah to become dependent on prescription drugs. Through her women's group she will soon be able to make this connection and to look at the serious impact it has had on her life: both on her intimate relationships and on how she learned to think of herself and her sexuality both apart from and in relation to others.

Danielle: Alcoholic and Liberated

Danielle has just joined Sarah's women's group. She ran in the park for three miles before the session, hoping to work off some excess energy, but she's still nervous and overly eager to tell her story. She's a little uncomfortable around women, although she doesn't want to admit it. She wonders what she's doing here anyway. Women like Sarah, married and supported by their affluent husbands for years, weren't exactly what she was used to, nor what she felt she would find she had much in common with.

At twenty-six, Danielle is happy in her choice of career as a technical writer. She grew up with computers and is competent at her work. Short and intense, with curly red hair, she is proud of her body and almost never wears a bra. Sarah thought Danielle could have stepped right off a page of *Self* magazine because she looked so well put together. In fact, magazines like that are where she gets much of her information about how life should be lived. She carefully watches female characters on television and in movies, paying close attention to how they interact with men. Danielle's female friends do the same, and they enjoy discussing the latest fashions and scandals together.

Danielle thinks of herself as a liberated woman, and by many standards she is. A daughter of the sexual revolution, she grew up with all the technical information she would ever need to have a happy sex life. "Hey," she begins, "when I was six years old I was playing outside my house and my neighbor asked me where my mom was. I replied very seriously, 'She's upstairs fucking and she doesn't want to be disturbed.' Sex was always a part of my life growing up. It was there—people 'did it'— my mother 'did it.' "

Danielle was astounded to hear about Sarah's experience in the bathtub. Her memories are quite different. "I took baths with my friend Ryan until we were seven. We'd get soap all over each other, then we'd get our moms to spray it off. We saw each other naked at least once a week from the first year of our lives and never thought much about it. Of course eventually there came a day when we learned we were supposed to be embarrassed—and as a consequence, we were. And that was the end of that. I'm not scarred for life or anything." Danielle learned to be embarrassed from the messages of the society around her, which eventually counteracted her upbringing and contributed to her current self-image.

Danielle settles back into her chair as she tells the group about her drinking history. Her parents, Marianne and David, were children of the

1960s. They took their counterculture lifestyle with them into adulthood, working for the rights of migrant workers and other oppressed
minorities. They were vegetarians, wore natural-fiber clothing, and had
been recycling for almost thirty years. Marianne and David smoked
marijuana and sometimes took psychedelics, but they rejected alcohol as
the drug of "the establishment."

A natural part of Danielle's adolescent rebellion against her parents
was to have her hair cut professionally every six weeks, wear makeup,
and drink. She drank heavily from the age of fifteen for nearly ten years
and began having blackouts in her second year of drinking.

At the end of her drinking, Danielle acknowledged to herself that
she was having what she termed "sexual blackouts." "I'd remember having dinner with some guy I barely knew or had just met, and the next
thing I knew it was morning . . . I'd wake up in bed with this stranger. I
was terrified because I couldn't remember what had happened . . . I knew
we'd had sex, but God knows what I'd said or done. I'd lost this whole
block of time and it scared me." Danielle connected these experiences
with her earlier alcoholic blackouts, and she knew she was in trouble.
But it wasn't only the blacking out that bothered her—it was also the ac-
cumulation of emptiness and isolation she felt, and how she found herself behaving.

While Danielle is able to feel physically gratified in sobriety, sex
leaves her emotionally empty. She's not sure what's missing. In an attempt to fill the void, she avidly reads women's magazines to learn how
to get a man, how to please a man, how to be sexually fulfilling and ful-
filled. She enjoys these articles, because they often mention various
techniques and include step-by-step instructions on how to make a man
happy by being a sexy woman.

Danielle truly believes that today's woman is not only allowed to
be but is *supposed* to be sexually active and to like it this way—to be good
at pleasing men and to be attractive and desirable. This belief focuses her
exclusively outside of herself, on the needs of her partners. She has lost
or ignored a vital part of herself: the emotional content of sexuality. She
must rediscover it so it can become a part of her sexual self.

Theoretically, Danielle does what she wants. Recently, however, she's been feeling that her sex life in sobriety is not what she had hoped it would be. It feels out of balance with the rest of her life. She's still been sleeping with many men, without feeling connected to any of them. Lately, she rarely feels like even seeing someone for a second date.

Without the alcohol, she realizes she doesn't go to bed with these men because she likes or really wants them. What she longs for is the feeling of connection—the emotional response that transforms "having sex" into sexual intimacy, something very different.

Danielle uses sex as a fix. She understands physical desire and is able to act without shame or guilt, but she does not know how to begin to integrate intimacy with sex in order to experience love. "I haven't had a real, long-term, honest-to-God boyfriend in years. I'm not even sure I've ever had a real relationship with a man. Sometimes I feel like shit. This isn't the way I thought it would be."

Having sex is the only way Danielle knows how to feel connected to a man—maybe even to feel connected to herself. Yet these encounters leave her empty. They sharpen her awareness of the lack of connection. Anonymous sex with strangers was not working for her. Her drinking allowed her to fool herself again and again into thinking and acting as if the physical act of having sex would provoke an emotional response. She thought that was the equation for intimacy. But she had it reversed: intimacy develops from a connection that begins at an emotional level and may progress to include sex.

Theresa: Sexually Abused and Codependent

Theresa has her Hispanic mother's long, shining dark hair and dramatic eyes. She's outgoing, articulate, and a pleasure to be around. But her lovely and engaging appearance gives no indication of her emotional reality. Theresa has had an especially difficult life and until quite recently depended on alcohol, Valium, and cocaine.

On Theresa's thirtieth birthday her boyfriend, Jeff, gave her an ultimatum: if she didn't get some help with her addictions he would leave.

Because she loved him, and he really seemed to care about her, she took his advice. For the past six months she has been in individual and group therapy and has been abstaining and attending Twelve-Step meetings.

In therapy Theresa has begun to talk about her childhood for the first time. The memories are painful, and now, as she allows herself to cry when she tells her story, she often pauses to compose herself.

Theresa's childhood was full of contradictions. She grew up in a well-groomed, middle-class home that successfully camouflaged the family's chaos. Her mother, Carmen, was a sweet, convent-educated woman who was also a prescription pill abuser. She was in and out of mental hospitals during Theresa's childhood, but it was never clear whether she was actually mentally ill or whether her psychiatric problems were the result of prescription drug use and abuse. Carmen was "in the system," and her doctor—like many doctors—chose to overprescribe rather than provide therapeutic intervention.

Carmen was also the victim of her oppressive Roman Catholic family system, in which she learned to feel guilty and ashamed of voicing needs and wants that differed from those allowed by the church. When she divorced Theresa's father, a childhood friend, to live with Bill, a non-Catholic, her family cut her off completely. Although Carmen continued to take Theresa to church every Sunday, she felt excluded by the parish because of her status as a divorced woman.

Her new boyfriend rendered Carmen's isolation complete. Her family, which had provided at least the illusion of support, was no longer in her life. And Bill, a handsome, successful businessman who Carmen thought would provide her and her daughter with a safe, respectable life, was in fact an alcoholic who was completely unresponsive and insensitive to her needs.

When Theresa was nine she was gang raped by her mother's boyfriend and some of his drunken friends. Bill was well respected in the community because of his business success, but he was a menacing and dangerous drunk. It was a painful and terrifying experience, and Theresa mentally dissociated from her body during the experience; it was the only way she could protect herself. Theresa kept the rape a secret. She knew her mother had no power over Bill, and she feared that if Carmen knew about the rape it might upset her enough to cause her to go back into the hospital. Theresa forced herself to "forget" the experience, and Carmen died of a barbiturate overdose when Theresa was sixteen, never knowing the violence her boyfriend had done to her daughter.

Theresa grew up to be a woman who knew how to give men what they wanted. Her early socialization about male and female roles was fairly stereotypical, because of both her mother's passivity and her background, which was influenced by the macho elements in Hispanic culture. According to her world, the models were clear-cut: men were active, assertive, aggressive, and competitive—all-powerful. Women were soft-spoken, obedient, polite, demure, and passive—all-powerless.

Theresa's abuse, combined with her socialization as a passive, compliant female, offered her no options of self-empowerment. Instead, she looked outside herself for power, for the man who would rescue her. Movies, magazines, and advertisements showed Theresa the image she would need to reach her goal: a beautiful, sensual toy that any wealthy and powerful man would be lucky to have. The internal conflict this goal produced, however, was excruciating. While society told her to be good in bed, her Roman Catholic upbringing told her it was a sin.

Theresa's first voluntary sexual experience was at fourteen, with a boy she never saw again. She was devastated, because she had naively assumed that he loved her and that they would "go steady." But she knew how attractive she was, and she soon learned some necessary skills. "I knew exactly, instinctively what would please a man, in bed or out. I knew what he wanted, and that's what he got.

"I did this for years—my whole sexual life. I was giving my sexual partners exactly what they wanted without paying any attention to myself." As she speaks her voice tightens, and she twists strands of her long hair into tight spirals. "I knew what I was doing. Being able to please can get you a lot of ego strokes. I was a great lover. I was right in there participating. Now I see how I was using control and manipulation. Yet whatever attention I got didn't seem to be enough. Now I know that what I was getting, what I thought I wanted, wasn't what I wanted or needed."

Although Theresa's physical appearance is meticulous, she is in a continual struggle for balance. She has not experienced that "pink cloud" of early sobriety. In fact, things seem to be getting worse. Though she has been clean and sober for six months, she is now dealing with the ramifications of things that happened when she was using. She is mourning the loss of her ten-year-old son, Robbie, who was removed from her custody at age two because of her cocaine and alcohol use. And she recently lost her job at a public relations firm as a result of making too many errors that she seemed incapable of preventing. The realization that she and her life are out of control is hitting hard.

Theresa is fortunate to have Jeff in her life during this difficult time. He is a successful attorney, he has no substance-abuse problems, and he genuinely cares about what happens to her. Lately he has been particularly concerned, because Theresa has begun to experience terrifying flashbacks to her rape while making love with Jeff. This is a common reaction among incest survivors, but it took Theresa by surprise.

"Sometimes I just seem to float away from my body during sex," Theresa told her therapist. "I mean, I'm there, I'm doing it; but I don't feel a thing. That's pretty bad, but what's worse is that sometimes when I look at Jeff's face I see that bastard Bill. I can't remember Jeff at all, and I'm right back on the floor at age nine. It's a nightmare, a nightmare."

Mimi: Alcoholic and Lesbian

Mimi is a lesbian who enjoys a successful career as a professor of sociology in a large university. She's worked hard to get there. Her students see her as a witty and incisive lecturer; she is the head of her department; she has received a number of teaching awards and enjoys a good reputation because of her research publications. At age forty-five she swims laps daily in the university pool and is an active member of the opera guild.

Mimi has been in recovery from alcohol abuse for three years. To her dismay she has discovered the extent to which she had depended on alcohol to allow her to be sexually assertive. Now she feels fearful about starting new relationships. Recently, in an attempt to separate her drinking behavior from her sexual expression, she began to talk in therapy about her early childhood.

Mimi was born in West Virginia and grew up in a white, working-class family. Her birth came as something of a surprise to her parents—her two sisters were thirteen and fourteen when she was born.

"My dad was very traditional, the real patriarchal head of the family." Mimi smiles as she remembers. "He loved to hunt and fish, but he never did this with my sisters, because this just wasn't something girls did. He'd always missed having a son to share these things with, and when I came along I guess deep down he saw me as his last chance. So he taught me to tie flies, and he taught me to shoot. We played ball together and had a good old time."

Mimi loved her life and saw nothing unusual about it at all. But as an adolescent she became aware that she was different from the other girls in school. The way she moved her body was somehow "wrong." The way she wanted to dress didn't seem to fit. She got good grades and had a lot of friends, but she also carried a lot of shame to which she couldn't put a name.

"I was like many adolescent lesbians, I guess," reflects Mimi, her musical voice low and sad. "Many of us simply repress our sexuality altogether and channel our energies into sports, drama, band, or studies. We become invisible nonparticipants in the dating game. I was always one of the crowd, but the guys never thought of me in sexual terms."

Mimi felt envious of her girlfriends' boyfriends but didn't know why. She was not interested in dating boys; her relationships with her female friends were the center of her life. She didn't understand that she was jealous of their boyfriends; she didn't know what she was feeling except pain. She tried to giggle and flirt with boys in an unconscious attempt to be included by the other girls. But she had no sexual encounters in high school, and her life was pervaded by the isolating feeling that she was different.

College, with its stimulating intellectual atmosphere, came as a welcome relief. It was there, at nineteen, that Mimi had her first sexual relationship—with her roommate, Linda. Mimi grimaces when she thinks about how innocent she was. "We made love together for a year and a half before I realized that what we had was a lesbian relationship. Naturally, being the budding academic that I was, I found this out by reading about it in a book."

Mimi's and Linda's confusion was fostered by society's heterosexual bias. Heterosexuality is the only option our society offers young people. Lesbian relationships are not only not offered; they are usually not spoken of out loud. This lack of accurate naming by the dominant culture makes it that much more difficult for us to name accurately our feelings and experiences in all sexual areas.

"I was pretty excited by my discovery and told Linda," Mimi continued, "but she thought I was nuts. She patiently explained to me that we were just really good friends, and that we were practicing for when we got married—we were *improving* our sexual technique for the Prince Charming who would certainly come along! Actually, Linda did get married and have a family after college. Who knows what was going on for her."

Mimi credits her own high achievement to the fact that she was brought up to live in a man's world. It simply never occurred to her that there was any other way to be. The impact on her sexual life was more problematic, however. "I was ready to acknowledge that I was a lesbian, but I wasn't exactly facilitated in that identity at the university—especially in 1963! You know, the traditional male-female model was so strong that women loving women was not even seen as an option. It barely is now in a lot of places. Alcohol made it much easier for me to act on my sexual feelings for women. I could be as assertive in my private life as I was in my academic life. It was wonderful."

When Mimi stopped drinking, the alcohol-induced sexual bravado that had worked so well for her disappeared. "When I was drinking, I thought I was some kind of a sexual goddess. But when I stopped, I was terrified. I had no idea how to act, or what would happen if I was rejected. Finally I just stopped having sex." Now, after two years of celibacy, Mimi is ready to begin trying to understand what it means to be sexual sober.

Discovering Our Sexual Selves

Sarah, Danielle, Theresa, and Mimi are struggling with their unique experiences and the tangled messages they received from their families' legacies and from our society while growing up. Yet they share a fundamental and common experience and identity: they are all women trying to negotiate their way in a society that does not value women or encourage them to discover and enjoy the uniqueness of female sexuality.

Sarah learned early that physical appearance is important, but she received contradictory messages about sexuality: it's important to be concerned about how your body looks, but there is one part of your body that must remain unnamed and untouched. Consciously, Sarah does not want to be like her mother, Laura—an overly critical, narcissistic woman who, like many of her peers, was raised to see her children as an extension of herself. Nonetheless, her life is affected by her mother's views on what a woman's life should be like. Sarah's unconscious solution has been to disconnect from herself and her sexuality through drugs that dull her body's responses and repress the cumulative pain of her fragmented experiences.

Unlike Sarah, who had been raised to "save it" for the man she would marry, Danielle was socialized to be sexually active. Her mother, Marianne, tried hard to raise her daughter in a permissive atmosphere that encouraged exploration and openness. As a consequence, while Danielle is at ease with physical sexuality, the emotional content is missing. She moves from relationship to relationship without ever making a real connection. In recovery she, too, is finally beginning to recognize this pain-inducing void in her life and to struggle to reconnect her emotional life with her body and sexual activity.

Theresa learned early that she could use her beauty and intelligence to get other people to take care of her. This is not just something sexually abused women learn. It is one of society's implicit messages to women, which mothers often unwittingly pass down to their daughters: for women, passivity and manipulation is the key to getting along in the world. As a consequence, women like Theresa have difficulty owning their feelings and needs; their power is as reactors, not as actors. They have little direct access to anything, especially to themselves and their own inner lives.

Codependence is the word used to describe this dynamic. The hazard of this label is that women often accept this diagnosis as individual pathology. It is important to understand that codependence originates from unmet childhood needs, abuse, and the influence of social/cultural conditioning.

Mimi was at first confused and then stigmatized by her sexual orientation. She grew up without words to identify her feelings and experiences. As a result of what is traditionally seen as male socialization, she became assertive and achievement-oriented. She knew instinctively how to succeed in a man's world without catering to men or having to be with them as lovers. In recovery, however, she became aware of how important this assertive identity was to her and how afraid she was to feel vulnerable in a sexual relationship. She was hiding behind a wall that kept her from connecting with other women, sexually and otherwise.

The message implicit in these women's experiences is that sexuality is much more than sexual behavior. It's an identification, an activity, a drive, a biological process, an orientation, an outlook. Its content is physical, emotional, psychological, and spiritual. Sexuality is a lifelong process of discovery, a totality of who we are and how we are in the world. As you move with these and other women on their personal journeys of sexual recovery, I hope you will begin to become aware of the components of your own sexuality: its complexity, its history, and its uniqueness. These are your legacies to claim and explore.

Chapter 2

The Great Lies

Truthfulness has not been considered important for women, as long as we have remained physically faithful to a man, or chaste. We have been expected to lie with our bodies: to bleach, redden, unkink or curl our hair, pluck eyebrows, shave armpits, wear padding in various places or lace ourselves, take little steps, glaze our finger and toe nails, wear clothes that emphasized our helplessness. . . . We have had the truth of our bodies withheld from us or distorted; we have been kept in ignorance of our most intimate places. . . . In lying to others we end up lying to ourselves. We deny the importance of an event, or a person, and thus deprive ourselves of a part of our lives. Or we use one piece of the past or present to screen out another. Thus we lose faith even with our own lives.

—Adrienne Rich, *On Lies, Secrets and Silence*

Sexual denial comes in many guises: You may pretend not to understand a dirty joke. You may claim you're a virgin when you're not. You may "forget" to bring your diaphragm on a date, even though you have every intention of having sex. You may tell yourself you only had sex because you were drunk. You may fake an orgasm to please your lover.

You may continue to perform the sex act even when it's never left you satisfied. Performance, a put-on—that's what it's often about.

Our sexual lies are as varied as we are, but they all have the same effect: They separate us from our inner selves. Sexual denial is evidence of our inner struggle toward reconciliations with the outside world.

Many women, and virtually all recovering women, have so distanced themselves from their sexuality that they despair of ever being able to bring their inner and outer sexual selves into harmony. This was my experience. Being in recovery affected my sexuality as much as it affected the other aspects of my being. It was only then that I began to realize the degree to which my alcoholism had anesthetized and distorted my sexuality.

The saddest part was that during my early recovery no one told me that I would need to explore my sexuality. No one pointed to the sexual problems that I might encounter in sobriety, and no one reassured me that most women had similar experiences.

Denial of sexual concerns extends to recovery counselors and Twelve-Step groups. No one seems to be able to talk about sex or to want to try, and it's rarely discussed even in therapy. Yet, as we know, only when denial is examined and replaced with truth and understanding does change become possible.

It is important to become aware of the relationship between our inner process and our outer actions. We become whole by making our behavior consistent with our feelings. The recovery process demands that we become familiar with our inner lives and that we express our inner selves authentically in the world. If we are unable to see the relation between our thoughts, feelings, beliefs, and interactions with others— and stay consistent on all these levels—we will be unable to live our lives with meaning and fulfillment.

America's moralistic attitude toward sexuality is so deeply ingrained that it is often invisible. Understanding that we live in a moralistic society in which sexual desire and expression has been systematically attacked or diminished, while it is flouted in the media, helps us to understand why so many of us learn to close our hearts, minds, and bodies to our sexual needs. We function today as products of this history.

Blessed Ignorance

When Sarah's group first began to discuss sexuality, she was amazed at how open some of the women were. Danielle, for example, had no qualms about describing the size and shape of her various lovers' penises. She was even able to refer to them as "dicks," which made Sarah very uncomfortable.

When she began to think about her sexual relationship with Scott, she realized that she hadn't given it much thought in a long time. In fact, she tried not to think about it. They don't have sex much any more, but she isn't sure why. She knows he wants sex, and she wants to please him, but it never seems to happen.

Scott complains that when he comes to bed she's already asleep. Sarah has asked him to wake her, but the times he's tried she's been unresponsive. Now he figures, why bother? On the other hand, Sarah blames Scott for his compulsion to work. She feels that he's never home, so what can he expect? Neither of them realize that part of the problem is that the pills Sarah takes "to relax" actually interfere with her ability to wake up or be present. It's easier for them both not to think about any of it: the pills, the inability to connect, or the lack of time even to have sex.

Sarah is in denial about her pill addiction. She is also lying to herself when she thinks that perhaps that's just the way married life is after a while. Also, the model from her own parents was one of little affection and contact. She is settling for what she's been taught to expect, but it isn't enough. She lies to herself that it is. On some deeper level Sarah has begun to realize that she is going to have to focus on her sexuality, and she finds the idea terrifying.

Sarah's reticence even to think about her sex life is not unusual. In our society women are valued for their ignorance of sexuality. "Nice" girls aren't supposed to know about sex. Men seem to want women to be innocent and inexperienced—at least we hear that's what they want. So we become guilt-ridden and feign ignorance about and inexperience with masturbation and sexual encounters. But the reality is that we do have sexual feelings, and we do act on them. For women, the guilt and shame that follow expressions of sexuality contribute to the defensive construction of a denial system that surrounds sexual knowledge and thwarts the development of an emotional sex life.

Our cultural role as women is to nurture and hold together, to maintain the ideal values that create empathy, compassion, and tenderness in a world driven by self-interest and dominated by competition and aggression. We want our sexual interactions with others to be about caring and tenderness, acceptance and joy, but often they aren't. Sometimes telling the truth seems brutal and unloving—and it is true that honesty without sensitivity is brutal. Yet being honest, especially with ourselves, is a necessary first step toward changing our dysfunctional patterns.

Sarah was socialized to embrace romantic ideals about sex. She believed that sex before marriage was okay if you were going to marry the person. She slept with her first husband, Max, in what she liked to call "a moment of passion"—that is, "I didn't mean to do it, I just got carried away"—and then felt obligated to marry him. Even after they were divorced she continued to operate in the same way: she viewed every man she dated as a potential life partner, in order to justify having sex with him.

Most recovering women are familiar with the "no-talk rule," which is the prime mechanism that protects denial in dysfunctional families. But the no-talk rule is also a familiar fixture in our sexual lives. This rule has a variety of forms: If you need to talk about sex, it's not okay; it's no good if you have to ask. If your partner really loved you, you would get just what you wanted and needed in bed. When the right person comes along, it's going to be perfect. If it's not perfect, it must be my body or my technique. These rules can prohibit us from ending an unsatisfactory relationship, from asking for what we want, and from taking responsibility for our own sexuality.

Blessed Manipulation

Theresa learned to manipulate men sexually in order to get her basic needs met. "I knew that if I kept myself attractive I'd get men with money who would take care of me. I held onto them by knowing exactly what they wanted in bed and giving it to them." Her relationships were not mutually empowering, caring interactions; they were commodity transactions. She was socialized to expect men to take care of her financially, and in return she gave them the use of her body. There was no place in this pragmatic reciprocal arrangement for emotional connections or fulfillment. Between the ages of twenty and twenty-six, Theresa went out exclusively with unstable and dangerous men whose wealth came from illegal or questionable activities.

Theresa paid a high price for her dependence. One of her lovers, a cocaine dealer, set her up in an apartment and bought her a sports car. He viewed her not as a lover but as an appendage, and he toyed with her in his own abusive style. At one time he even kept her locked in a closet for three days, feeding her cocaine under the door. Another lover was a gambler who occasionally beat her.

In recovery Theresa became painfully aware of the extent to which she focused on her dependence on men to the exclusion of her own sexual and emotional needs. In effect, she was trapped in the role of a little girl, weak and lost. "I gave them what they wanted, but they never asked what I wanted. It never occurred to me that they should. And it never occurred to me to ask myself what I wanted."

Now she feels the effects of those years of abuse. She has been used, degraded, and dismissed as being nothing more than a warm body, and she is determined never to go back to that life. She is living alone in a small studio apartment and takes whatever job she can get, even cleaning houses—a far cry from her high-powered public relations job—in order to support herself. Theresa struggles daily to learn new self-growth and recovery skills, and she has begun to have feelings of self-worth that reinforce her commitment to recovery.

Denial about sexual behavior begins early. Children are very curious about their bodies and sexuality. When parents act secretive, embarrassed, or ashamed in answering questions, as Sarah's mother did, children begin to feel they've done something wrong by asking. Eventually they begin to believe that sex must be disgusting and dirty, something to be denied or dismissed or at least to be kept a secret.

The behavior of alcoholic, addictive, or otherwise dysfunctional families may seriously affect a child's developing sexuality. Touch, for example, is a vital component of sexual experience. Alcoholics, however, give touch inconsistently and inappropriately, often withholding it altogether. Physical and sexual abuse, as in Theresa's home, is an extreme experience but unfortunately not an uncommon one.

Affection is another critical area. Some alcoholic parents are affectionate only when they've been drinking, so children often learn to connect affection with intoxication. Children carry this confusion about the nature and place of affection into their adult lives. One woman remembers, "What's most important to me is affection. I supposedly had a great sexual partner, my children's father. And with him I didn't get any affection. He rarely held my hand or put his arm around me. I realize now that I was never touched unless he had a sexual need and wanted something from me."

Blessed Permissiveness

Danielle's childhood message regarding sexuality was, in effect, "Go for it. Sex is great, and it's nothing to be ashamed of." This overt message was her progressive mother's response to her own repressed childhood. She didn't want her daughter to grow up with the sexual taboos that she had endured, which had produced feelings of guilt. So she made sure that Danielle understood that her body was a wonderful thing and a source of pleasure—but she failed to address the emotional aspect of sexuality. As a consequence, although Danielle was able to enjoy the physical pleasures of sexuality, she felt an absence of emotional connection and content that she was unable to explain. She tried in vain to deny this inner longing and compensated for it by having more sex with more men.

Social Lies

Social lies are the lies that society teaches us; they are rooted in the soul of our culture. All of us, men and women, are affected by these myths. Social lies even become institutionalized—they are reflected in family systems, schools, religions, legal systems, and governmental policy. It is important that as women we become aware of the detrimental effects these lies have on our lives.

Addiction Is Immoral

Society places a greater stigma on the addicted woman than it does on the addicted man. While the behavior of a drunken man is often overlooked, excused, or even encouraged, being intoxicated or high is considered—to say the least—very "unladylike" behavior.

Drinking or using drugs threatens women's sexual reputations, and addicted women are often stigmatized in sexual terms. They are routinely called "sluts" and "whores," and they are assumed to be sexually loose and promiscuous. Drunken women, unlike drunken men, can never be "good old boys" out for a night on the town. Although the disinhibition theory about alcohol is inconsistent, this is the cultural expectation. It becomes an excuse for men to act out but a device to level blame on women. Because women experience more stigma, they have greater denial about their drinking or using.

This is unfortunate but not surprising, because addiction is above all a disease of denial. Denial enables us to continue in our addiction—

whether it is to alcohol, to drugs, to food, or in other distorted relationships—often in violation of our values. This conflict increases the denial.

The same denial processes that are involved in addiction are also present when we deny our sexual needs. People who are addicted have two primary beliefs: (1) that they are not addicted and (2) that they are in control. In the same way, in order to feel good about ourselves, we often believe that our sex lives are fulfilling and satisfying on all levels and that we are in control of our sexual behavior.

To defend these mistaken premises we often deny both our feeling world—the shame, guilt, and embarrassment—and our physical experience—sexual behaviors that violate our value systems. For example, while actively drinking Danielle insisted her sex life was just fine: "I fucked a lot of really great-looking guys." But in recovery she came to see how her denial enabled her to ignore her emotional needs and make them invisible.

Breaking denial starts with a willingness to look at things with a new awareness; this is as true in the denial of sexuality as it is in the denial of a problem with drinking or drugs. Without awareness we remain trapped—unable to change and unable to see the need for change. When we are in denial we are unaware of our thoughts, feelings, desires, and motivations and how they relate to our behavior. They become blocked and block each other. To move away from the protective mechanism of denial means to become more aware of who we are, what we feel, what we think, and why we do things. We may reconnect with our inner selves or connect for the first time; doing this gives us more understanding of why we act the way we do, and we gain integration and motivation to stay connected.

Sexual recovery starts with a decision to expand our consciousness. It proceeds because of a willingness to become and to remain attentive and receptive to our true selves. Moving away from denial allows our sexuality to awaken and blossom. It takes courage to begin to strip away the layers of denial built up over the years and to look with a clear eye at our experiences, behaviors, and patterns. But acknowledging the truth and facing the pain begins a process of healing. And as we heal we can begin to let our true sexual selves emerge.

Homosexuality Is Perverted

We live in a heterosexist society in which boys and girls are conditioned and trained to be heterosexual. No matter how liberal we may profess to be or believe we are, we unthinkingly accept this attitude as the norm. For example, parents never suggest that their young teenagers might benefit from dating both boys and girls to see which they prefer.

This bias is deeply embedded in our society. According to author Barbara Walker, "Female homosexuality was generally regarded as a virtually unthinkable threat in patriarchal societies. Christian Europe regarded lesbianism as 'a crime without a name,' and sometimes burned lesbians alive without trial."* With this legacy, the need to deny and to conform to the dominant heterosexual model runs deep and is powerfully communicated.

When we're talking about homosexuality, we're talking about a minority that's oppressed solely by its choice of sex partner. Gay men and lesbians are generally not the product of family groups that include other gay men and lesbians. Mimi, who had a traditional, conservative childhood, did not even have a language with which to describe her sexual feelings. She had no access to her feelings or to this vital part of her life.

Many lesbians have not had the opportunity to develop a positive self-image. Some women use alcohol or other drugs to deny their erotic feelings for other women. Others, who are aware of their attraction to other women, are able to act only if they allow themselves to "lose control" through intoxication. Still others—like Mimi's roommate Linda, who believed she was honing her sexual skills for her future husband—

---

*Barbara G. Walker, *The Woman's Encyclopedia of Myths and Secrets* (San Francisco: Harper & Row, 1983), 535–36.

are able to deny completely their feelings of attraction and connection to another woman even in the midst of the experience.

Pleasure Is Forbidden

Many women have had to deny their sexual selves in order to conform to the strictures of traditional religions. Many women, especially those raised in fundamentalist faiths, feel shame and guilt about their sexual lives. Eventually they learn to think of themselves as being bad, even unredeemable.

To many women the word *religion* seems full of hypocrisy. Theresa's memory of the room in which she was raped by her mother's boyfriend and his friends includes a large crucifix hanging on the wall. Another client told me, "The only things the nuns told us in school about sex was, 'Never kiss a boy with your mouth open.' Of course this was the first thing we did when we got the chance to be with a boy."

Formal religious rules regarding sexuality are usually absolutes and often negative: "Don't touch yourself there, it's a sin." "Don't have sex before marriage." "Don't fall in love with a member of the same sex, it's a perversion." "Emulate the Holy Virgin"—who had a husband and son without any experience or acknowledgment of the act, much less the sexual pleasure.

The crucial element of spirituality is often completely left out of the discussion about sexuality. Sexuality and spirituality are frequently seen as polar opposites. Many women, even women raised in "religious" homes, are unfamiliar with the meaning of spirituality. Spirituality is the transcendent feeling that imbues the process of becoming our truest, deepest, most wise and knowing selves. It is not about rules or absolutes imposed on us from some outside authority. It is not opposed to sexuality; it is the element that allows passionate lovers to momentarily transcend time and space.

Sexuality is our own human expression of the creative energy of the universe. Each of us is a unique sexual being manifesting spirit in a human form. Being who we are means embodying that divine spark, communicating the essence that is especially ours with physical acts of touching and connecting. As we start the journey of recovery, however, that divine spark is often dimmed. Years of sexual repression, denial, and dishonesty repress its vital forces. The centrality of our sexual energy is diminished or lost.

Who we are—our innermost self—becomes hidden, both from ourself and from others, during the descent into addiction. But recovery, though sometimes a long and painful journey, can also be a journey of great joy. As we become who we are, tremendous energy is released: our lights begin to shine again, and we become empowered both sexually and spiritually.

It is possible to restructure and reestablish the connection of our erotic passion, desire, and fulfillment to spiritual life forces. Each complements the other. The energies are interactive and share the same origin.

Healing emotionally encourages and allows both our sexual and our spiritual selves to develop. While locked in denial we hear only the negative messages derived from our socialization. As we break through the bonds of denial, we begin to hear the voice of our own inner wise woman. This voice of intuition and power sounds from deep within us. As we listen to that voice, we learn to grow and change.

You Should Not Be Sexual

Many women find it difficult to recognize and accept sexism as a continuing, thinly disguised fact of our lives. Our schools, television, movies, and advertising all reflect a male-valuing society that subtly or not so subtly denigrates the female. Even our careless treatment of Mother Earth reflects the destructive nature of patriarchal norms and values. This pervasive attitude affects the sexuality of all women in our culture to a greater or lesser degree. Realizing this can be disturbing, but it can also begin to connect you with your inner sexual feelings.

The following short fantasy was written by Theodora Wells in 1970 and remains valuable today. It illuminates in a startling way the powerful effects of sexual socialization.

To get the full impact, I suggest you have a friend read it to you, or read it onto a tape and play it back with your eyes closed.

There is much concern today about the future of man, which means, of course, both men and women—generic Man. For a woman to take exception to this use of the term "man" is often seen as defensive hair-splitting by an "emotional female."

The following experience is an invitation to awareness in which you are asked to feel into, and stay with, your feelings through each step, letting them absorb you. If you start intellectualizing, try to turn it down and let your feelings again surface to your awareness.

Consider reversing the generic term Man. Think of the future of Woman which, of course, includes both women and men. Feel into that, sense its meaning to you—as a woman—as a man.

Think of it always being that way, every day of your life. Feel the everpresence of woman and feel the non-presence of man. Absorb what it tells you of the importance and value of being woman—or being man.

Recall that everything you have ever read, all your life, uses only female pronouns—she, her—meaning both girls and boys, both women and men. Recall that most of the voices on radio and most of the faces on TV are women's—when important events are covered—on commercials—and on the late talk shows. Recall that you have no male senator representing you in Washington.

Feel into the fact that women are the leaders, the power-centers, the prime movers. Man, whose natural role is husband and father, fulfills himself through nurturing children and making home a refuge for woman. This is only natural to balance the biological role of woman, who devotes her entire body to the race during pregnancy.

Then feel further into the obvious biological explanation for woman as the ideal—her genital construction. By design, female genitals are compact and internal, protected by her body. Male genitals are so exposed that he must be protected from outside attack to ensure the perpetuation of the race. His vulnerability clearly requires sheltering.

Thus, by nature, males are more passive than females, and have a desire in sexual relations to be symbolically engulfed by the protective body of the woman. Males psychologically yearn for this protection, fully realizing their masculinity at this time—feeling exposed and vulnerable at other times. The male is not fully adult until he has overcome his infantile tendency to penis orgasm and has achieved the mature surrender of the testicle orgasm. He feels himself a "whole man" when engulfed by the woman.

If the male denies these feelings, he is unconsciously rejecting his masculinity. Therapy is thus indicated to help him adjust to his own nature. Of course, therapy is administered by a woman, who has the education and wisdom to facilitate openness leading to the male's growth and self-actualization.

To help him feel into his defensive emotionality, he is invited to get in touch with the "child" in him. He remembers his sister's jeering at his primitive genitals that "flop around foolishly." She can run, climb, and ride horseback unencumbered. Obviously, since she is free to move, she is encouraged to develop her body and mind in preparation for her active responsibilities of adult womanhood. The male vulnerability needs female protection, so he is taught the less active, caring virtues of homemaking.

Because of his clitoris-envy, he learns to strap his genitals, and learns to feel ashamed and unclean because of his nocturnal emissions. Instead, he is encouraged to keep his body lean and dream of getting married, waiting for the time of his fulfillment—when "his woman" gives him a girl-child to carry on the family name. He knows that if it is a boy-child he has failed somehow—but they can try again.

In getting to your feelings on being a woman—on being a man—stay with the sensing you are now experiencing. As the words begin to surface, say what you feel from inside you.*

Most women find that this short fantasy conjures up many images, along with many feelings and questions. You might want to think about the following:

---

*Theodora Wells, "Woman—Which Includes Man, Of Course," *Association of Humanistic Psychology Newsletter,* June 1970, 2.

- What would it feel like to be a woman in this scenario?

- What would it feel like to be a man?

- What kind of sexual person would a woman be in this scenario? What kind of sexual person would a man be?

- Who would be vulnerable to sexual abuse? To depression? To unexpressed rage?

- Who would feel victimized?

- Who would feel powerful?

This role-reversal exercise illuminates the emotional impact of being raised as a female in a society that puts primary value on the male. When, as women, we hear these powerful but unfair messages repeated for ten, twenty, thirty, forty years, they become part of our consciousness. Their effect on our lives is enormous but often unexamined. Young women today are still being profoundly affected by this aspect of the socialization process. It affects what we study, how we behave, what we wear, how we talk, whom we love. And it has a profound impact on the nature of our sexuality.

We don't even notice these cultural norms, because they are so embedded in our society; yet when we reverse them, they suddenly seem ludicrous. Only when we are confronted by the seeming absurdity of a social system organized around and dominated by women—while retaining our traditional norms—do we begin to question what we have so readily accepted about the current male-centered and male-valued system. It is time to create balance in our lives, both as individuals and as legitimate participants in a larger society. And the place to start is within ourselves.

Gender Is Irrelevant

Many of us are overwhelmed when we first confront the reality that women and girls are targets of sexual repression and abuse simply because of their gender. The implications of our socialization as females are tremendous; this socialization deeply affects and distorts how we feel about ourselves, how we see ourselves sexually, and how we interact with others.

I have heard women say, "I've never been treated differently because I'm a woman. I'm an alcoholic, not a woman alcoholic." As comforting as those thoughts may be in early sobriety, they simply are not true.

As women, whether or not we abuse drugs or alcohol, each of us is directly influenced by the place we occupy in our society. The statistics are chilling: 38 percent of American women have been sexually abused before the age of eighteen; 42 percent have been sexually harassed on the job; and every seven minutes another woman is raped. These statistics are even higher if the woman is or has been chemically dependent. According to one well-known study, 100 percent of alcoholic women experienced their first assault before they began to drink.*

As we begin to reconnect with who we really are and who we want to be, we must also try to break through this confining shield of our shared socialization. Most of us have learned to be "feminine" and to act in ways that are acceptable for women—even when those ways may not be congruent with our inner selves or reflect our own self-generated desires.

Women Should Whisper

Most women have learned that placing other's needs ahead of our own is a virtue. We are taught to defer to others, especially male others, to not choose what to eat for dinner, to not choose when to have sex. The unspoken message we internalize is: "I am less important than you are." It is a message that gets reinforced over time as we live our lives in accommodation to others. We repeatedly hear versions of this message,

---

*Idee Winfield, Linda K. George, Marian Swartz, and Dan Blazer, "Sexual Assault and Psychiatric Disorders Among a Community Sample of Women," *American Journal of Psychiatry* 147:3, March 1990, 339.

and we see other women conform by deferring to another's wishes. Denying ourselves by not giving voice to our own thoughts and preferences eventually removes the idea that choices are in fact being made—but not by us.

In our sexual lives—as in every other part of our lives—when we deny the reality of our sexual needs, we relinquish our power of discretion and our power of choice. To recover our power we must give voice to our needs and wants.

The first step is to concentrate on finding your voice. Just like the women in Sarah's group, most women have had little practice talking about sexual issues. It can seem embarrassing and intrusive, like "airing dirty linen in public"; but sharing ideas and experiences about sexuality with women who are ready to listen and communicate can be an incredibly liberating experience. You may learn things about yourself you never suspected, and you will begin to appreciate other women and the similarity of our shared experiences.

If you cannot connect with a group of women, start with a close female friend. If that feels too uncomfortable, you may want to begin by reading material on sexuality that is addressed specifically to women (see appendix C for a list of such material). Begin wherever you can; begin where you are.

The Hope of Truth

Women in recovery almost unanimously express dissatisfaction with their sexual lives, but few have the tools to implement the changes that will allow them to become contented. Sometimes we hide our unhappiness and disappointment in denial. Sometimes we're stoic about the dreariness of our sex lives. Sometimes we're angry and resentful because we aren't having the kind of sexual experience that we want. Sometimes we're so grateful to be sober that we pretend we can live without other things—like a good sex life. But rarely do we have the opportunity in treatment programs, in Twelve-Step meetings, or in therapy to talk about our sexual dissatisfactions. There are few places available to women in recovery where we can learn how to discover our sexual lives and integrate them into our recoveries.

The first step in a sexual recovery process is to be honest about your sexual feelings, even if you are not encouraged and supported by your society, your family, your partner, or your recovery counselor. Being honest takes courage and the willingness to find out what it is that you want and feel, and to discover a way to express it.

Awakening Your Sexuality is about healing and growth. It is about exploring the process of creating for yourself the kind of sexual life that you want. I hope to provide you with tools for recovery. These tools are designed to allow you to discover your sexual feelings, to bring your actions into congruence with those feelings, and to become the healthy sexual person that you are inside.

Becoming who you want to be sexually is about becoming whole; it is about becoming a woman with choice, empowered to risk and change. It is about fluidity, about integrating your feelings and actions into a seamless web of self, bridging the gap between your inner feelings and your outer actions. It is about rekindling your inner light and letting it shine. It is about finding wholeness and consciously welcoming into being the person you already are.

Chapter 3

The Flow of Desire

Desire is not simply a desire of each self for its self pleasure. But what is it for?

Possibly, if it is for anything, desire is for the experience of journey toward and joining in something that thereby becomes greater than the separate selves. . . . Desire in the larger sense affirms our connection and being "a part of" rather than "apart from." It leads to expansion rather than satisfaction; the former suggests growth, life, and openness; the latter suggests stasis.

—Judith V. Jordan

My love for you is mixed throughout my body.
— Ancient Egyptian love song

Sexual desire describes the powerful mix of sexual urges, stirrings, and interest that we feel and express toward a lover. Even though we hear desire discussed freely and can recognize it in others, our own desire often eludes us and goes undetected. This is especially true for many recovering women. Learning to recognize and express desire—knowing when you feel desire, being relatively comfortable expressing it, and being sexually assertive and direct—are vital steps on your journey toward sexual empowerment.

What Is Desire?

Socialization has a profound effect on the way men and women experience desire. For men, being sexual, which includes having intercourse and achieving ejaculation, is both a rite of passage and the continuing proof of masculinity: feeling sexual desire is touted as absolutely necessary to being a man. When a man wants to hurt another man, he speaks of emasculating him, of "cutting off his balls." Virility—that is, male sexual prowess, vigor, and irresistibility—is about power.

For women, on the other hand, sexuality is not about feeling or acting all-powerful. Women usually describe sexual desire as the longing to be joined with a particular partner in a loving and caring relationship, not as "needing to get laid." For women, then, sexual desire often seems to be more concerned with relationship and the emotional joy of sexual connection than with physical need, the act of intercourse, and the achievement of orgasm. While there are undeniable physical differences between women and men, the reason for this dichotomy is not preordained by nature as much as it is determined by society.

In a traditional view of female sexuality, the feelings of power connected with sexual energy and with passion have been seen as a negative for women and have even been denied women. As Lois Wyse so aptly put it, "Men are expected to apologize for their weaknesses, women for their strengths."* These differences in socialization leave men and women to live out the old saying that men profess love to get sex, while women use sex to get love.

Sexual desire often propels women into dangerous territory—unwanted pregnancy, a reputation as a "nymphomaniac," or feelings of having been used. Thus women often renounce their right to desire, leaving the mysteries of sexual desire and initiation to men. While the association of power with sexual energy and passion is a rite of passage for men, the same does not hold true for women. We have cultivated

---

*Lois Wyse, *A Woman's Notebook III* (Philadelphia: Running Press, 1983), 36.

instead the arena of response and reaction. We allow ourselves to invite desire but not to express desire.

One consequence of this behavior is that women often send sexual signals without feeling sexual at all. Consciously or unconsciously, we have learned that it is possible to manipulate men in this way; and many women routinely act coy and flirtatious with men—whether they are transacting business, shopping for groceries, or having sex. With this orientation, few women are aware of or able to separate their own sexual desires from the desires of their partners. Heterosexual women in particular learn to recognize the signs of male arousal and sexual interest, and fail to value their own sexual needs.

Developing a comprehensive model of human sexual desire, then, has been a difficult problem for researchers. Most theories of sexual desire, including Freudian drive theory, have used male desire as their base, as measured by male reports of sexual fantasies, thoughts, incidents of masturbation, and partner activities. Women's desire is frequently reported as a variation of "real" desire—that is, male desire—or even as a series of deficiencies in desire. Thus, traditional theories are often of little help in understanding women's desire.

More recent research suggests that men and women experience desire differently:

> Overall, it does appear that men have a more insistent and constant sexual appetite, which is readily accessed through a large variety of internal and environmental prompts. Women, on the other hand, have less intense and more sporadic sexual desires, which they are more likely either to suppress or ignore if a host of conditions are not met. The pathway between desire and execution seems to be longer—with more byways, detours, and obstacles—for women than for men![*]

To compound the problem, rapidly changing cultural mores affect our perception of what sexual desire "should" be. Thus in the late 1960s

---

[*]Sandra R. Leiblum & Raymond C. Rosen, ed. *Sexual Desire Disorders* (New York: Guilford, 1988), 12–13.

and 1970s, decades in which sexual freedom was espoused, "lack of desire" was seen as the problem. In the late 1980s and 1990s, however, with the focus on addiction and AIDS, the problem has been redefined as "too much" sexual desire. So the question still remains: What is sexual desire?

Desire is generally described as having three components: physical, mental, and emotional. In every experience of desire, it has been said, all three components exist, although to varying degrees.

- The physical component is what we call lust, "horniness," or sexual appetite. We want to have sex because we want to experience pleasure.

- The mental aspect of desire encompasses sexual fantasies, ideas, and thoughts about what it's been like before, what we think it will be like this time, and how we think our partner will behave.

- The emotional component of desire is the drive for attachment, the need to feel close to another by connecting physically during sex. This aspect is what most women refer to when they describe sexual desire. It is an expression of women's desire for mutuality, an impulse away from separateness, toward joining and feeling joined: it is an urge toward mutual pleasuring and the creation of bodily union.

An important stage precedes desire: willingness. According to therapist and author JoAnn Loulan,

> This is the decision to have sex for whatever reason. You do not even have to want to have sex. . . . It is not a passive stance. It is not meant to be looked at as, "Oh well, I guess I'll lie here and go through with sex." Rather, this is a very active stage, at least in the mind. You are consciously deciding that you do want to have sex and you are willing to do so even if you have no physical or emotional desire.*

---

* JoAnn Loulan, *Lesbian Sex* (San Francisco: Spinsters Ink, 1984), 42.

Most sex therapy books define sexual desire as the specific sensations that push us to seek out or become receptive to sexual experiences. Unfortunately, that description of desire may not be helpful to us as women. We may seek out or become receptive to sexual experiences for many reasons other than desire.

Theresa, for example, learned to use her sexuality as a lure for men and as an exchange for financial support, drugs, or security. She didn't consider whether she actually desired the man or the sexual experience, but used sex as a barter for the needed commodity. This ensured her disconnection from her own sexual wants and needs. She became expert at getting men and pleasing men; she was alert and responsive to their sexual needs and desires; but she did not know what pleased her, or whether or not she was feeling sexual desire.

Recognizing Sexual Arousal

Few women can readily identify when they are feeling sexual desire. Society, as we have seen, does not encourage us to express our desire. Unlike men, who cannot fail to understand the implication of an erect penis, women have little impetus to learn to be aware of the meaning of more subtle physical clues, such as vaginal lubrication, to tell us when we're sexually stimulated.

Knowing when you feel sexual desire is something you will probably have to learn consciously. Knowing that it is perfectly natural and reasonable to feel sexual and to express that sexuality is the first step. The ability to experience sexual pleasure is an integral part of being human, and initiating that experience cannot be left to only one-half of the human race.

As you learn to recognize your own sexual arousal, you can begin to act from it. As you begin to accept yourself as a sexual being who feels desire and has wants and needs, then you will feel more comfortable initiating sexual experiences. And as you assert your right to pursue sexual pleasures on your own behalf, the shame and guilt for feeling desire will fall away. Accepting and asserting your right to sexual desire is crucial to your sexual awakening.

Physical Problems and Desire

Virtually all women are capable of feeling sexual desire. If you do not feel sexual desire, you can discover what is blocking its expression. Lack of energy, abuse, gynecological problems, stress, and crisis are all contributors to the lack of sexual feeling and desire.

Lack of Energy in Early Recovery

Many women experience a decrease in sexual desire during the first two years of sobriety. Early recovery can be an intense time, requiring you to mobilize all your resources. You may simply not have the energy available for sexual interests. I have heard many clients echo the sentiments of this recovering alcoholic woman: "I was exhausted when I quit drinking. All I wanted to do was sleep. I had zero interest in sex—I felt like I was recovering from a long illness."

Women in early recovery also have to deal with the physical effects of alcohol abuse. Being physically debilitated naturally affects sexual desire. Desire is most available when we are healthy, physically active, and energetic. During early recovery we may be involved in the process of regaining our health and energy. We have to establish new patterns of nutritious eating and learn to sleep well without the aid of chemicals. Some women have exhausted their adrenal glands and experience a deep sense of fatigue. Other women will be healing from ulcers, respiratory ailments, and the effect of alcohol on the liver. During early recovery, it is not uncommon to experience a diminishing of sexual desire for diverse reasons, physical or emotional.

Abuse

The number one impediment to sexual desire is a history of sexual or physical abuse. Women who have been raped, sexually abused in childhood, beaten, or otherwise violated inevitably connect sex or touching with pain and fear, guilt and shame. This is a natural reaction:

> If your softball coach pinched your breasts in the locker room after every game, you may not want your lover touching your breasts today. If your stepfather violently raped you, you might experience pain in your vagina today, or you might be scared of intercourse.*

If you are a survivor of abuse, it is important to get counseling with a professional trained to work with abused women. As Theresa found out, when women begin to identify and recall details of their abuse, they may begin to reexperience the old feelings of pain and shame, numbness, or lack of connection, and they may also have flashbacks or rage. There are strategies to help you cope with these effects, and your counselor can suggest actions you can take to help yourself heal from the abuse.

Gynecological Problems

Lack of sexual interest may also be related to gynecological difficulties and vaginal infections. Alcoholic women experience more gynecological difficulties during both active drinking and recovery than nonalcoholic women, probably from the chemical effects of alcohol on the body.

In early recovery it's important to get a thorough gynecological exam, paying special attention to possible yeast infections. The three most common forms of vaginitis are yeast infections, bacterial infections, and trichomonas, all of which can make sexual activity extremely unpleasant, if not painful. Even a mild infection can radically decrease sexual desire.

Stress and Crisis

Early recovery can be a time of stress and crisis. Recovery brings change, and even positive change is stressful. Getting a massage, taking a hot

---

*Ellen Bass and Laura Davis, *The Courage to Heal: A Guide for Women Survivors of Sexual Abuse* (New York: Harper & Row, 1988), 240.

bath or sitting in a hot tub, exercising regularly, eating well, and getting plenty of rest can all help you cope with stress. Meditation, prayer, and reading devotional literature may provide you with the spiritual resources to make it through a stressful period. It takes time to reduce the stress in your life. As the stress abates, desire will often return.

Emotional Problems and Desire

In addition to the physical problems that contribute to the lack of desire, there are emotional conditions that can interfere with desire as well. Lack of trust, depression, loss, and grief impact the natural ebb and flow of desire.

Trust

Most women find it difficult to feel sexual desire when they do not sense a mutual need for emotional connection. I have heard many women express variations of the following statements:

- "My partner never listens to me, hears me, or sees me. Why would I want sex?"

- "He sits behind a newspaper all night, not saying a word. Why should I suddenly feel sexual just because we're in bed together?"

- "I can't feel sexy on the spur of the moment. I need to feel intimate before I feel desire."

- "He touches me for three minutes and expects me to be aroused. He doesn't understand that sex isn't something two people do to each other, it's something that happens between two people."

- "I don't feel full of desire after we've been bickering and fighting all day, but she does."

All of these statements imply a lack of trust between partners. In order to feel sexual desire, most women need to trust that their partner values, respects, and cares for them. Typically, male sexual desire is characterized by the satisfaction of an individual want, a fragmented, biological urge to "get off." For women, sexual desire is an integral part of an interaction with another person. It's usually not about doing or having it done; rather, sex is an engagement of two desirous people.

If you are having difficulty experiencing sexual desire, then it is important to look first at the relationship between you and your sexual partner. If you do not feel close and trusting, or if you have unresolved conflicts, then you may not be able to feel sexual desire.

Depression

Women are also more prone to depression than men, and alcoholics are more likely to be depressed both during active drinking and during recovery than nonalcoholics.

Depression has a negative effect on sexual desire, one widely demonstrated in studies of all types of women. In fact, depression is usually listed as one of the major causes of inhibited sexual desire. Depression is often related to feelings of powerlessness, helplessness, and unexpressed anger. Women frequently feel this way when they see no options for themselves and feel trapped in their life situations. You may feel almost continually depressed, down, and sad; or you may feel "blue" for a few days or weeks at a time, with more or less normal periods in between. In either case you may truly be clinically depressed, and it is important that you get a diagnostic evaluation. Individual and group therapy can often help women see possibilities for change that they hadn't been aware of, first in others and then gradually for themselves.

Depression is marked by the presence of at least three of the following symptoms:

1. You are unable to sleep (insomnia) or you seem to sleep all the time (hypersomnia).
2. You have low energy and a chronic tired feeling.
3. You feel inadequate, have very little self-esteem, and are prone to self-deprecation (putting yourself down).
4. Your effectiveness and productivity at school, work, or home decrease.
5. You find it difficult to pay attention, concentrate, or think clearly.
6. You withdraw socially.
7. You lose interest in or enjoyment of pleasurable activities.
8. You are always irritable or express excessive anger toward others.
9. You are unable to respond with apparent pleasure to praise or rewards.
10. You are less talkative or active than usual, or feel slowed down or restless.
11. You are pessimistic about the future, brood about past events, or feel sorry for yourself.
12. You always seem to be tearful or crying.
13. You have recurrent thoughts of death or even suicide.

Loss and Grief

Loss and grief have a negative impact on sexual desire. It is common for women in early recovery to experience grief over the loss of alcohol as their constant companion and comfort. Women who have lost years of their lives to chemical dependence will have many accompanying losses: loss of family, loss of adolescence, loss of career, loss of loved ones.

During the process of grieving over these losses, women may experience little sexual desire and an almost total loss of sexual interest.

This is a common experience during any grieving process, whether for the loss of another person or for the loss of parts of yourself. As you heal from your losses, your desire will return.

Ebb and Flow of Desire

No one has the same level of sexual interest all the time. If you have a trusting relationship, and there is no unresolved conflict, then you may simply be in a period of low desire. Throughout our lives we feel an ebb and flow of our desire, just as we do other forms of physical or intellectual energy. At some points in our lives we may feel more sexual and have more interest in being sexual, at others less. This constant ebb and flow is natural and normal.

Your level of sexual interest may be related to your hormonal cycle; it may be greatly affected by pregnancy, nursing, and menopause. Sometimes it is related to a fear of unwanted pregnancy. Many women report that menopause was a sexually freeing experience for them, and that desire flowered after fifty. Some women report that their desire increased with age as they felt more secure in their bodies and less self-conscious. Other women say that their desire mellowed and became less insistent with age. Some women report desire as less genitally focused and more diffuse with age, and others say the opposite.

Rekindling Desire

As you become physically healthier and more stable in your recovery, you will probably experience a gradual increase in desire. If you do not, there are a number of steps you can take to rekindle desire. You may need a period of celibacy in order to recover your sexual feelings, but this needs to be stated and affirmed between you and your partner.

If you're in a relationship and are frustrated by your lack of desire, or your partner is frustrated by it, you will need to make the sexual part of your relationship a priority. You will need to make talking about sex—what it means to you, what you want from it, how it feels to you—a basic part of your communication.

If you and your partner are having differences or conflicts, you need to deal with them. For many recovering couples, unexpressed anger and unresolved conflict are a major block to the flow of desire.

Putting a priority on your sexual relationship also means allotting time for erotic activity. Many times we schedule every other activity— time with friends, time with children, time for household chores—not realizing that we haven't allowed time to connect physically and emotionally with our partner. Being sensual and sexual requires genuine relaxation. If you're not rested it's hard to feel playful. Pressure to perform, to squeeze sex into the last thirty minutes of your day, isn't conducive to pleasure.

If you have no partner and are frustrated by your lack of sexual interest, ask yourself some questions. Are your unresolved feelings, especially anger, sabotaging your sexuality? Are you healthy, rested, and getting enough exercise? Do you feel good about your body? Do you feel sexually attractive? Do you have time to cultivate a sexual connection with someone? Are you involved in activities that will put you in contact with potential partners?

If you can answer these questions positively but still feel frustrated with a relative lack of sexual interest, you may also want to consider counseling.

Our socialization as women greatly affects our ability to feel, recognize, and act on sexual desire. Once we become aware of this, however, we no longer need to let it define, dictate, and dominate our lives. We can learn to notice when we feel desire, and we can choose to break through the limits of socialization to express it.

Sexually Sober Without Fear

Being sexual without the aid of alcohol or drugs is a concern for most recovering women and is frightening for many. Like Mimi, some women have never had sex sober. In addition, many women had unfulfilling and dissatisfying sexual experiences when they did have them while sober.

Mimi's fears, for example, were on three levels: (1) she was afraid because she had never been sexual sober, and she didn't know what the experience would be like or what her responses would be; (2) she was afraid that sex wouldn't be satisfying, and that as a sober person she would have dissatisfying sex—or no sex or not enough sex—for the rest of her life; and (3) she was just plain scared to have sex. In therapy Mimi began to understand that sexual responses are learned responses. Facing the fact that she was frightened to have sexual experiences sober was actually her first step in learning how to have more satisfying sex.

In early recovery Mimi was blocked. She found herself unable to date without the facilitation of alcohol. She simply could not think of herself as a sober, sexually active woman. After a while she settled for celibacy and went on with the rest of her life.

One day Mimi attended an academic conference in a nearby city. She felt safe and unpressured in this familiar environment, where she was perceived as competent and confident. "After my presentation this woman came up to me to request a citation. We seemed to have common academic interests, and we exchanged business cards—you know, the usual meaningless "Let's have lunch.""

Several weeks later Sheila came to Mimi's city on business and they planned a dinner meeting. Throughout the evening Mimi felt comfortable and connected, and she enjoyed their easy camaraderie. "Dinner was delightful. We had a lot of shared experiences, and we laughed together over everything. I suddenly realized I was actually having fun with this woman!"

After dinner Sheila expressed her attraction to Mimi. Mimi—much to her surprise—did not immediately respond with fear or a compulsion to control. And she hadn't even been the one to initiate! Mimi was able to stay in the moment and recognize her own attraction to Sheila. She felt comfortable and found herself letting go. For the first time what was happening at the moment was enough.

Sheila ended up going home with Mimi that night. At first Mimi was afraid, but she was able to talk about her fear. "Sheila was able to accept and acknowledge my fear. She gave me the sense that she wanted to continue what had been a wonderful evening, and that she wanted to be close with me whatever my limits. I was so relaxed I actually fell asleep in her arms."

As the weeks progressed and as Mimi became more confident and secure, their relationship became sexual and increasingly passionate. As Mimi's desire increased, her fear diminished. Sheila's playfulness in bed and enjoyment of pleasure without focusing on performance allowed Mimi the possibility of rediscovering her sexual self.

A Safe Environment

Like Mimi, becoming aware of your fear of having sex sober can help you avoid getting into sexual experiences that are anxiety provoking in other ways. If sex is already frightening because you are going to engage in it sober, then it is crucial to reduce your other anxieties about sex.

Start by trying to figure out what makes a sexual experience comforting and secure for you. You may need to know your partner for some time and explore extensive touching before you become more sexual. Or you may want to be sexual only in the bedroom when the children are asleep. You may need to promise yourself that you will never be sexual out of reaction to pressure from your partner.

Being aware of what you need, now that you're sober, will help you get in touch with what makes a sexual situation comfortable for you. Give yourself permission to do whatever makes the sexual experience feel as safe as possible.

"When I got sober," Theresa recalled, "I had no idea it would affect my sex life. I just thought I'd quit drinking and that everything else would stay the same. It came as a rude shock to me to find that I couldn't tolerate going through life the same way any more. Suddenly I had feelings about everything.

"The strangest thing to me was my fear of sex. I just couldn't imagine being sexual with Jeff 'straight.' I hadn't had an orgasm the whole time I'd been with him, but I never let him know. I concentrated on pleasing him, I didn't tell him what I wanted and needed. Hell, I didn't even know myself. I realize now that I didn't get any pleasure out of sex.

"It wasn't Jeff's fault, he tried his best. I just wasn't there. And then the memories of my rape kept coming back. I felt overwhelmingly angry at all men—Bill, my boss, my 'loving' boyfriends—and I took it all out on Jeff.

"Well, once I was sober, I couldn't hide any more. I was there whether I wanted to be or not. And mostly I was there in stark terror."

The Courage to Relearn

As you are sexual sober more and more times, you will learn how to be more and more comfortable with sex in sobriety. Your anxiety will decrease with experience over time. As your body begins to give you clear feedback, you will start to become aware of your sober sexual responses and be better able to predict them. You will learn what pleases you, what feels good, and what you want more of. You will, in fact, relearn how to have sex.

One night when Sarah stopped taking sleeping pills, she was very agitated. She no longer knew how to fall asleep on her own. As she lay awake reading, waiting for Scott to come home, she grew angrier and angrier. At least if he was here we could have sex, she thought, and then I could get some sleep.

The longer she waited, the more she thought how nice that would be. And then she realized that beneath her feelings of agitation she actually did want to have sex. Scott may not be home, she mused, but I am. And suddenly masturbation seemed like a great idea. With only a slight twinge of guilt left over from what her mother would think, she began to learn that she could take care of some of her own needs.

A Second Adolescence

AA folk wisdom says that you stop growing emotionally when you become chemically dependent. On some level, addiction seems to impede sexual development as well as the personal growth process. It's certainly harder to integrate the two while drinking.

In recovery you may feel very young and immature. You may discover that you feel like a teenager sexually, that you don't really know what you want and you don't know what kind of touch feels most arousing. You may feel that you need to experiment sexually in terms of both techniques and partners. Many women in early recovery act out sexually in ways they never did when they were addicted.

Such experiences are not unusual for newly sober women. If you started drinking or using during adolescence, you never had a chance to get to know yourself sexually; your sexual responses were often filtered through a chemical haze.

Now you may need to go through that period of sexual development and experimentation as an adult. You may feel ashamed and embarrassed to find yourself acting like a sixteen-year-old, and you may also feel cheated and angry that you have to go through sexual self-discovery as an adult.

Allow yourself to feel your feelings and to be exactly where you are in the process. Comfort yourself with the fact that although chemical dependence prevented you from learning about yourself sexually, now you can choose to change that. You can do what you need to do to feel safe as you explore your own sexual growth.

Chapter 4

Accepting Your Body

Before going to bed that night, I looked in the mirror above the bathroom sink and when I saw only my face staring back—and that it would always be this ordinary face—I began to cry. Such a sad, ugly girl! I made high-pitched noises like a crazed animal, trying to scratch out the face in the mirror.

And then I saw what seemed to be the prodigy side of me—because I had never seen that face before. I looked at my reflection, blinking so I could see more clearly. The girl staring back at me was angry, powerful. This girl and I were the same. I had new thoughts, willful thoughts, or rather thoughts filled with lots of won'ts. I won't let her change me, I promised myself. I won't be what I'm not.

—Amy Tan, *The Joy Luck Club*

Women's bodies come in all shapes and all sizes. No two are alike. Yet most of us carry an ideal image in our heads, and it's usually one we can never reach. If we're tall we want to be shorter, if we have big breasts we want them to be smaller. Skinny women want to be rounder, muscular women want to be lithe and delicate, delicate women wish they looked sturdier . . .

If you've spent any time in a women's locker room, at an aerobics class, or at a swimming pool, you have probably seen many different kinds of bodies. Most of us can appreciate the infinite variations in physical types and regard them without judgment—as long as we're talking about somebody else's body. When it comes to our own body, we are less accepting. We know exactly where our "bad" points are, and we figure everyone else does too. When someone disagrees with our judgment of our body, we know it's only because they didn't look closely enough.

Our culture, based as it is in Judeo-Christian notions of morality—which instruct that sex is primarily for procreation and mandate that women hide parts of their body in public—holds extremely negative views about the body in general, even though it gives lip service to a more positive image of the body. The traditional Christian view of the body is that it is the source of all temptation and sin, both the sin of the flesh and that of the mind. No one is immune. Rather than being considered a sacred vessel of the divine, the body is seen as a vehicle for the profane, with a relentless potential for sin.

Seventeenth-century scientific rationalism introduced the concept of mind-body dualism that we continue to embrace and that defines the reality of our modern lives. In this view, mind and body are independent entities that only connect via the brain. The mind is seen as the seat of rationality, governing choice, will, and responsibility. In contrast, the body operates by purely mechanical, physical laws, which we can discern, predict, and manipulate with "objective" scientific methods. This view is evident in the "wisdom" of Western medical science: it is a collection of techniques that treats the physical body solely and separate from the thinking and feeling self. Symptoms may be eradicated, physical lives are saved, but as for ideas of healing the whole person or developing treatments for the noncorporeal self, for the mind and the soul— these were discarded three centuries ago.

This culture's prohibition against women knowing their own bodies is extreme. The most basic form of knowing anything, especially ourselves, is to touch. Touching ourselves, and feeling around "down there," has been discouraged for many of us for as long as we can remember. It seems that the only time it is acceptable for us to touch ourselves is if we have toilet paper between our fingers and our skin. Men, curiously, do not receive the same kind of messages, and most are not inhibited at all about touching themselves.

Consider, for example, the difference between what's acceptable for men and women in sports. Whether on the baseball field or the tennis court, men constantly scratch their chests, adjust their jock straps, rub their thighs, and pat each others' behinds. In contrast, a female tennis player rarely touches any part of her body except her face and hair. It is jarring to imagine a female tennis player adjusting her underwear because it's gotten stuck in her crotch. Typically, women do not even play contact sports like football or rugby. Looking at gender differences in sports, and how men and women differ in their behaviors while playing them, we can see one example of the ways in which we are encouraged as women to be disconnected from our bodies.

However we may feel, one thing is undeniably true: Every woman has a body, and every woman has some sense of her physical being and image. Self-acceptance at any level depends in part on accepting our body as it is, not as it isn't. Admiring it and reveling in what it can do rather than focusing on its shortcomings or perceived flaws comes on the heels of this acceptance; it may happen more quickly for some of us than others, again depending on our unique combination of experiences.

If we want to reconnect with the person we are internally, we can't reject bits and pieces as "not okay": we need to begin to accept every part of us. This includes our minds, our spirits, and, yes, our bodies. Without these wonderful vehicles—miracles of movement and pleasure—the rest of us would have no place to live. We need to stop identifying with the "imperfect" parts of our bodies and begin to accept our bodies as inextricable parts of ourselves. They are not the enemy, and getting to know your body is the key to unlocking many other doors.

In my sexuality workshops I have found that most women are chronically dissatisfied with their physical selves and are all too quick to criticize their bodies. They say things like, "My stomach is too flabby," "My breasts are too saggy," "I'm too old for that," or "Maybe if I were ten pounds lighter . . ." Generally, not one woman in the room feels secure enough about her body to want to reveal it.

It is not an overstatement to say that all women in America dislike some part of their bodies. Our negative feelings about our bodies reflect our culture's emphasis on the importance of women's appearance. America's ideal is the slim, smooth, hairless, flawless, airbrushed centerfold, with generous curves permitted only in a few key places. Not even beauty queens totally accept their bodies, and the most beautiful actresses are the ones who keep plastic surgeons in business. The rest of us do our best with clothes and makeup and exercise and diets, but mostly we end up feeling bad about our bodies.

Feeling flawed on the outside leads to feeling undesirable on the inside. We resign ourselves to living lives of longing, settling for less because we secretly fear that we are undesired by others. Our body image has a tremendous impact on the quality of our sexuality. Author Sheila Kitzinger says that "sex has to do with the way we express ourselves though our bodies . . . and from physical well-being springs sexual energy."* If you view yourself as unshapely and unattractive, you will be much more likely to want to have sex late at night, in the dark, and under the covers. And deep down inside you will suspect your lover of cataloging your body faults even as you are making love.

The feeling of being undesirable—and thus, undesired—can gradually change. This change happens as we learn to adjust the messages we give to ourselves and begin to believe we are all desirable in our unique way. It isn't something we need to earn; it doesn't accumulate partner by partner. Our desire and desirability are part of who we are and what we bring to any sexual relationship.

---

*Sheila Kitzinger, *Woman's Experience of Sex* (New York: Viking Penguin, 1985), 27.

Addiction and Body Image

While actively in addiction, many chemically dependent women neglect, ignore, or cover up their bodies. A few, like Danielle, focus on keeping their bodies "perfect" in order to hide their addiction. Women who have been socialized to behave codependently, like Sarah, are often very focused on their bodies and keep themselves looking good, not from a sense of loving their bodies or caring about themselves, but to attract partners. Recovering women need to acknowledge how they feel about their bodies: they need to look at them, decide to accept them, and maybe try to change a little through moderate diet and exercise.

Let's look through the eyes of two women to see how body image is an issue in their lives: Sarah, who is in denial about her dependence on prescription pills, and who wonders about the lack of sex in her marriage; and Paula, who has denied that she has any sexual feelings at all yet is completely preoccupied with her body and its size.

Sarah

Last week Sarah burst into her women's group fifteen minutes after it had started. She dropped into her chair with a rueful grin and apologized for being late, explaining that she had been at her doctor's office getting a prescription. When the women expressed concern that she was sick, she explained, "Oh no, I just had to get a refill for my sleeping pill prescription." The women in her group, some of whom were in recovery from chemical dependency, pursued this explanation, asking her more about her pill use. They were concerned about her possible dependence, even if she wasn't concerned. They prodded Sarah to tell them more. As she spoke, Sarah began to put together some things about her life in ways she never had before—things that she had ignored.

The complex array of the facts of Sarah's life—prescription drug use, poor body image, and unsatisfactory sex—appeared to Sarah to be a tangled web whose strands of connection were ambiguous but strong. Sarah is only beginning to unravel them. As we learned earlier, Sarah's mother regularly took her adolescent daughter to the doctor to get her diet pills—amphetamines—to control her weight. Sarah internalized her mother's concern and tried to get her body to match the images in the magazines.

Recall that Laura, Sarah's mother, had been greatly influenced by the idea that the correct medication would remedy any problem. In the 1950s and 1960s, new drugs like penicillin and a vaccine for polio were seen as miraculous cures; the use of new tranquilizers like Miltown was so prevalent that it showed up in jokes told on the Ed Sullivan Show. Laura always had a well-stocked medicine chest, saved old prescriptions, and carried her stash of pill bottles with her wherever she went. She often gave medicine to Sarah and her brother, Nate, from her supply. She seemed to have something for everything and everyone. Sarah learned to take pills from the time she was a little girl. She thought of it as part of everyone's normal daily activities.

In college, like many students, Sarah continued to use uppers to study for exams, this time obtaining them from her friends. In her first marriage she justified the need for more pills to keep her weight down. As a consequence, she would still be feeling the effects when she went to bed. Often she would be sexually assertive, but her needs didn't come from her own sexual feelings; rather, she was experiencing a chemically induced form of anxiousness that she mistook for feeling sexual. Gratification eluded her. She tried to use the release of sex as a kind of tranquilizer. It didn't work, because it wasn't about a sexual feeling coming from inside. Still, she persisted. She didn't know why, especially because sex never really helped her feel better, or more attractive, or loved.

Now she is in her second marriage. Her husband, Scott, doesn't come to bed until very late. So Sarah doesn't even have the familiar but ineffective relief that she thought sex provided. She has begun to use medication to calm her down at night.

In addition, she has been increasingly anxious over her relationship with Scott. He seems to spend more time at his office or working at home than he does with her. She doesn't feel he notices her, much less tries to find out how she's feeling or what she wants. Her concerns about their conflicts over parenting roles, her hypercritical mother and alcoholic father, his increasing preoccupation with his job, and their almost nonexistent sex life seem never-ending and are all stress producing. Over-the-counter sleeping pills seemed harmless, and until recently, they worked.

Of course they are not harmless. Sarah has developed an addiction. When Scott does come to bed Sarah is too groggy to really wake up. Although she's asked him to wake her, when he finally gets to bed, he can't. If she does awaken, she is prevented from responding by the level of toxic chemicals in her system. She feels isolated, neglected, and unattractive. Scott has given up trying to approach her. He feels that it's just too much work; it doesn't work too well anyway. Neither one of them recognizes that Sarah is addicted and that this is a major component of their sexual difficulties and alienation from each other.

Lately Sarah has found that the four or five pills she had been taking nightly do not provide the effect she used to get with two. She's had to switch to prescription sleeping pills. To make sure she doesn't run out, she gets different prescriptions from her internist, her gynecologist, and even her children's pediatrician.

Sarah suddenly stopped talking as she realized what she had been saying. My God, she thought, how can I be addicted to pills and not even know it? Without another word she collapsed into heaving sobs.

Sarah thought she had been making progress, coping better with her life, and developing a sense of herself. She had recognized her father's alcoholism and was able to see its effect on many different parts of her life. She was working diligently on these issues both in therapy and in her women's group. She couldn't understand why she had not been able to see this before, or how she could have gotten so far along in her cycle of pill dependence.

It's not surprising that Sarah was able to deny her addiction to pills. After all, Laura and Doug were her primary role models. Her mother was self-medicating and always appeared to be in control, presenting a perfect external appearance. It was the family belief that everyone took pills. You got them from your family doctor. Her model for addiction was her alcoholic father, a quiet man who became loud and embarrassing when he'd had too much to drink. Sarah wasn't like that at all. She knew she had some problems . . . she was an adult child of an alcoholic. But she almost never drank, so how could she be an addict?

Sarah is an adult child, trained from childhood to conform her behavior to the expectations of others. So it is not unusual that her focus in her marriage is on Scott, and on pleasing him rather than herself. This includes sex. She couldn't make love and experience the pleasure of her own feelings, because she never knew what they were. Though almost completely unacquainted with or knowledgeable about her own body, she certainly knows how to give Scott what he wants and is ready to cater to his sexual needs if she is awake. Now that they are rarely sexual with each other, however, she can't even do that. She can't focus on Scott, she doesn't know how to value herself, she's using a lot of pills that distort her perceptions, and she's frightened and panicked.

Paula

Paula looked down at her nails, bitten to the quick again. She really hated that about herself, but she did it so unconsciously that she could never seem to stop. Her therapist was asking her about her sexual relationships. She took a moment to consider. "I don't know," she replied, "I honestly don't think I have any sexual feelings." As she said it, she thought about what a strange statement that was.

Paula is a competent medical doctor who prides herself on her ability to help other people heal, yet she is unable to accept or nurture herself. Several years ago, to counteract what she perceived as temporary stresses in her life, she got caught in a tightening knot of addictions: alcohol to reduce the tension, amphetamines to counteract the fatigue, and diuretics and laxatives to keep her from getting "fat." Paula has the characteristics of an incest survivor, but no clear memory of any incest activity.

Paula, a wisp of a woman, has never been in any danger of becoming overweight. Yet she was obsessed with the idea of staying thin and small. At an unconscious level she was trying to prevent herself from becoming a mature woman by refusing to develop and grow into a woman's body. This was a serious problem for her—at one time she nearly died of starvation because she refused to feed herself. Although she is no longer anorexic or chemically dependent, she is still tiny and pale. With her plain straight hair and clothes, she still gives the impression of being more like a child than a professional woman.

Emotionally, Paula has also done everything she can to ensure that she stays childlike. She managed to sidestep most of the ordinary experiences of growing up. Raised in the affluence of southern California, the supposed birthplace of sexual freedom, Paula remained completely untouched by the abundance of sexual messages around her. Her wealthy, alcoholic parents were rarely available physically or emotionally, and they were totally absent as a source of sexual information.

She was ignorant of her own body and was scared when she began to menstruate at age thirteen. Her housekeeper gave her a sanitary pad, and for the next twenty years that's what she used—she never thought about changing brands, and she had no close female friends who might have told her about tampons.

Paula has been living with Tom for three years. This has been her only relationship since she left home. Tom, however, is sixty-four—older than her father—and his sexual energy reflects that of an aging man. This suits Paula's needs, because it allows her to keep up the pretext that she is still a little girl, ignorant and unsullied by sexuality. In addition, on the rare occasions that they "do it," she feels even more like a child because of the contrast between their ages and levels of energy.

Paula has channeled all of her life force into her intellectual and professional life, cutting herself off from her body and its needs. Paula's task now is to reconnect with her sexuality and give birth to herself as a woman. To do that she needs to get a sense of her body and then to grow into it, grow up, and assume the power of choice that she has a right to claim as an adult woman.

It is a big step for Paula to understand the extent to which she has been disconnected from her sexuality. She has been in psychotherapy two times a week for two years, trying very hard to understand her needs and to learn to nurture herself. She has begun to grow and change in the process. Paula is beginning to discuss with her therapist the need to bring her sexuality to life. She knows this is what she wants, but knowing it intellectually is just the beginning. She must continue to work on learning to feel—a long leap from thinking about feeling.

Paula is scared. It is time to let go, to grow up, to become a woman. At thirty-three, she thinks wryly to herself, it's about time I tried.

Learning About Your Body

This chapter offers some practical techniques for making friends with your body. The mirror exercise that follows is a good first step toward self-acceptance.

Find a time when you are alone and undisturbed. Take off your clothes, including your jewelry, and stand naked in front of a full-length mirror. Use a hand mirror or a second full-length mirror to see your back.

If you find the idea of looking at yourself naked a bit scary, you're not alone. Many women find it difficult to look at their bodies without the camouflage of clothes. Many others look carefully only at their hair and faces, and glance quickly over the rest. Keep trying, and be patient with yourself.

Paula's therapist suggested that she try this exercise. On her first attempt she spent half an hour working up the nerve to take her clothes off, knowing she would then have to look at herself "unarmed" in a mirror. When she did finally get them off, she was able to look at herself only for a few seconds. Her heart was beating wildly and she honestly thought she might faint.

When she described her experience to her therapist, she was gently reminded to start slowly and be easy with herself, beginning with one part of her body at a time and extending that area a little bit each day. As she followed her therapist's suggestion, Paula felt considerably less threatened. After several months she was able to look at her body in the mirror without flinching. She recognized it; she found that it could look different depending on the light, the shadows, and how she stood. Most important, she began to connect how she viewed her body with what she was thinking about or what she was feeling.

This was a revelation, a real breakthrough in understanding. Paula's body—and how it looked to her—did have a relationship to the "rest" of Paula. They were irrevocably connected.

When you have begun to try to look at your body without repulsion and without concentrating on some alleged imperfection, you are ready for the next step: to begin to accept your body. Once you have some idea of how you look, let go of the need to chastise yourself for what you think are "ripply" thighs, "tiny" breasts, or a "scrawny" neck. Take a calm, objective, nonjudgmental breath. Say aloud to your reflection in the mirror, "You're fine. I like you just the way you are. This is okay. This body's okay."

Now go slowly over your body, expressing love to every part, as you would to the body of a beloved child. First do it verbally: thank your body for being there, express appreciation for what it does for you. For example, you may thank your feet for helping you to walk and run and dance. You may thank your neck for allowing you to look behind you. You may thank your spine for allowing you to bend over. You may thank your breasts for allowing you to distinguish yourself as female, for giving you sexual pleasure, for feeding your baby.

Paula was able to do this portion of the exercise for only a few moments before she felt overwhelmed. She had never given herself any love or nurturing, and she found it almost unbearable. She was, however, a woman of great determination. As she kept practicing over the passing months, she actually came to look forward to her time with herself. The pain of really being with herself gave way to anticipation of this new ritual she had claimed for herself.

One day Paula's therapist mentioned that Paula's presence had changed—she seemed more substantial, more powerful. Paula nodded her head in rapid agreement. "I know this is going to sound crazy," she said, "but I think I always lived in a two-inch square, right at the front of my forehead. The rest of me might not have been there at all, for all I cared. Now I actually have a sense of myself as a three-dimensional person. I'm aware of myself from the front and the back at the same time. I can feel the wind blow all around me when I walk down the street."

Loving our bodies is a difficult task for most women. You may have days when you are satisfied with how you look and days when you despair over having to look at yourself at all, much less of ever accepting your reflection with love. On these days it is important to remind yourself that these feelings are natural; many of us have spent years emotionally disconnected from our bodies. We are not encouraged to do otherwise. Learning to love yourself is a progression over time. After you are able to really look at your whole self naked in the mirror—for the first time without dismay and disappointment—gradually you may feel a sense of familiarity and tolerance, maybe even reassurance. Finally the acceptance and love for your body—as you now know it and feel about it—will develop: this is a major step toward sexual recovery, one that you have made happen.

If you would like to take this exercise a step further, you can begin to make friends with the inside of your body. Lie down and close your eyes, and begin to feel what's happening inside of you.

Feel your breath moving in and out. Feel how it fills your lungs and empties out again. Feel your chest rising and falling. Feel the beat of your heart. Listen for the sound it makes as it pumps blood throughout your body. Feel your blood circulating to every part of you, keeping you alive and vital. Give your body your appreciation for doing this all by itself, without needing any help at all from your conscious mind.

Many of us are not able to accept our bodies overnight, but eventually, with practice, we will begin to appreciate and even enjoy our uniqueness. You don't have to change your body to feel good about yourself. You can decide to accept your body, feel okay about it, and be grateful, knowing it is precious just the way it is.

What About Your Genitals?

Many of us struggle to find a proper way to talk about our genitals. We have slang words that males use—pussy, cunt, beaver, box, hole—but these words have an offensive edge that leaves women feeling embarrassed, uneasy, angry, ashamed, or like a commodity. We also have technically correct words—vulva, labia majora, vagina, clitoris—but these are medical-sounding terms, so clinical that they may actually serve to distance us from our genitals. Some women have resorted to euphemisms and flowery terms—inner flute, labia flower, Mound of Venus—which may sound contrived and function to cover up the physical aspects of our genitals. Recently, some women have begun to use the word *yoni* (yo-nee), a Sanskrit term associated with beautiful erotic paintings from India, in order to have a word that feels both positive and warm.

Our society doesn't offer us positive images of female genitals. People may laughingly call the Washington Monument a phallic symbol, but the term *phallic symbol* has a positive ring to it that suggests power and assertion. Skylines of major cities, such as one finds in Manhattan and Chicago, are virtually filled with monuments extolling the symbolic phallus, their high-rises stretching endlessly into the sunset. The softer, rounder, more complex images of female genitalia aren't reflected in such landscapes.

We are so used to seeing these forms that it may come as a surprise to discover that the masculine emphasis in art and architecture is a relatively recent historical event. Exciting new archaeological research reports that a thriving female-centered culture flourished for many thousands of years in Neolithic Europe, about 25,000 years ago. In her book *The Language of the Goddess,* the respected archaeologist Marija Gimbutas

includes photographs and drawings of nearly two thousand symbolic artifacts from this era based on the female form and specific genitalia*.
These artifacts served every area of life, from pottery to decoration and
even to burial. For example, according to Gimbutas, Irish Neolithic
tombs, called "court cairn" tombs, "show that the 'court' is the space between the Goddess's open legs; the corridors or chambers beyond are
her vagina and uterus." These are among hundreds of similar tombs discovered worldwide, evidence that the shapes and images of women's
bodies once influenced the most fundamental forms of civilization.

As patriarchal cultures became dominant, however, these images
faded and were replaced by images based on the external female form.
The women we are used to seeing in art are the naked Greek goddesses,
the sensual odalisques, and other "alluring" females, such as virgins, an-
gels, and slave girls. It is only in scientific textbooks that we see drawings
of female genitals, and then the labels do not explain the role of the various parts in the sexual experience. In the twentieth century, Georgia
O'Keeffe's paintings of flowers became metaphors for female genitals,
and they carry a powerful message because of this bold connection
made by a woman about a decidedly female image.

If we don't know what our genitals look like or what to call them,
and the very thought of them makes us blush, it is not surprising that we
have a difficult time enjoying ourselves as sexual creatures. "Touch me
here, don't touch me there" may be about as specific as we can get. And
if we don't want to or cannot look at ourselves, we're not going to be
comfortable with a lover looking at us. Nor is it easy to seek out or create
spaces where we feel sexual all by ourselves.

Many women have never looked at their own genitals. As young
girls, curious about their genitals as they are about other parts of their
bodies, some women may have done some self-exploration. Yet frequently we learn early in life that this is not permissible, and so we don't

---

*Marija Gimbutas, *The Language of the Goddess* (San Francisco: Harper & Row, 1989), 154.

do it or we feel guilty when we do. Then there are the messages we hear from advertisers: that we need a douche or deodorant spray and that panty liners keep us "fresh." Many women begin to acknowledge this part of their body for the first (and maybe the only) time during pregnancy and when giving birth.

I recently read a letter to an advice column in the newspaper from a woman who said one of her labia was twice as big as the other. She complained bitterly that this had ruined her life. She was so ashamed of this "defect" that she didn't want anyone to see her, and as a consequence she had absolutely no sex life. She was becoming increasingly obsessed with this size difference in her genitals, to the degree that she wanted to have plastic surgery to "make them perfect."

Clearly, like many women, this woman had never seen another woman's genitals. Men see each other's penises in gym class and public bathrooms, comparing size and shape. But women's toilets have doors; women wear layers of underclothes; women are taught to be defensively modest, especially with other women. The woman in the column did not know—and had no way of knowing—that the same variation that occurs among other body parts also occurs among female genitals. For example, most people have one foot that is slightly larger than the other, and no one's ears are in perfect symmetry. Some women have breasts of two different cup sizes. Certainly no two noses are alike. Why would our genitals be any different? The truth is that female genitals come in different sizes, shapes, and colors.

Because we have so little access to the variety of female genitalia, we tend to take some textbook drawing as the only possible way a woman can look, or the way every woman should ideally look. An excellent antidote is Betty Dodson's series of graphic and informative drawings in the book *Sex for One: The Joy of Selfloving* (see appendix C). Looking at the variations in these drawings and then looking at your own genitals is an excellent way to begin to appreciate the beauty of your own body and its uniqueness.

Exploring Your Genitals

Do this exercise when you are alone and feel safe and undisturbed. You can approach it with two objectives: to see what's there and to feel what happens when you touch various parts of yourself.

For this exercise you will need a hand mirror and a flashlight. Sit propped on your bed with pillows behind your back and your knees bent and open. You may want to put pillows under your knees to help you maintain this position comfortably.

Begin by looking at your genital area when you're not excited. How many different parts can you see? Can you name them? Do you know what their function is physically and sexually? Refer to one of the books listed in appendix C if you need help answering these questions. Do this exercise once a week for a month; and if you are a premenopausal woman, begin to notice how your genitals change as your menstrual cycle progresses. Relax and enjoy your exploration of this exciting new world within you.

Because Paula is a medical doctor, she was familiar with the technical aspects of the female anatomy and its function. Yet she was genuinely surprised to realize that she had never connected this academic information with her own body. When she looked into her own vagina she had the feeling of looking at a completely unknown world.

Paula looked at herself with utter fascination. She noticed that the outer lips were a light, purply pink, and smooth, while the inner lips were redder—like a blushing cheek, she thought. And so wrinkly! As she did this week after week, she noticed that sometimes she was dry, and sometimes more moist, according to where she was in her cycle.

It was some time before she was able to touch herself. She was horribly embarrassed, even though she was alone. Paula was so disconnected from her body that she had no conscious memory of ever touching herself, except when she washed herself or wiped after urination.

As she began to touch herself, she found herself pulling her finger away instantly. She felt guilt and shame—the remnants of early childhood messages. Slow down, she told herself, slow down. You can do this. *It is okay to do this.*

She touched each part gently—the outer lips, the inner lips, the clitoris, the vaginal opening—and tried to notice how each felt. She began to ask herself questions: Is it slippery? No, more like a petal, dry and smooth. Oh, that's kind of bumpy. I wonder if it's always like that?

When she was able to relax, Paula began to notice how the rest of her body felt when she touched each area. Touching her vagina, her clitoris, the inner and outer lips—each gave her a slightly different and unique sensation. It certainly felt different than when Tom did it. This, she began to think, might even be pleasant.

Giving Yourself Sexual Pleasure

If you had trouble with the last part of that exercise, read on. You'll see that you're not alone.

Most women in recovery, and codependent women in particular, have spent their whole lives trying to figure out what other people want. They pay little or no attention to what they want for themselves in much of their lives, let alone when it comes to their own sexual needs, fantasies, or desires.

Again, denial works in many ways here to undermine our knowledge of ourselves. We may deny we have sexual feelings, we may fake orgasms. We may emphasize the physical activity of sex with no connection to our emotional self. We have no model for growth or understanding. Just getting a partner to "do it" to us or with us is supposed to be enough, but the rest doesn't take care of itself. When we ask ourselves what satisfies us sexually, we genuinely may not know.

The ability to give ourselves sexual pleasure is an important part of developing positive feelings about ourselves as sexual beings. We all had different childhood experiences concerning touching ourselves. Sarah, as we have seen, never let her hand stray "down there." Danielle, in contrast, had discovered the joys of her clitoris by the time she was three. Mimi didn't really discover her sexual self until college. And Theresa understood only what it meant to satisfy men.

Some women would like to masturbate but feel guilty even thinking about it. In fact, one study showed that half of the women who said they masturbated felt guilty about it.

In the 1970s, researcher Shere Hite asked three thousand women whether they masturbated regularly, and 82 percent answered affirmatively. Only 62 percent of the women that Kinsey interviewed in the late 1940s reported that they masturbated, so the numbers of women exploring their own touch may be increasing. But these figures still contrast strongly with the more than 90 percent of men who report they masturbate at least weekly. It may be that men masturbate more because they have reasons to touch themselves daily: they hold their penises to urinate, they adjust their testicles to fit into their underwear, and they see their genitals when they undress.

Historically, women have received many negative messages about masturbation. We may be told that any sexual activity not aimed at reproduction is a sin, or that masturbation is really self-abuse. Some religions believe that masturbation is a carnal activity that debases your moral character or fiber. These kinds of ideas seem to affect women more than men. We are also told that masturbation is only for women without partners. It's something you do as a last resort, and even then it's "abnormal."

I've heard women express the fear that if they masturbate, they won't want partnered sex, even though most women have plenty of sexual energy for both masturbation and partnered sexual activity. The causes of dissatisfaction when having sex with a partner generally have more to do with the quality of the relationship than with whether or how often one of the partners masturbates.

By contrast, the reasons to masturbate are few but powerful: One, it feels good. And two, the more you know about how your body responds, the more you know what you like. This can help you to help your partner give you pleasure. There are other reasons to masturbate: it can provide a good release for vague anxieties, it can help you relax for sleep, it is good for your fantasy life, it is a good way to love yourself, and it is fun to see what happens.

Most women who masturbate reach orgasm, and many times those orgasms are physically more powerful than an orgasm experienced with a partner. This is because no one else knows your body as well as you do, and no one but you can know what you are feeling from moment to moment. There is no one else's pleasure to think about and distract you. If you don't like what you're feeling, you can stop or change immediately. If you're pressing too hard, you can lighten up. If you need to go more slowly or quickly, you can. And you don't have to waste a moment agonizing over or negotiating how to explain it to your partner.

Most women are physiologically able to experience orgasm, but many have not had the kind of stimulation that can bring them to orgasm. Women who have been alcoholic or chemically dependent have probably had a depressed sexual response and need to learn that they can have a satisfying sexual experience. Women who have been sexually abused may also experience conflict and have difficulty with sexual pleasure and orgasm. For them, sexual pleasure is often associated with guilt and shame. The capacity to trust and enjoy is severely threatened. Sex and sexual impulses may even feel dangerous for women who have been abused, but these women can learn to feel safe again.

Masturbation is the best way to begin to reconnect with your sexual responses. Masters and Johnson found that the orgasms produced by self-stimulation occurred more dependably and more rapidly, and were of greater physical intensity, than those achieved through stimulation by a partner, although the experience of sharing sexual intimacy with someone else may be more emotionally and physically satisfying. Thus, by stimulating yourself gently and with care, you can learn how you respond to different forms of touch. If you have had abusive sexual experiences, it is very important to be particularly gentle and caring with yourself.

Conscious Masturbation

Begin the touching exercise described in the last section, but this time do it while you masturbate. Stop at various points and look at yourself. Notice how the color changes with arousal, note the engorgement of both your inner and outer lips. You may notice an increase in lubrication. Does it feel different in consistency? You will be able to see when your clitoris enlarges and becomes erect, then later retracts and becomes hidden.

When Danielle began this exercise, she thought, this won't be hard for me at all. She had been masturbating with orgasms—multiples, even—for many years, and knew how to stimulate herself. But as she began to touch herself with the awareness required by this exercise, she was surprised to find that there were many aspects of giving herself pleasure that she had been ignoring.

She had always concentrated on getting to the orgasmic release as quickly as possible. Now Danielle began to enjoy the sensuality of her skin, touching and stroking her breasts, her stomach, her hips, teasing her own body as she might that of a lover. At the same time she discovered that areas other than her clitoris were also sensitive, and she gave attention to these as well—gently massaging the rim of her vaginal opening, brushing her hand lightly over her pubic hair.

After several months she grew to know her responses in a way that amazed her. She learned that right before her period started she felt really sexy; the slightest touch brought her exquisite pleasure. But the first few days following her period she was sometimes unable to achieve orgasm. Her body seemed to need time to build its reserves of feeling. She was fascinated with the new depth of her sexual response, and she began to share her knowledge with lovers. As she became able to please herself, and able to ask others to please her, she began to open the door to the fullness of sexual experience she had missed for so long. Finally, her physical pleasure had connected to her feelings.

Unlike Danielle, who came to this exercise with enthusiasm and experience, Paula had never had an orgasm. She had only recently learned that she could have any pleasurable sensation about herself connected with her body, much less one from her genitals. When her therapist informed her that masturbation is the best way for preorgasmic women to learn how to have an orgasm, she was frightened. She had learned to look at her body in the mirror, and even to accept what she saw. She had learned to touch her genitals. But those seemed like clinical exercises. This was much more threatening. She was beginning to feel uncomfortable about the time she was spending with her own body.

Like Paula, you may need to deal with feelings of repulsion about masturbation before you are able to move toward a more satisfying sexuality that includes orgasm. Or you may need to work through old feelings of guilt and shame. Three good books about orgasm and masturbation are Betty Dodson's *Sex for One: The Joy of Selfloving,* Lonnie Barbach's *For Yourself: The Fulfillment of Female Sexuality,* and *Becoming Orgasmic: A Sexual Growth Program for Women,* by Julia Heiman, Leslie LoPiccolo, and Joseph LoPiccolo (see appendix C). Each of these books talks about techniques that are used in groups conducted for preorgasmic women.

When you learn how to bring yourself to orgasm, you can take responsibility for your own pleasure. To interact more knowledgeably with your partners while pleasuring one another means having this sense of what feels good or not so good, a sense that allows you to feel connected to your body and your feelings. When your partners no longer have to guess at what you're in the mood for, and are relieved of the full responsibility of satisfying you sexually, they too are freed up to be more experimental and more responsive. When you know what excites you and what brings you to orgasm, you can begin to communicate this clearly to your partners. This greatly increases your potential to have a satisfying sexual relationship and enhances the connections of your mind, body, genitals, and emotions.

PART TWO

ACTIONS:
THE OUTER JOURNEY

Just as the inner journey of early recovery requires us to be honest about our thoughts and feelings, the outer journey requires us to look honestly at the patterns of our relationships and sexual interactions. Although it may seem easier to explore our patterns of behavior, it is often very difficult and painful to acknowledge what has happened and what is happening in our lives today. We need to take this process step by step, recognizing that self-care during this process is recovery in action. The following are some of the issues we must address:

1. Exploring childhood and family sexual issues. How did your family deal with sexual issues? How did they talk or not talk about sexual issues? What did they call things? How did they explain things?

2. Honestly naming the sexual events of your personal past. This includes developing your own history and naming the events accurately.

3. Looking at your own sexual behaviors, including charting the sexual/chemical lifeline. How did your sexual experience and chemical dependencies influence and interact with each other?

4. Looking at your selection of sexual partners. Who have you been sexual with and why? What were the characteristics of the relationship?

5. Learning to live in the present. This is absolutely essential to sexuality.

Chapter 5

Exploring
Sexual Behavior Patterns

Self-knowledge is the subtlest art of all. This is forced upon
us sooner or later and the more we evade the issue the more
layers will we have to penetrate before we reach the core.
—Malvina Hoffman, *Heads and Tales*

The outer journey of sexual recovery involves looking at our lives from a
fresh perspective. Now the inner work we have done bears real fruit: we
are capable of seeing more and of being more honest with ourselves
about what we see. Our understanding of our past actions and present
interactions continues to deepen as our recovery unfolds. As denial
melts away, we begin to understand the motivations behind our past actions and to see what we can do today to nurture sexual growth and expansion.

Emerging Patterns

Patterns of sexual behavior that you were only dimly aware of in early
recovery will now begin to emerge with greater clarity. Looking honestly at your sexual past is absolutely essential to sexual recovery. Only
when you can see the patterns in your sexual relationships can you begin to understand them and change. In recovery there is a link between
seeing and understanding who you have been in relationship to others,

and growing into who you want to be sexually. Without looking honestly at where you have been and where you are now, you will not be able to choose who you want to become. Understanding the past is crucial to creating the kind of life you want.

You may find many reasons to avoid looking at your sexual history. Over and over again, in both group counseling and private sessions, I've heard female clients express these reasons for avoidance:

- "My old life is over and done with. What's the point of stirring up old memories?"
- "My past hasn't affected me. Anyway, I'm starting fresh now."
- "I'm clean and sober now, and my past sexual actions were part of my addiction—why should I look at them?"
- "My life is too stressful now. I'll look at my sexual relationships later, when I'm feeling more stable."
- "My life is finally getting comfortable. Looking at my sexual patterns will just bring on more pain."

All these reasons boil down to one: denial. We deny that our sexual past has the power to affect our present sexual behavior. We deny that understanding how we've been formed allows us to change. With that denial, however, we also deny ourselves the future possibility of sexual freedom and choice.

Theresa had great difficulty accepting that there was a pattern of abuse in her adult relationships. Her story illustrates how long it can take us to be willing to see patterns in our relationships, especially if they threaten the sense of self we've built so carefully.

Theresa resisted talking about her sexual past in therapy. She had taken great pains to construct an image of herself as confident, bright, and articulate, and she was shocked to hear her therapist apply the world "abusive" to her relationships. "I hated the idea," she said later. "I couldn't stand the thought of being an abused woman. My image of an abused woman was a weak, weepy sack who couldn't stand up for herself. It felt like my whole sense of myself as strong and independent was under attack."

Talking about her sexual patterns brought up painful material that had been buried for many years. "It was hard enough dealing with my childhood incest experiences; I didn't want to have to start thinking of my adult relationships in a similar light. I almost left therapy, I was so upset."

Theresa had used alcohol and drugs since adolescence to avoid facing the reality of the abusive patterns of her life, and to give herself confidence. Now that she was clean and sober, the bleakness of her relationships felt overwhelming. "I just couldn't accept that I wasn't the strong person I thought I was. It took me months before I could say out loud that my relationships with my boyfriends and my first husband had been abusive."

Once these old memories and experiences began to surface, without being filtered through chemicals, Theresa experienced their full impact. Between therapy sessions she began to have anxiety attacks and flashbacks about her rape, especially during sex.

"I know it's hard on Jeff, but he tries to be supportive of my therapy and recovery." Theresa visibly relaxes as she marvels at this fact. "I'm incredibly lucky to have him, especially given the men who came before. I know my situation bothers him, but he's still able to be gentle and comforting when I have the flashbacks. I can share my feelings of pain with him. He's the first man I've ever told about early childhood experiences.

"No more will I choose someone who feels good by putting me down. I finally feel free to choose someone who's good for me, someone not at all like my mother's boyfriend, who only wanted to use me, to hurt me."

Theresa's willingness to finally look at her relationships as an adult woman and see their connection to her incest experiences was the key: this attitude and the ensuing process enabled her to develop and maintain a healthier relationship. Only when she had the courage to be honest and tell the truth, naming her past as what it was—violent and abusive—could she sustain a growing relationship with Jeff.

Acknowledging your sexual history can be painful. Looking at the patterns in your sexual interactions may bring up a multitude of feelings you may not be able to anticipate and don't want to have. Even so, I cannot overemphasize the importance of taking a clear-eyed look at your sexual past. It will help you move on to a healthier future. It requires a measure of faith, a leap of sorts—in yourself, in the process, and in the resilience of your inner self.

Childhood and Family Sexual Issues

The first task of the outer journey in early recovery is to seek out the truth of your early childhood and family sexual experiences. Your sexuality, which includes your most basic ideas of what sex is and what it means, was formed in the crucible of your early family experiences. Here you began to absorb the messages about sex that stayed with you the rest of your life. But in early recovery you can begin to bring those messages out of your unconscious, make them explicit, look at your beliefs about sexuality, and recognize where you got them.

Memories

Begin with your memories. Remember and say aloud what you experienced related to sexuality in childhood. The behaviors and attitudes of your parents, grandparents, aunts, and uncles have greatly influenced your feelings about your body, your sexuality, and your relationships. Recalling those behaviors and attitudes and being specific about particular incidents will lead to more memories and insights about the connections between your family's attitudes and your own.

If you are not in therapy or in a women's group, writing in a personal journal may be your first step toward acknowledging the role sexuality played in your family. Ask yourself some specific questions, for example: How did your parents express their sexuality toward each other? Were they affectionate in front of you? Did Dad make jokes about how hard it was to get Mom into bed? Did Mom act as if sex were a burden she had to endure? What did your parents say when cousin Bill "had" to get married? How did they treat his new wife? What did they say about Aunt Pat, who'd lived with a woman "friend" for forty years? What didn't they say?

Your answers to these sorts of questions will begin to create a rich picture of the sexual messages you received and how they were conveyed. Now go deeper and explore the emotional tone. Were sexual messages expressed as warnings and admonitions, or were they more implicit, contained in silences and holes in the conversation? Remember how you felt during these times.

You may not be able to remember anything about sexuality in your family. When you try to remember when you first learned about intercourse, for example, you may draw a blank. This inability to remember is a strong message in itself. Many women who can't remember any childhood family sexual experiences later discover that they had experienced a family sexual trauma. Forgetting painful experiences such as incest is the way we protect ourselves as children from emotional events we are too vulnerable to handle. As adults, however, we can develop the strength to remember and confront these events.

If you were sexually abused, or suspect you might have been, individual therapy is indicated. Seek out a counselor who is experienced in working with repressed sexual trauma and knows how to help clients recover from childhood abuse. Often women's centers and women's treatment programs can recommend therapists who are skilled in this area. A skilled therapist can help you recover your past and help you to emerge empowered rather than devastated. This will allow you to move further along the path.

Checking with Other Family Members

Talking to your brothers and sisters about what they remember experiencing as children can be helpful. You can ask them how they recall Mom and Dad talking about sex; how they perceived the way Mom and Dad touched each other; how Mom and Dad responded to the children's adolescent sexuality; and how the family handled their sex education. You may get validation of your own feelings, and you will certainly get insights into how others in your family experienced a similar situation. Or you may not even recognize the characters in their memories, because their perceptions or experiences were so different.

In some circumstances, however, it may not be helpful to talk to your siblings about their childhood sexual experiences. If they are actively drinking or using, if they are actively codependent and invested in their own denial, if they molested you as a child, or if you were molested by a parent and your siblings are unwilling to accept that fact, it is important to think carefully about this step. You may choose not to talk to your siblings because you are not ready to talk about your own molestation by a family member with another family member.

It will probably not be helpful to talk to a parent who is still drinking, using drugs, or interacting codependently with the other partner or with you. But talking to a nondrinking, nonusing, noncodependent parent may be enlightening. Your parents may find it easier to reveal their discomfort and uneasiness about sex and the way they raised you now that your childhood is over. They may even feel remorseful about their sexual attitudes and how they passed them on. They may welcome the opportunity to express their retroactively felt dissatisfaction with their own child-rearing practices, and they may share in greater detail how they themselves were raised.

Sometimes the value of talking to a parent is not in getting validation or information, but in the process itself. Being direct, candid, and assertive can be an important lesson regardless of the response.

Your goal in talking to your parents about their sexual attitudes when you were a child is to learn more about the sources of your sexual beliefs. If you enter a conversation with expectations about changing your parents' beliefs, you will probably be disappointed. If you expect an apology for what you regard as their harmful attitudes during your childhood, you probably won't get it. But if you earnestly desire to learn more about the sexual climate in your parents' home, you may come away from the conversation understanding more about your own sexual attitudes and where they come from. The ability to communicate with others about these attitudes will function as a key to your own understanding, acceptance, and growth.

For several weeks Danielle's women's group had been discussing sexual attitudes and how they were formed by the family. Danielle had always believed that she and her mother, Marianne, had no sexual secrets, but now she began to realize there was a lot she didn't know about her. She was especially curious about Marianne's childhood experiences with sexuality.

"My mom gave me all the information we needed—she even took me to the gynecologist to get birth control pills in high school," Danielle said with a laugh. "She and my dad were always fondling each other in front of us kids and talking about their sex life at dinner. So I learned that sex was permissible.

"But they never talked much about love, or commitment, and now that I think about it they never just hugged for the hell of it. Their affection always had some sort of sexual reference."

Because Marianne had always been so open, Danielle thought it would be easy for her to talk about her own sexual experiences. She was surprised at how angry Marianne became as the story poured out of her.

Marianne and her two sisters had been raised in a small town in Kansas as strict Fundamentalists. There was no dancing, no singing, and life was very serious. Her father was a factory foreman, her mother was a full-time housewife. Both parents were hardworking God-fearing people who didn't talk much about anything, and never about sex.

Marianne's mother protected her daughters from what she saw as a dangerous world. She viewed sex as a duty that women were supposed to get through as quickly as possible. "She wouldn't allow me to date until I was sixteen," Marianne recalled bitterly, "and then she only wanted me to go out with boys from our church. She constantly monitored where I was going and what I was doing." Danielle shivered when she tried to imagine her mother's gray, somber life as a girl, depleted of any warmth or pleasure in connection to sex or sexual impulses. "How in the world did you finally break away?"

"When I went to college, I rebelled with a vengeance. It was the 1960s, and it seemed like you could do whatever you wanted. I started smoking pot and being sexual all at once. My sexuality just seemed to explode. It was so intoxicating to be out from under her watchful eye. The drugs and the sex were part of the landscape.

"I felt guilty and angry and happy all at once. When you came along, all I knew was that I wanted you to know that sex was okay, that your body was okay, that pleasure was okay. I was trying so hard to get away from all that God stuff, sin and hell and damnation. I guess I made a real point that your body's pleasure was all that mattered, because deep inside I wasn't so sure. I still think about what my mother would say if she were alive to see me, or if she had known the truth about what I got into."

Marianne's conflict between her rigid upbringing and her permissive life-style made her uncomfortable with her own sexuality. Permissiveness and repression are unsatisfactory alternatives; these two ends of the spectrum leave out all the subtle nuances in between. Marianne happily gave her daughter the technical, body-oriented information she had been denied, but she shied away from questions about feelings, because she had no answers. She seemed to say, "Ask me anything," but she was also projecting the attitude, "Don't get too close."

Danielle came away from the conversation with a deeper understanding of her family's approach to sexuality. "I always thought our family was so hip, so free. My mother seemed as though she was being very open, very liberated about sex. Now I see that is only partly true—I see her more clearly."

Danielle felt shaken by this realization, but it allowed her to see why the emotional content seemed to be missing from her sexual relationships. "In my mind sex and making love have become two distinct things. Sex is more mechanical and making love is, well, making love. I feel like in sex there's something left out. It's a flatter experience than making love."

Dysfunctional Sexuality in Family Life

Sexual problems don't exist in isolation; they are a symbol of the lack of wholeness within the family. A healthy family includes a certain level of affection and explicitly sexual energy detectable between parents or other adults. When the family no longer functions at a healthy level, sex will be affected. This lack of healthy sexual functioning indicates a lack of integration in the family system.

Because sexuality is so polarized, distorted, and emotionally overladen in American society, it's unlikely that your parents' child-rearing practices related to sex—however well meaning—were always positive. For example, in reaction to her own repressive childhood experiences, Danielle's mother wanted to make her daughter's childhood different. Taking her daughter to get birth control was realistic; teenage Danielle was sexually active and needed to know about birth control. But she also needed to know about the emotional aspects of sexual involvement, and that was information Marianne was unable to provide.

Like Sarah, you may have grown up in a family that gave you incomplete and confusing information about your sexual development and what you could expect during sexual experiences. Your parents may have been less oblique, withholding information about sex but telling you repeatedly to cover your body, and you may have internalized feelings of shame about your body parts as exposed liabilities. Women who experienced constant criticism about how they looked as teenagers often become self-conscious about their appearance as adults and view themselves as objects in continual need of repair.

You may have been made to feel ashamed for having sexual feelings, even as a very young child. One woman told me, "One day my mother found me playing doctor with my friend Eileen. It was all pretty innocent—we were only four years old—but she beat the living daylights out of me and never let me play with Eileen again."

Adults in your family may have made inappropriate sexual remarks to you, been overtly sexual in your presence, or invaded your boundaries by asking you about your sexual experiences. An adult family member may even have touched you in a sexual manner or forced you to be sexual, as Theresa's mother's boyfriend did. These events can have different effects on different women, again depending on other facts unique to each woman's life.

Or your family may have ignored any outward signs of sexuality entirely, never hugging or displaying physical affection in front of you. One client told me, "My parents had separate beds, separate bed tables, separate lamps. The beds were always perfectly made, as if no one had ever slept in them. I can't imagine how they ever got close enough to one another to conceive me!" Growing up in this kind of family can lead a child to think that "normal" sexuality means *no* sexuality.

All of these are examples of how developing sexuality can be distorted by families with varying degrees of dysfunction. Many otherwise constructive, healthy families simply falter when it comes to sex. It is a powerful, difficult issue. As family life deteriorates, sexuality is one of the first areas to suffer. Healthy sexual functioning requires honesty, clear communication, and intimacy. It is an integral part of a healthy family system.

The Violation of Physical and Emotional Space

One of the most common traits of the dysfunctional family is the absence of healthy boundaries—those physical and emotional barriers that separate us from others and from the world. Boundaries say, "This is where you end and I begin."

When someone stands too close to you for comfort, you feel that your physical boundaries have been violated. You may keep stepping back to get the right amount of distance for your comfort. Emotional boundaries operate in the same way. For example, you may feel emotionally violated when someone tells you that you shouldn't feel the way you do.

Boundaries are about limits and protection; we need firm boundaries to define us and prevent our merging with others in sacrifice of our selfhoods. If your boundaries have been violated repeatedly, you will probably have problems with setting limits. And others seem to be able to sense this overly permeable state; perhaps this contributes to how we get into unhealthy relationships.

In most dysfunctional families, physical boundaries are either overly rigid or enmeshed. Rigid boundaries are like walls between parents and children. "No one ever touched in my family," one woman told me sadly. "When my parents hugged or kissed me, it felt like a duty. Remember the invisible shield they used to talk about on toothpaste commercials? That's how it was with my parents and affection—like there was an invisible shield between us." The lack of communication in this woman's family left her feeling distant, isolated, and lonely. As an adult she felt really safe only when she was disengaged and shut down emotionally. She had great difficulty learning how to be intimate.

Families with enmeshed or overly permeable boundaries, like Sarah's, produce children who don't know where they end and others begin. Parents with a blurred, unclear sense of their own and others' boundaries behave in overly intrusive ways. This engenders an unhealthy form of closeness and intensity of feeling. One client told me, "My mother was a psychologist, so you'd think she would have known better. She always wanted to know what I was thinking, what I was feeling. And then she'd analyze my thoughts and explain that I wasn't crabby because I was coming down with a cold, but because I was avoiding my feelings! It felt like she was always inside my head. She imposed her own version of reality onto me, instead of validating and respecting what I was experiencing." Children raised in such families don't know how to define their limits and are unable to protect their rights. They lack a healthy sense of separateness and individuality that might enable them to know and to say what feels okay and what doesn't. Such children grow into adults who unconsciously violate others' boundaries and allow others to violate theirs.

Sexual boundaries are often blurred in the dysfunctional family. Parents may be intrusive and rigid at the same time. Teenagers may lack privacy in the bathroom, yet at the same time be forced to submit to unrealistic regulations about dating. Parents may express horror at inadvertent nudity, yet tolerate inappropriate touch; some will touch each other and their children with utter impunity. According to one client, "When I was twelve my father was always making remarks about my breasts—that they were bouncing around and I should wear a bra. It was really embarrassing and made me quite self-conscious. But when I tried to talk to my parents about sex, they told me I wasn't old enough to know yet." This level of hypocrisy and the various forms it takes are systematically communicated to us as we develop into mature women. The effect can be devastating; it obscures truth while paralyzing us, in effect predisposing us for fragmented ideas about sex and about ourselves as sexual beings.

Parents may also be intrusive without being rigid—opening their children's mail and becoming friends with their teenager's dates. Or they may be rigid without being intrusive—always requiring their daughter to be home from a date at 10:00 P.M., even if a movie doesn't get out until 10:15.

Children who are unclear about sexual boundaries become adults who express confusion about what is appropriate sexual behavior when dating, and who may have difficulty saying no to pressure from others. Few parents are able to help their teenagers understand what kind of sexual play is "okay" with a date. Even less common are parents who are equipped to help their adolescents develop a sense of appropriate sexual expression when what started as a date progresses into a caring relationship. Children who have very confused boundaries may even need to cut themselves off from others in order to feel safe.

It is important to take a good look at the physical, emotional, and sexual boundaries in your childhood. Where were they? When did you feel they were violated? Did you yearn for more closeness and less rigidity? Or did you need more clearly defined limits? Your answers to such questions may give you insight into how you define your boundaries now and whether you'd like to change, and to understand how change might look and happen in your own life.

Naming the Personal Past

Naming your adult sexual experiences is crucial to developing honesty about sexuality in recovery. But saying aloud what happened and what didn't happen and naming it appropriately is often a painful process.

As you begin to look at your sexual past, you may find, like Theresa, that you have minimized the abusiveness of your sexual experiences. Theresa explained, "There were many times in my relationships when I had sex even though I didn't want to. And that's how I thought of it—having sex when I didn't want to. Now I see that I was rationalizing it. What was really happening was that I was being forced to have sex against my will." It's very important to be able to see something as it really is and to label it accordingly. When Theresa was able to name her experience correctly, it helped her see that in fact she was not in control—deciding to have sex even though she didn't want to—but in an abusive sexual relationship that echoed her childhood rape.

Naming the past can be a painful experience. Like many women, you may have survived by shutting out the awareness of the reality of your sexual behaviors. But as you grow in recovery, you will find that moving beyond old behaviors means telling the truth about where you have been.

If you find that truthfully naming the past brings up unmanageable feelings for you, don't hesitate to seek help. Self-help groups, support groups, and individual therapy can all help to support you in confronting the reality of your past sexual experiences.

Joining a Women's Group

Naming your past may be easiest to do while in a women's recovery group that includes sexuality as an issue. In such a group many women feel safe for the first time in their lives to talk about and name what actually happened. You may discover that your experiences with sexuality aren't unique and that other women know and understand exactly what you are talking about.

"For the first time I saw that I wasn't alone," marveled Joan, a recovering alcoholic, to her group. "I'd carried a lot of shame and guilt about my sexual past, and I guess I thought I was the biggest slut in town. But the women in my group showed me that other women have gone through similar sexual experiences and have come out of it alive, even healthy!"

Being in a women's group can help remove the tremendous burden of individual responsibility that women often feel about their sexuality. Many women come to see that their unhealthy ways of being and acting are part of our legacy as women. In a group, women can begin to accept the ways their sexual expression has reflected low self-esteem and self-worth, and to be truthful about how they've used their sexuality to try to feel good about themselves.

"I was at a meeting once," continued Joan, "and I was obsessing about all the men I'd slept with. I guess I was going on and on and blaming myself for all the sins of the world. And this other woman in my group said, 'Why don't you open the phone book, and look at all the names of men you haven't slept with?' Well, that put it in perspective for me in a hurry."

Unfortunately, many women's recovery groups have an unspoken agreement not to talk about sex. This leaves women feeling that sex must not be important in sobriety, since no one's talking about it. Or they may fear that no one else is having sexual difficulties and problems, and that there's something very different about them.

If you are a member of a group in which sex isn't mentioned, you may need to break the ice by suggesting sex as the topic for a particular meeting. Sexuality is one of the most difficult subjects for women to talk about. But when given the chance, it's amazing what women need to say, want to say, and have to say.

Often women come to my recovery groups not understanding why they're specifically for women. Pat, a recovering alcoholic in her mid-forties, initially couldn't see any value in going to an all-women's group, but she soon changed her mind. "I've never liked women much. They always seemed to be talking about unimportant things, and being around them got on my nerves. At the bank where I work I spent most of my time with men—they were more interesting. Joining Stephanie's group was my first experience with women's lib kind of stuff, and I was pretty skeptical.

"Then my new boss started coming on to me. He'd ask me to go out for a drink after work, and I'd say that I didn't drink. Next he suggested that we go to a conference together, though it was out of his way and inconvenient for him to pick me up. When I pointed that out, he backed off, but I had a sense he would try again.

"I was quite worried, but I didn't know what to do. I'd just been promoted and I wanted to keep the job. I wondered how to humor him, but I didn't have any intention of getting involved with him. So I talked about it in the group. Everybody was outraged. They definitely thought he was taking advantage of his position over me. In fact, they called it sexual harassment."

When Pat heard that her experience had a name, and it was abuse—sexual abuse—her entire perception changed. "I was surprised. I'd had no idea it was that serious. It was only after the group got so mad on my behalf that I could get in touch with how I felt. I realized then that I was very mad at him. He was taking unfair advantage of me. And because he was my boss I didn't feel free to tell him to bug off."

Pat changed her perceptions of what was happening to her because she was in a women's group that validated her experience. The other women knew what it felt like to be sexually harassed in the workplace and to feel that they had no way out. They supported her to become aware of her own feelings of anger. Pat began to value her own perceptions of her reality more easily because of her experiences in the group.

The decision she made to choose not to disregard the voice of her inner self enabled Pat gradually to regain an ability to trust her intuitive response to people and situations. This was the response of Pat's authentic self, one empowered and committed to discerning reality and to proclaiming the legitimacy of her understanding. Here is an example of how a woman who started without the capacity to hear her inner self or to feel that her view of reality was valid found herself. She now knows that her inner voice deserves—and she herself deserves—to be listened to and respected.

Recovery Programs

Because of a new consciousness on the part of many women who are now working in the recovery field, a number of treatment programs are beginning to have regular groups for women. Almost invariably, women express how important these groups are to their recovery and how appreciative they are of their existence. There is something inherently empowering in a group that focuses on women's lives as women experience them.

This empowerment helps women name their experiences truthfully. If you work in a treatment program that has no women's group, you might suggest that one of the regular groups be separated by gender at least once a week. Treatment programs that have created women's groups and seen how effective they are have made them a part of their standard program.

Chapter 6

Identifying Dysfunctional Sexual Behavior

In face of the great unknown that surrounds and permeates much of our sexual experience, perhaps the most common human response has been to make it safe and comfortable by fashioning an ideal image of "how it should be." Since these images and ideals have varied greatly from epoch to epoch as well as across different cultures it is clear there is simply no one way it "should" be. In fact, this very attempt to live up to some ideal has led to much of the unconsciousness and distortion in our sexual exchanges. Perhaps the great challenge for us today is to learn to bring a finer and deeper awareness to sexuality, so that we can discover it freshly, as vibrant expression of the mysterious communion.
—John Welwood, *Challenge of the Heart*

As women we are rich, complex beings, and sexuality is a central facet of this richness. It does not exist in isolation, apart from the rest of life. Whether we have had a good day or a bad day, are chemically dependent or in recovery, or are working inside or outside the home, our sexuality will be affected just as our mood will be. Instead of blaming ourselves for problems with sexuality, we need to take a good look at how we use sexuality to express what else is going on in our lives. Recognizing these connections can open up a whole new level of self-understanding.

At the heart of sexuality is our ability to express love. The way we relate sexually to others is a very real expression of who we are. Our feelings about ourselves—about our self-worth and self-esteem—are manifested in the way we relate sexually to others. If we do not love ourselves it is immensely difficult to love someone else or to believe that others love us.

When you begin to tell the truth about your sexual past, to give accurate names to your experiences and stop judging yourself for your actions, you will also begin to look deeper into what you were looking for or seeking to communicate through your sexual behavior. You will begin to acknowledge your longing—to be held, to be touched, to be loved.

Women who are confused by their distorted sense of self exhibit four common patterns through their sexuality: codependence, acting out, avoidance, and addiction. Each pattern is an expression of the way we relate to sexuality in our lives. Not one of these patterns is a form of healthy sexual relating, and each has its own accompanying difficulties.

As part of the inner journey of recovery you looked honestly at your sexual feelings and began to deal with your hurt and pain. The outer journey of recovery requires you to look honestly at your adult sexual patterns, to name your experiences on the way to hearing the voice of your inner self. It is a task that can be just as painful and just as easy to avoid. But it is an essential task of early recovery to examine your sexual behavior and identify these patterns, and I encourage you to move forward on your journey in this way.

Codependence

The term *codependence* is used here to describe a pervasive problem. Women in our society are actually socialized to be codependents; that is, we are socialized to feel satisfaction and fulfillment only from meeting the needs of others, from putting others first in our lives. Women learn to center their lives around the needs of partners, spouses, children, or aged parents at the expense of their own lives. Even women who rebel against this concept are affected by it, because they are made to feel like "bad" or "selfish" women whose nonconformity is dangerous to everyone.

Women who do not learn how to define and meet their own needs depend on others for their sense of self and self-esteem. They are unable to set limits because they fear abandonment. Sexually, women express a codependent way of relating to others by consistently putting their partner's sexual needs ahead of their own—engaging in sex when they're not aroused, allowing penetration before they're sufficiently lubricated, having intercourse when they're feeling angry, giving in to their partner's pattern of having sex even if it doesn't meet their needs.

Sexually codependent women have trouble identifying and asserting their sexual limits and boundaries. Because they didn't learn in childhood that they have a right to be treated with dignity and respect, they have lost the ability to hear, respect, and value their own sexual needs.

Valuing a relationship does not make you a codependent; in fact, it creates balance and intimacy. It is the lack of mutuality that often results in codependent behavior.

Veronica, forty-four, identified herself as a sexual codependent early in treatment. She was raised in North Dakota in a working-class family. Her mother was very passive and had gotten married at eighteen to get away from her own abusive family. Veronica also fled from her family, through education as well as marriage. She knew she needed financial stability to get out of what she felt was a stifling environment, so she worked very hard to win scholarships and otherwise earn the means to educate herself. She now works as a biologist in a county medical laboratory.

When Veronica looked at her family and how she learned about sexuality, she recognized some familiar patterns. "I was raised in the 1950s when nobody—I mean, nobody—talked about sex. My mother didn't even tell me about menstruation until I came crying to her when I was eleven because I thought I was bleeding to death.

"When I got married at nineteen, I was pretty ignorant about my own body and about sex in general. I had masturbated since I was a little girl, and I knew how to have an orgasm, but I didn't know that you could have one with a partner too. During the ten years I was married, I never had an orgasm. I just thought intercourse was different than masturbation—more satisfying in some ways, less in others.

"My husband was an alcoholic. I'd drink with him in the evenings. We'd have sex in the missionary position and I'd fall asleep either high or drunk. The next morning I'd have a terrific headache, but I always attributed it to the drinking. It didn't occur to me then that my headache could also be caused by my frustration and despair and the way I was lying to myself about my life.

"I had no idea of learning about and asserting my own sexual needs. I thought that in marriage your job was to please your husband and that you'd better do it or he'd leave you, and justifiably so. Now I look back at all those headaches I had and say, of course! I must have built up tremendous unreleased sexual and physical tension as well as resentment."

Acting Out

Sexual acting out includes engaging in sexual behaviors that violate our sexual values. Alcoholic women are prone to acting out during both active drinking and early recovery.

Alcoholic women often report that they drink as a way to decrease their sexual inhibitions, and women who drink often find themselves in sexual situations that they would avoid if sober. Mimi, for example, used alcohol to give her the bravado she felt she needed in order to be sexually assertive. After a few drinks she felt in control and able to approach a potential partner with confidence. In early recovery, without the alcohol, she became very frightened, felt vulnerable, and was fearful about how sexual relationships would work.

Research also indicates that men associate a woman's drinking with her sexual availability. When a man sees a woman drinking, he perceives her as willing to have sex. This creates the following alcoholic sexual situation: men become more sexually aggressive; women expect their sexual inhibitions to be lowered; the judgment of both is impaired; and women end up in sexual situations they often regret.

Jackie, twenty-six, had experienced a meteoric rise in a major corporation. She was a striking woman, tall and athletic in the exquisitely tailored clothes she wore. Her appearance, combined with an MBA from Stanford University and her thoughtful, methodical style, clearly marked her for success. She had been in recovery for a year when she told the following story to our women's group.

"My most outrageous example of sexual acting out happened at my company's anniversary buffet and dance. It was very fancy and I felt quite uncomfortable, so I started drinking before I even left my house. By the time the dance band started playing, I'd been drinking steadily for about four hours. I remember dancing, but not much else. The next morning I felt so bad that I knew I must have really tied one on.

"When I got to work, many of the women in my department avoided me, sort of disappearing around corners when I came around. I didn't know what was wrong or what to do. Finally I grabbed my best friend at work, Allison, and dragged her into the bathroom and begged her to tell me what I had done.

"She had a hard time telling me, but finally I got the picture. I'd made out on the dance floor with another manager—while his wife was watching. They were even friends of mine; I'd bought their kids birthday presents.

"I was mortified. Not only could I not remember what had happened, but everybody else had seen it and they remembered fine."

Jackie was acutely embarrassed as she recounted her sexual acting out. Her behavior at the party was very different from that of her usual sexual persona. Although she was single, she was somewhat introverted and rarely dated. She spent most of her time working or jogging. After dredging up this story, however, she decided it told her something about her sexual feelings. They might be repressed, she thought, but I cannot continue to ignore them, especially when they're in danger of coming out unpredictably and in a form completely disconnected to my values. She decided to examine this neglected aspect of her life more closely.

Avoidance

Women repress their own sexual energy for many reasons. A few, like Paula, have shut down their sexual feelings so completely that they are wholly unaware of their own desire and incapable of fulfilling it. Sexuality also becomes obliterated for other reasons, including alcoholism, personal boundary violation, sexual trauma, fear, and shame.

Women express sexual avoidance in many ways. One woman may be involved with an alcoholic partner who has more and more difficulty being sexual. Another may involve others in her relationships— having in-laws live in her home, letting friends stay overnight, drinking with a group until she passes out. Still another woman may choose partners who are sexually unavailable, workaholics, compulsively unfaithful, or chronically ill.

Social Factors

Social factors often play a role in sexual avoidance. Since so much fear and shame surrounds women's sexuality in general, simply not being sexual may seem to be the easiest course to take. Many women find it extremely difficult to face society's disapproval of women's sexual expression. Sheila Kitzinger puts it succinctly:

> We live in a society in which men get serviced and women provide the service. Women are the nurturers. It is assumed that men go out to work and provide economic support in return for housekeeping, child-rearing and sexual availability and they are active and dominant, while women are relatively passive and submissive,

having been led to expect men to know best how to satisfy them. Many people do not live like this, of course, but everything we believe and do is affected by that basic template from our culture which shapes and limits our choices, and which often makes non-sense of them because, as social beings, we find it hard to act completely independently of it.*

Alcoholism

Drinking suppresses the physiological responses of sex organs, which means alcoholic women have a harder time being responsive to touch, lubricating, and achieving orgasm than nondrinking women. Getting aroused and achieving satisfaction sexually while actively drinking may thus seem futile, and many women just stop trying. Or so much energy may be focused on drinking, controlling drinking, and thinking about the next drink, that little energy is left to invest in developing sexual relationships. A woman's sexuality—powerful, confusing, and influenced by the ambivalence of our culture and the often garbled lessons of our family upbringing—is often among the first things a woman neglects in order to conserve her time and energy for drinking. It is not hard to understand why something that is such a source of conflict is so readily repressed.

When Mimi stopped drinking, her sex life stopped too. She knew how to be only one way sexually: the one who was assertive and in charge. In early recovery, however, she felt frightened and very unlike her usual confident self. In the first months of her recovery she tried to maintain a sexually dysfunctional relationship, because she knew that otherwise she'd be alone. That relationship fell apart six months into her recovery, and as a defense—not a choice—she became totally celibate. She felt so vulnerable sexually that she simply stopped dating in order to avoid even the possibility of binding herself in a relationship. It wasn't until she met Sheila that she began to open up to her sexual self once again.

---

*Sheila Kitzinger, *Woman's Experience of Sex* (New York: Penguin Books, 1985), 10.

Boundary Violation

Women who were raised in families in which their personal boundaries were not respected may also tend to avoid sex. Boundary violations occur on a continuum from lack of privacy to covert or emotional abuse to actual abuse. A violation incident need not be sexual to have a negative impact on a woman's sexuality. For these women, sex may feel threatening and unsafe and be so anxiety producing that they would do almost anything to avoid sexual situations. Many women who are afraid of sex are in a double bind: they opt not to have sex at all, but then they feel ashamed about their celibacy, because they live in a society that puts so much emphasis on sex.

Carolyn, a social worker in her mid-thirties, came to therapy because of the lack of sexual expression in her current relationship. She had been sober for six years and had a solid recovery in AA, but she was unhappy because she didn't feel very sexual in sobriety. She realized that she had always avoided sex, only rarely getting past her avoidance and then only when drinking.

"My family was the stereotypical upper-middle-class WASP ideal," she began. "Outside we looked great; we were all talented and successful. We all played sports and were popular at school. But at home, no one seemed to respect the others. After dinner, always an ordeal, we would each go to our separate rooms and read or watch TV. I never knew when my brothers would barge into my bedroom or the bathroom without knocking. And I am sure my mother listened to phone conversations.

"When I started having sex, I was scared and I couldn't even get near someone without a lot of alcohol in me. Even now, after being sober six years, I still have a hard time warming up to someone. I have to know a person a long, long time in order to get the utmost level of trust in them I need to be sexual. It's not easy for me to be sexual, even when I want to."

Carolyn works in a family service agency. About a year ago she began working with a colleague, Jan, to develop a grant for a new peri-natal drug program for mothers. Through the intensity of the research project they became friends and began to go to dinner and occasional movies together. She had heard the rumors around the office that Jan was a lesbian. Although Carolyn had had several sexual encounters with women while drinking, she would not allow herself to have any sexual fantasies or feelings about Jan.

Even though they liked each other and enjoyed being in each other's company, the two women had never discussed their personal lives with each other. They opted instead to repeat their family-of-origin patterns of superficial contact and lack of communication. This familiar but inherently unhealthy way of relating to each other was the reflexive response of women who were out of touch with their desires and needs. "I worked with Jan for nine months before I even considered that I was attracted to her. Even then—typical of me, I guess—Jan had to make the first move . . . and it took her quite a few moves to get me to respond. This relationship is important to me. I'd really like to learn how to be more sexual."

Sexual Addiction

Sexually addictive behavior can be any sexual behavior that feels compulsive, and thus out of control, regardless of how many sexual partners you have.* For example, you may be sexually addicted in a relationship if you neglect your job and risk losing it in order to meet secretly with a lover. Or sexual addiction can be operating when you have more than one affair at a time, or when your sex life is only a series of one-night stands and casual liaisons. Compulsively masturbating as a way to relieve tension and anxiety is also a form of sexual addiction.

Being sexually compulsive is often associated with other addictions, such as chemical dependence. Sexually compulsive women cover

---

*I am using the words *addiction* and *compulsion* interchangeably. There is a continuing discussion among professionals about the similarities and differences between these behaviors and their causation. In the future, this distinction may have an impact on how we treat these disorders.

their pain or seek to fill their emptiness by addictively seeking out sexual partners and engaging in sexual experiences. The constant intrigue of looking for and seducing a new person can temporarily reduce anxiety and stress as well as increase your feelings of power and well-being. Women often report using seduction as a way to feel good about themselves. They use their sexuality, sex appeal, and prowess to control and manipulate others and to get what they want.

Women who have been abused as children—commonly accepted to be 38 percent of all women and over 70 percent of alcoholic women—are likely either to avoid sex entirely or to become sexually compulsive. These women have learned to sexualize all relationships, particularly relationships with authority figures. Their personal boundaries have been violated, and as adults they have difficulties setting sexual limits. This reenactment of their childhood abuse through compulsive sexual behavior is a cry for help. If heeded, it may actually help the woman to identify early childhood abuse and allow her to find ways to heal from the experience.

Sexually compulsive behavior is often coupled with drinking. Many women report the thrill of going out and looking for a partner. They love the ritual of getting dressed up, putting on makeup, and choosing which bar to start at. The hunt, the chase, or the process of getting another person to pursue her provides the needed rush. The intrigue itself—along with all its trimmings—becomes the drug of choice.

Danielle's experience illustrates sexual compulsion: her alcoholism and sexual addiction were intimately connected. In recovery for eighteen months and finally getting comfortable calling herself an alcoholic, she found that she also had to face her addiction to sex and its continuing destructive presence in her life.

Danielle was fortunate to be able to talk in her women's group about why she thought her sexual behavior was like an addiction. As she began, she crossed and uncrossed her legs and spoke quietly. "You know, lately I've been wondering if my sexual behavior might be as addictive as my drinking was. I mean, I seem to think about it all the time. And when I'm not thinking about it, I'm doing it.

"I look at every man I meet as a potential sex partner, and I know from their reaction that they can sense my availability. I've slept with three guys at work, which is very uncool, and lately I've watched myself coming on to guys other places—in my AA meetings, and even when I'm jogging through the park. When I go shopping, I find myself buying clothes that I know are seductive." She paused, suddenly aware of the high-cut shorts and Spandex tank top she was wearing.

"I've been thinking that maybe I'm going after sex to avoid thinking about myself and the inner work everybody tells me I'm supposed to be doing. " Danielle's insight was correct. She was at a point in her recovery at which she was encouraged by her therapist and her treatment program to keep her attention turned inward to focus on herself. Because this was frightening for her, she responded by becoming more outwardly focused, obsessing about sex. It was an external "fix" to an internally generated set of feelings.

Danielle is finding that she has to work just as hard to come to terms with her sexual addiction as she did with her alcoholism. Even though the two were intertwined when she was drinking, her sexual addiction didn't simply fade away when she stopped drinking. In fact, the number of repeated sexual liaisons with men she hardly knew was increasing. This realization eventually led Danielle to enter a recovery program that treated sexual addiction in addition to continuing with her AA meetings for her alcoholism.

The Sexual/Chemical Lifeline

Filling out a sexual/chemical lifeline is the best way I've discovered to see clearly the relationship between your chemical use and your sexuality. The chart is crucial to understanding how your chemical dependence has affected your sexual behavior.

As you look back through your past to identify your sexual experiences, you may remember incidents that you had forgotten, or you may be surprised at how painful many of your memories are. You may also become aware of certain patterns, especially interactive ones between the chemical and the sexual activities. For example, your drinking and your sexual experiences may get closer and closer together. Or your sexual experiences may have become more and more infrequent as your drinking became more unmanageable. You may also identify incidents of sexual acting out that were associated with particular drinking bouts.

It is important to fill out this chart; don't just read about it. After you have read the explanations for the way Theresa filled out her chart (Figure 1), it will be easier to fill out your own chart (Figure 2). Please feel free to fill out your chart right in the book. If you are going to share this book with friends, you may want to photocopy it instead. Or you might even want to copy it onto a larger piece of paper so you can include more experiences.

Creating a lifeline with your sexual experiences plotted along one line and your chemical experiences plotted along another can be particularly revealing. Seeing how the lines intertwine, the ways they affect and reflect each other, can provide insight into how your sexual behavior and chemical dependence have interacted. Understanding this connection greatly enhances your chance to create the kind of sexual life you want in recovery.

Only when you can see clearly and graphically what your sexual behavior has been during your childhood and your active chemical dependence can you choose to work on changing the patterns that have developed.

Theresa's Sexual/Chemical Lifeline

Figure 1 shows Theresa's sexual/chemical lifeline. Theresa has drawn a line with the years of her life marked off at five-year intervals. The space above the line has been designated for pleasant experiences (marked from 1 to 10) and the space below has been designated for painful ones (marked from -1 to -10). Theresa has indicated her sexual experiences with a solid line and her alcohol/drug experiences with a broken line. Let's take a closer look at her experiences.

Sexual History ——————
Chemical History ‑ ‑ ‑ ‑ ‑

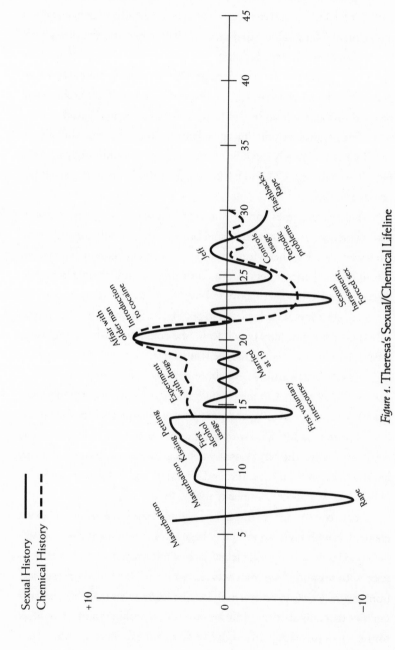

Figure 1. Theresa's Sexual/Chemical Lifeline

Sexual Experiences. Theresa begins by charting her sexual history with a solid line. As you can see, Theresa first masturbates at age eight. It is a positive, pleasurable experience, guilt-free because she doesn't yet have a name for what she is doing.

Her incestuous gang rape at age nine is a sexually traumatic experience that she keeps to herself as a horrendous secret. During the actual rape she dissociates from her body as a way of protecting herself.

She begins masturbating again between the ages of ten and eleven and finds it a relatively positive experience. She masturbates to soothe herself at night, to relax and fall asleep. Sexual contact with herself becomes a comfort.

Kissing becomes part of Theresa's experience at age twelve, with kissing games at parties, and kissing boys on the schoolyard and in the janitor's closet. Her need for attention and physical contact is satisfied through sexual encounters. Around this time her self-esteem begins to be connected to being attractive to boys.

At age thirteen kissing leads to petting, and both are positive physical experiences. She likes how it feels. She competes with other girls for attention from boys and knows she is attractive.

Theresa feels ambivalent about her first voluntary sexual experience at age fourteen. On the positive side, she wants to satisfy her own sexual desire and curiosity, and peer pressure mandates that she have a boyfriend and be included with the group. On the negative side, she is devastated when the boy doesn't want to go steady with her and drops her the next day. In the background are vague and disturbing memories of her rape, which she continually tries to forget.

Between the ages of fifteen and eighteen she has a variety of sexual encounters with high school and college boys. Often she is the more experienced one, although she feigns lack of information and prior experience with sex and sometimes acts like a virgin. These relationships last from several weeks to several months. She learns what males like and often tries to manipulate or subtly arrange sexual positions and encounters for her own pleasure, although she does not ask directly. She often comes home from a date that included sex and masturbates to sleep.

When Theresa is nineteen she marries Joe, a man with little sexual desire. They frequently fight about their sexual relationship.

At twenty Theresa becomes involved in a sexual relationship with an older man. Sex is very intense. She experiences multiple orgasms and more variation in sexual activity than she has with her younger lovers.

Her affair precipitates a divorce, and she is granted custody of her son.

After her divorce, and for the next five years, Theresa chooses as sexual partners men who live "on the edge" in our society, "earning" a living through gambling, cocaine dealing, and so on. She is financially taken care of by each successive partner.

In these relationships she needs alcohol or cocaine in order to be sexual, and her social life revolves around and includes both. She drinks alcohol and snorts cocaine at parties, at home, and on dates. She buys very few drugs; most are provided by her partners. Her life revolves around drugs; she seems to have no separate life. All her female friends are the girlfriends of her male partners' friends, and they are all using.

Joe becomes angry about her alcohol and drug use and charges her with neglect. At age twenty-two she loses custody of her son.

The same year Theresa is sexually harassed on the job, and her employer forces her to have sex when she is under the influence of alcohol, a humiliating experience.

At age twenty-six Theresa meets Jeff, a dependable, solid, professional man. Theresa covers up her drug and alcohol use and hides a good deal of her chemical history from Jeff. She attempts to control her usage. Her gynecologist prescribes Valium to her for nervousness—she is continually crying about the loss of her child and about problems at work. Valium becomes an important part of her daily life. Although Jeff seems like a savior—she says he is the healthiest man she has ever known—his tendency toward addiction is not obvious to her. Jeff grew up in a dysfunctional, chemically dependent home. He reacted to his family by refusing to drink or use drugs as an adult. Instead, he focuses his attention on work.

He and Theresa have a strong physical connection. He's shy and likes her outgoing nature and ease with other people. He likes to be alone, so their social life is limited. She's fun, upbeat, and brings out the child in him, and she is very responsive sexually. He's always been somewhat afraid of women and has had difficulty initiating sexually. Theresa makes few demands on him emotionally, which creates a balance in their relationship.

Chemical Experiences.   Now let's see how Theresa's sexual experiences interacted with her chemical history, as shown by the broken line. Theresa uses alcohol at age fourteen with her first voluntary intercourse. She loves the high and continues to drink, with no particular negative experiences. Periodically she gets drunk, but she suffers no consequences that she's aware of. She finds that alcohol makes her feel more comfortable with people and makes it easier to make conversation and have social interaction. Alcohol numbs her emotional pain and helps her to "forget" the rape.

Joe, Theresa's first husband, does not like her drinking, particularly her need to drink before sexual encounters. He is sexually inexperienced and has little desire. While intoxicated Theresa neglects to use birth control, has an unplanned pregnancy, and gives birth to a son at age twenty.

At this time she is also experimenting with various drugs that are given to her by friends at parties. She takes many of them without knowing or asking what they are.

She is introduced to cocaine by an older man who is very sexually experienced. She loves cocaine and sex with this lover. In a short period her alcohol and cocaine use escalates. She has cravings and blackouts, and she is anxious and irritable without drugs. Her tolerance for alcohol decreases and she gets drunk faster. She has multiple negative consequences: she is arrested for drunk driving, she loses her child due to neglect, her husband divorces her, she chooses inappropriate or dangerous sexual partners, and she is forced to have sex while intoxicated.

When she meets Jeff she begins to try to control her usage, although she doesn't know that she's addicted. She has problems with periodic loss of control—she arrives late for their dates, forgets to call him on evenings when they are not together, passes out in bed, is hung over, misses child visitation times, makes errors on the job, and has decreased work performance.

On Theresa's thirtieth birthday Jeff gives her an ultimatum: "You aren't managing this. Get help, or our relationship is over." She knows she has hit bottom and agrees to get professional help.

In the first few months of recovery, she begins to have flashbacks during sex to her childhood experience of incest.

She knows she is having sex with Jeff, but in her mind it is, inescapably, Bill—and vivid memories flood her with pain and rage. In therapy she learns to open her eyes during sex in order to get into the present and see who she is really with. She learns to stop being sexual when she feels frightened.

After a while she begins to hate all men. She projects all the anger she feels toward her mother's boyfriend and his friends, her fourteen-year-old boyfriends, her cocaine-dealer lover, and her employer who forced sex on her, onto Jeff. She has to learn to separate the past events from her present life and deal with the wounds from her childhood.

In therapy she learns about the concept of the inner child. This is the idea that we all carry a child within us; our childhood self lives on in our adult bodies and still carries our pain. Unresolved wounds will be triggered by events in our adult lives. Theresa and Jeff have a strong bond, and in their sexual relationship her painful sexual memories come back. She needs to heal that inner child. No longer can she use alcohol and other drugs to numb the pain and anesthetize the memories. She needs to reparent herself, to create a safe environment with Jeff where her inner child can learn to trust.

The Sexual/Chemical Lifeline Chart

Now you can fill in this blank chart according to your own sexual and chemical experiences. As I mentioned before, the patterns that emerge on the chart can provide the information you need to begin to change those patterns today as a part of your recovery.

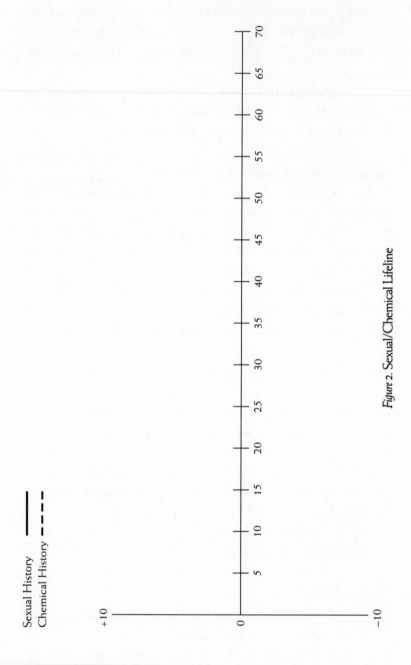

Figure 2. Sexual/Chemical Lifeline

Chapter 7

Understanding Partner Selection

"Coming to Meet" (Hexagram 44) describes a correct relationship as one in which two people come to meet each
other halfway. Halfway means that both are open and receptive to each other. Coming to meet halfway also must be
mutually voluntary, based on the principle of spontaneous
attraction described . . . as the "essential principle of related-
ness." We must maintain reserve in our relationships until
the coming to meet is mutual . . . coming to meet halfway is
possible only between people who are mutually honest and
sincere in their way of life.
                —Carol K. Anthony, *The Philosophy of the I Ching*

Do you choose your sexual partners, or do they choose you?

This can be a difficult question to answer. Since the combination
of unmet childhood needs, abuse, lack of mutuality, and socialization
causes us to relate to others in codependent ways, we tend to see ourselves as reactors: we stand willing to react to those who select us rather
than to actively choose those with whom we want to engage. The great
fairy tales of our culture that embody this ideal, inert posture for maid-
en-women—Snow White, Sleeping Beauty, and Cinderella—have
planted deep within us the image of the sleeping or unformed woman,
wakened and transformed by the chaste kiss of a charming prince. The
idea that we could be free to choose our own mates seems alien and suggests that if we have to go looking it is because no one wants us.

The truth is that we do choose our sexual partners—whether we do it consciously or unconsciously, or by actively seeking or passively accepting. Looking at the characteristics of people we have chosen, then, can be very revealing. For many women, this process may prove to be even more disturbing than looking at their own sexual behavior.

We often delude ourselves about the qualities of those we choose as intimate partners in order to enhance our own self-image. We recast our lovers, making them into the people we want them to be and perhaps into the people we need to have in our lives. Exploring the effects of this restructuring can help us to understand our own process of rationalization and denial. For example, a partner who constantly criticizes you is not seen as emotionally abusive, but is correcting you for your own good. A husband who spends almost every night "out with the boys" is not leaving you in isolation; he is just fulfilling the role of a man's man in which you want to see him. The lover who demands you spend every moment together is not needy, insecure, or obsessed, just madly in love with you.

It is as important to take a long, hard look at your partners' qualities as it is to look at your own sexual behavior. You may feel more inclined to look at your own behavior because you have control over changing it. You may wonder what good it could possibly do you to see the flaws of people with whom you've been intimate. But at least two good things can come out of it: first, even though you have no control over your partners' behavior, you can tell them what you need; and second, you can change how you interact with them.

You may feel that looking honestly at your partner would require you to change your present relationship, which may be an extremely frightening prospect. Before you choose to avoid looking honestly at your current partner, though, realize that honesty doesn't mean you have to make immediate changes. It simply requires you to tell the truth about what's happening now. Telling the truth allows you to assess your options, to see that there are choices. Then you can make the decisions that will help you to take care of yourself.

As you may have heard in your Twelve-Step meetings, early recovery is often not a good time to make major relationship changes. You need to find time to adjust to your recovery, to find out what your needs are, and to find out who your partner is. This does not mean that you should remain in a harmful relationship. Staying with a physically or sexually abusive partner will be more hazardous both to your sobriety and to your health than leaving. Leaving an abusive partner is *always* the best decision you can make for taking care of yourself and your children. (Check the appendixes for more information about battering and abuse, including information and resources about seeking other living situations.) Whatever the qualities and behavior patterns of your relationships, seeing your partner with clarity can only aid in helping you become a healthier sexual person.

The Ideal Lover and Recovery

Often the unresolved issues we have with our parents resurface in the adult partnerships we create. Chapter 5, "Exploring Sexual Behavior Patterns," explains how important it is to look carefully at the sexual behaviors and attitudes of our families of origin before we begin to look at our dynamics of choosing partners. Once you are clear about your family's sexual and emotional history, you will know more about which of your actions are motivated from present needs and which are rooted in the past.

Many times we look for those who seem to fit our image of the ideal lover. We carry within ourselves this ideal and end up projecting it onto others. That explains why we can fall in love at first sight and often fall out of love just as precipitously. As we come to know our partners better and better, they become real individuals to us, so that we can no longer project our ideal onto them. As we become less able to see our partner as our dream lover, we either move onto another partner or choose to build a more conscious relationship.

Women who are involved in an addictive process generally don't pay attention to their emotional issues or to those of their partners. Instead, they look for companions to be addictive with, not partners who are whole and in a process of growth. Women who change their addictive patterns and get into recovery may find their relationships floundering, because the addiction, not the person, has been the basis for choosing the relationship.

Alcoholics and Addicts

Women who grew up in dysfunctional families have been well trained to see dysfunctional ways of relating to others as being normal. Thus it is not surprising to discover that female alcoholics, addicts, and codependents tend to choose alcoholics and other addicts—including workaholics and codependents—as partners. In fact, 80 percent of women raised in alcoholic homes will become chemically dependent themselves or will marry alcoholics or addicts.

In a relationship in which one or both partners are addicts, the relationship is not between the individuals but between the individuals and the addiction. Their interactions are centered on obsessive ways of relating to people or to things. This is what is shared, rather than personal change and growth and relating honestly to one another.

Maintaining your recovery while with an actively using partner is difficult, if not impossible. Active alcoholics and addicts are not emotionally available in relationships. Their focus is on their addiction—the bottle or drug, work or gambling, sex or eating. They are simply incapable of meeting your emotional needs. There is no room in their lives for you and your needs. You are not the priority; yours is not the primary relationship in that person's life.

Codependence can also prevent partners from being truly present in relationships. When one partner is constantly focused on anticipating and meeting the needs of the other, there can be no real give and take, no emotional growth that comes from authentic mutuality.

Sarah's story expresses almost all of these factors. As discussed in earlier chapters, Sarah behaves in codependent ways; she is addicted to prescription pills, and her husband, Scott, is a workaholic. Both Sarah and Scott are emotionally unavailable to one another—Sarah is constantly regulating herself with stimulants or depressants; Scott, because he is consumed by his work, is rarely even physically available to her. Although the relationship is dissatisfying to both of them, each is stuck on his or her own parallel track.

As Sarah continues to recover from her pill addiction, she begins to see more clearly how Scott has made himself unavailable to her. She has tried to talk to him about the hours he works, but he becomes defensive and says they need the money, that she certainly doesn't bring any in. When she presses it further by talking about how empty their relationship feels, he becomes angry and blames her for her years of being detached and unavailable to him.

Scott's behavior is understandable in the context of his own family of origin. His mother was long-suffering, a martyr, her conversation frequently punctuated with deep, sad sighs. Her relationship with her son was enmeshed and intrusive, and he responded by pulling away physically and emotionally, a pattern he has continued with Sarah. Scott remembers her as kind but ineffectual; she never had any influence over his cold, distant father.

His father, a strict disciplinarian, traveled on business and was away from home much of the time. When he was home, Scott remembers him being angry and emotionally unavailable. The family rarely took vacations, and playfulness and having fun were low on the family's list of priorities. The only way Scott could get his father's attention was by excelling in his studies, and he applied himself to his schoolwork and extracurricular activities with such success that he was offered three scholarships to prestigious Ivy League universities. As an adult, Scott became a model worker, putting in extra hours on the job with no expectation of compensation.

Sarah fears that her personal recovery will destroy her marriage. She's never taken risks in any relationship before now, much less in the primary one with her husband. She certainly didn't get any sense from her own family that the best way to deal with feelings—especially painful ones—was to talk about them to the appropriate person. Sarah is very worried about what she should do.

Until—or unless—Scott can recognize and claim his part in the dynamics of their relationship—that is, see how his preoccupation with work functions as an addiction for him—Sarah's fears are probably well grounded. If he continues in denial, Sarah's recovery as a codependent may also be in jeopardy if she chooses to stay with him.

Sarah, like other women raised in dysfunctional families, has learned the skills she needs to coexist and to subordinate her needs to someone else's addictive behavior. It almost feels comfortable to her; at least it feels familiar. As she tries to unlearn these and learn new, healthy ways of relating, she would be greatly helped by a partner who is also trying to learn new skills. Scott and Sarah need to value and work on the relationship equally.

Abusers

Women who are chemically dependent or codependent typically have relationships with men or women who abuse them emotionally, physically, or sexually. Abuse can be expressed along a continuum. It includes not only rape and beatings but even continual small criticisms that gradually erode the spirit (see Figure 3).

Women who continually find themselves in abusive relationships were probably abused in some way as children. It's an odd fact of human nature that we tend to repeat familiar childhood patterns, even if they were humiliating and painful. They are an internal part of who we are and how we learned to behave and react to others. Some women even come to feel that they are so "bad" that they "deserve" abuse and are not even worthy of respect. This is never true.

Revisiting painful childhood scenes with conscious awareness has therapeutic value. When we are able to bring long-buried memories into consciousness, we can choose to bring some resolution and healing to our lives. But repeating these scenes without awareness only adds another layer of pain. Without the tools to resolve painful emotional memories, we continue to make poor decisions about partners. We repeat our ineffective coping strategies and remain locked in rigid cycles of continued abuse.

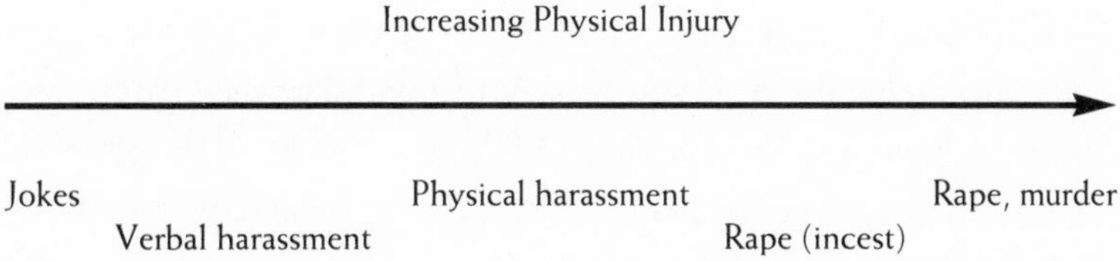

Increasing Physical Injury

⸻⸻⸻⸻⸻⸻⸻⸻⸻⸻⸻⸻⟶

Jokes   Physical harassment   Rape, murder
    Verbal harassment   Rape (incest)

Figure 3. The Continuum of Sexual Exploitation*

Self-help groups, women's therapy groups that focus on female abuse, and individual therapy can be of great help to women who come from abusive backgrounds. Theresa, for example, was helped by all three. "I didn't even realize I had been in abusive relationships until it was pointed out to me—first by my therapist, then in my women's group, and even my Narcotics Anonymous group!" At first Theresa refused to adopt this perspective because it threatened her image of herself as a woman in control of her life. But when she was able to correctly name her experiences, she saw them clearly.

"The relationship I had thought of as 'I sleep with Roger even though I can't stand him, because I know he'll give me a gram of coke for free, isn't he a jerk,' became 'Roger forced me to have sex with him and then bought it from me with a gram of coke. I'm the one who was used.'"

Theresa initially found this version of her life story depressing and disturbing, especially in combination with the flashbacks of her rape she had been experiencing, which were terrifying and excruciating in their power and vividness. Fortunately, her support network, including Jeff,

---

*From Kathryn Quina and Nancy Carlson, *Rape, Incest, and Sexual Harassment* (New York: Praeger, 1989), 11.

was able to help her get through these times until she had enough distance to begin to look at her behaviors without blame, guilt, or fear.

Her courage to take the risk of naming her past in order to forge a path of recovery through it rewarded her with a new sense of personal empowerment, the feeling that she really could determine her choices.

Setting limits and being willing to enforce them with those who are emotionally, physically, or sexually abusive is vital to remaining in and transforming those relationships. As demonstrated earlier, women in abusive relationships have trouble with boundaries, but they often find that counseling can help them set proper limits. Even more important, the woman's partner has to be willing to stop the abusive behavior. If your partner is not willing to seek help and make changes, you will need to leave the relationship. Otherwise the choice to stay is made at the expense of the self, and the cycle of abuse just keeps being perpetuated.

Some treatment programs have special aftercare groups for women who are struggling with abusive relationships. You can contact your local mental health resources for help, as well as the YWCA and battered women's shelters in your area. Books that are especially helpful are listed in appendix C under "Battering and Physical Abuse." The books listed are written in straightforward and informative language. They provide practical advice for how to deal with the police and legal system, and how to get support from your family, your friends, your church, or other community resources. Most of all, they can assist you in creating alternatives to a life of abuse and in finding places and people to sustain you during this process.

Unavailable or Distant Partners

Addictions and abuse definitely prevent partners from relating honestly and fully with one another, but people can be distant in other ways. They may be married to someone else or be involved in multiple relationships. They may have rigid boundaries that preclude intimacy. They may be depressed and unable to meet your needs. They may be profoundly narcissistic and refer everything back to themselves, denying you the right to your feelings or memories because they are wholly intent on the effect on themselves.

Distant and unavailable partners are not partners in the true sense. They do not and cannot bring equal sharing, intimacy, and commitment to the relationship. Sometimes this results from partners who accept an unspoken contract: "If you support me, I'll continue to overlook your affairs." Or, "If I can raise the children any way I want, you can concentrate solely on your career."

Clearly, contracts like these are not mutual, loving agreements. They allow adults to live parallel lives in the same house without ever actually being together or emotionally there for each other. Barbara's story is a good example.

Barbara, forty-three and recently divorced, explained, "When my husband suddenly left me for another woman, I was stunned and went into a deep depression. I thought we had it all worked out. I knew we weren't madly and passionately in love, but we had worked out a life. I raised and showed my dogs, he restored his old cars, and we had a great house that could accommodate all of that. Now I see that we simply lived our lives and left each other alone. We never talked about anything more serious than what to have for dinner. My therapist explained we were like two planets in different orbits that could never overlap."

Another common response to a distant partner is to become a pursuer. As our partners move away, fearing closeness, we rush after them, fearing abandonment and loss. This can happen over and over again, creating a nearly unbreakable pattern. "For years I thought the problem was men," said Becky, twenty-eight. "My girlfriends and I would complain endlessly about them, and how they were so afraid of commitment. You'd have a great date, they'd promise to call, and you'd never hear from them again. If you ran into them on the street they'd pretend they didn't see you.

"When I got into therapy I began to see that I might actually have a part in the problem. The minute I met a man I started fantasizing that he was The One. Then I'd think there could never be anyone better than him, how lucky I was to have found him, and how we would get married and have a wonderful life. Then I'd rush on to the depressing idea that he would leave me, that he really didn't like me at all, that he had another girlfriend he wasn't telling me about. All this in the space of about an hour!

"So by the time we went out on our date I'd be frantic. I'd have run through the entire relationship in my head all the way to its horrible end—before it had even started. Because I 'knew' he would leave me, I guess I clung hard while he was there. No wonder they kept running away!"

Becky eventually learned to stop moving forward so fast in order to allow her partners the space to move forward themselves. She needed to slow down and bring herself back to the present, to look at what was happening moment to moment with a clear eye rather than imposing a dark fantasy on events yet to come.

Because of our cultural conditioning, women are more likely to fear abandonment, while men are more likely to fear engulfment. Women and men often become polarized in their relationships, creating their own version of this exaggerated dance of pursuer and pursued.

However, this dance need not be gender-specific. Men and women can and do play either role. In fact, often, as the pursuer learns to pull back, the distancer moves forward to fill the space. Distancers need to reassure their partners that they don't intend to abandon them. Couples therapy can be helpful in learning to break this pattern.

Your Relationship Patterns

A relationship chart and a family genogram can be used to identify your relationship patterns. They are tools that can help you break through the denial that obscures your relationship history. When you begin to identify trends and patterns in your sexual relationship history and in your family tree, you will learn what you need to do in a program of sexual recovery.

The relationship chart will give you a picture of who you are in a relationship. When you have finished this chart, you will be able to see the history of your sexual relationships—the repetition of traits and patterns that originated with your parents and continues through adulthood.

Filling out a relationship chart is a graphic way to review the patterns in your relationships. It is difficult to remain in denial about your sexual relationship patterns when you encounter certain words and phrases repeated over and over again in the chart. By studying the chart you can get clues of what you need to do for sexual recovery. You will see the way you interact in relationships and the kinds of partners that you choose. Certain themes, feelings, and characteristics are bound to emerge as patterns. As you reflect on the predominant ones that seem to govern you, you will begin to have a deeper understanding of yourself.

The Relationship Chart

Figure 4 is a blank relationship chart. Filling out this chart can be painful. As you review the patterns of your past, you may become acutely aware of what you did not get in your relationships. You may also become aware of sexual behaviors you engaged in that you didn't really enjoy. Or you may become aware of the kinds of attention that you did want and didn't receive. It is important to acknowledge to yourself that filling out the chart is a major step in being honest about your sexual past. Give yourself credit for being willing to take that step. As with the sexual/chemical lifeline, you can fill out the chart right in this book or you can copy it, adding more spaces on a larger piece of paper if you need to. Again, do the exercise—don't just read about it. For the exercise to work, you need to fill out the spaces honestly, carefully thinking about your past relationships and their characteristics.

You may even want to fill out the relationship chart a number of times during your recovery. As you break through your denial, you will progressively come to see your relationships more clearly. You may

	1. Mother	2. Father	3. Relationship partner	4.	5.
Characteristics of person					
Characteristics of relationship					
Use of chemicals/ addictive behaviors					
Sexual qualities of relationship					
Sexual likes & dislikes in relationship					

Figure 4. Relationship Chart

become able to change the characteristics that you had previously identified as important or immovable; or you may begin to see certain patterns of interacting as being far more abusive than you had thought. Doing this chart several times will allow you to have a more complete view of your past. Naming your past in this systematic fashion is, again, the key that unlocks your capacity for healing. Choices that you have made will be clearer. They are choices you might be able to change.

Across the top of the chart are spaces for the names of people with whom you've had major sexual relationships. If you are currently in a sexual relationship, put that person's name in the last space. I've already listed father and mother as your first two relationships. If you were raised by primary caregivers other than your father and mother, mark out father and mother and put their names in the first two spaces. You may also add grandparents or stepparents, aunts or uncles, if they were significant to you in childhood.

Characteristics of Person. List the words that best describe the person emotionally. Paint a descriptive picture of the person. Examples of words to describe the person might include cold, warm, indirect, present, distant, affectionate, mean, caring, gentle, loyal, insecure, honest, reliable, sarcastic, or courageous.

Characteristics of Relationship. Use words that best describe your interaction with this person, that is, how the relationship felt to you. Examples might include caring, distant, fun, sympathetic, hopeless, warm, supportive, intense, uncommunicative, boring, deceitful, mutual, indifferent, critical. Also refer to the words listed above to use as characteristics of each person with whom you've been in a relationship. It is important to notice whether the words you use to describe the characteristics of the relationship are identical to the characteristics of the person you described. If they are, you can see the effect of your partner in that relationship. Where were you? What happened to the effect you had on the relationship? How did your self get expressed in that relationship? What does this say about your power in the relationship? If you feel that your characteristics did not determine the character of the relationship at least in part, this is an important fact to notice.

Use of Chemicals or Other Addictive Behaviors. Describe any use of prescription medicines, street drugs, or alcohol by you or your partner, as well as other addictive/compulsive behaviors either of you might have engaged in. Some suggestions might be:

- Alcohol
- Shopping or shoplifting
- Valium
- Workaholism
- Codependence
- Diet pills
- Compulsive exercise
- Marijuana
- Cocaine
- Gambling
- Anorexia/Bulimia

Sexual Qualities of Relationship. Pick words that best describe the sexual qualities of the relationship. Be sure to fill in the spaces for your parents. Were they supportive, open, respectful, seductive, voyeuristic, or repressive? Include not only the qualities of the relationship itself but your feelings about the sexual aspects of the relationship. They may be subtle, but if you felt them, record them. It is your sense of how things were that counts. The goal is to name qualities and feelings, even when they are vague or only nuances. For your partner relationships you might consider whether the relationship was mutual, passionate, one-sided, open, nonexistent, compulsive, accepting, shameful, tender, affectionate, routine, dutiful, or confusing.

Sexual Likes and Dislikes in Relationship. Go through the sexual qualities of the relationship that you've just listed and sort them into two categories: those you liked and those you didn't. Also include your likes and dislikes among the sexual activities you engaged in. These might include the following: nudity, telephone sex, massage, licking, bathing together, kissing, hugging, stroking, caressing, biting, sucking, penetrating, oral sex, bondage, using oil, anal intercourse, tickling, outdoor sex, reading erotica, masturbation, using feathers, French kissing, fantasies, experiencing orgasm, hot tub sex, sadomasochism, watching sexual videos, simultaneous orgasm, using sexual toys, sex with more than one person, and cuddling.

The Genogram

The genogram is a diagram of the relationships that exist between family members. It is another tool with which to look at your relationship patterns and get information on your sexual and emotional history. Sarah's relationship genogram, Figure 5, will give you an idea of how to approach recording and analyzing your own family history. Figure 6 is a blank genogram for you to complete.* Again, you may use it right in the book or make copies.

First note your family relationships as far back as you can, using the genogram symbols shown here in the text and in Figures 5 and 6. Then note next to each name the addiction symbol, if any, appropriate to that person. Finally, because this is a sexual/emotional history, use two to three words to describe each person and two to three words to describe each relationship. Refer back to your relationship chart for help.

---

*For more information on the genogram, see Stephanie Covington and Liane Beckett, *Leaving the Enchanted Forest: The Path from Relationship Addiction to Intimacy* (San Francisco: Harper & Row, 1988), 20–29.

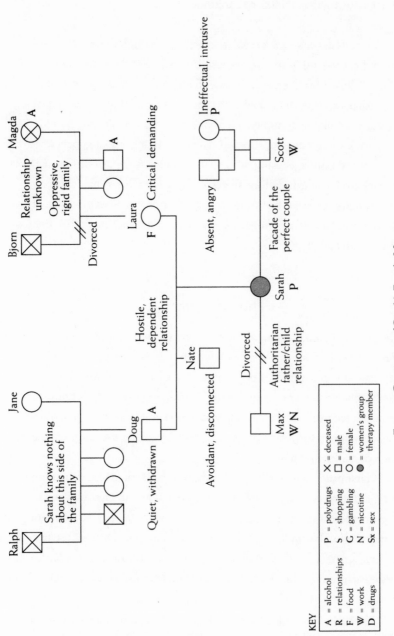

Figure 5. Genogram of Sarah's Family History

KEY

A = alcohol   P = polydrugs   X = deceased
R = relationships   S = shopping   □ = male
F = food   G = gambling   ○ = female
W = work   N = nicotine   ● = women's group
D = drugs   Sx = sex   therapy member

Genogram Symbols

Male = square   Deceased = X

Female = circle   Divorced = //

Addiction/Compulsion Code

A = Alcohol   S = Shopping

W = Work   G = Gambling

F = Food   N = Nicotine

D = Drugs   R = Relationships

P = Polydrugs   Sx = Sex

Sarah's Genogram

Sarah's maternal grandparents, Bjorn and Magda, had created a rigid, oppressive family life. Sarah knew nothing of their personal relationship, although she thought they had probably been as constricted in that as they had been with their children.

Sarah's father, Doug, had never communicated anything about his parents. His father, Ralph, had died before Sarah was born, and Doug had never mentioned his mother. As a child she had found it normal to have one set of grandparents, and she never questioned her paternal grandmother's absence. Now, for the first time, Sarah began to wonder about what lay behind her father's silence.

Sarah characterized Doug as quiet and withdrawn, addicted to alcohol. When she looked at her relationship with her own two husbands, she was startled to see that she had characterized both Max and Scott with similar adjectives: emotionally distant, unavailable, avoidant, and disconnected. With Max she had an authoritarian father/child relationship that echoed both her maternal grandparents' household and parents' hostile, dependent interactions. She and Scott had learned to project the facade of the perfect couple, replicating yet another facet of her parents' marriage: denial.

Finally, although neither she nor her husbands were alcoholics, she could see that the same addictive patterns were present. Scott was certainly a workaholic; Max, she remembered, also spent most of his time at work, and he smoked two packs of cigarettes a day to try to relieve tension and anxiety.

Sarah was shaken by her discoveries. No matter how hard she tried, it seemed she could not avoid repeating her parents' mistakes. Her therapist explained that cross-generational family patterns like hers are normal, because our families are our first and most powerful models for behavior. As children we cannot discriminate between what is "good" behavior and what is "bad" behavior; we simply absorb it all. Unless we have other models that are equally strong, such as an influential teacher, therapist, or friend, we will probably continue to repeat our family patterns.

Based on Sarah's model, you can now complete your own family genogram. Study it carefully. Do you see any apparent patterns? Look carefully for generational connections and repetition of the past in the present. Pay special attention to the blanks, the areas about which you know nothing. Those blank spots often conceal family secrets.

Living in the Present

Living in the present means that you are consciously aware of what is going on for you right now. You may say, "But of course I'm living in the present! Where else is there to live?" The fact is, however, that we spend most of our time either in the past, feeling guilty and worrying about things we've already done, or in the future, worrying about, planning for, or trying to control events that haven't yet happened.

When we spend our time in the past we carry our history around with us. We are burdened with expectations based on things that have happened to us, and we expect that these things will continue to happen to us. Or we may live in the future, like Becky, fantasizing each new relationship to a depressing conclusion before it even begins.

Healthy sexuality can take place only in the present moment, between two people who are really there—for each other and for themselves. If you are having sex with your lover but your mind's on what you

KEY

A = alcohol	P = polydrugs	X = deceased
R = relationships	S = shopping	□ = male
F = food	G = gambling	O = female
W = work	N = nicotine	● = You, the reader
D = drugs	Sx = sex	

Figure 6. Create a Genogram of Your Own Family History.

need to do at work tomorrow, you're not there. If you're meeting a new potential partner but your emotional expectations are based on your abusive ex-lover, you're not there.

The realization that we have spent the better part of our lives fantasizing about the past or future can be disturbing. We've lost a lot of time and experience. But no matter how much of your life you've spent elsewhere, you can learn to live in the present. And you can reclaim your past and not relive it. When you live in the present you will reconnect with your true self, because this is where she lives.

Your Observer Self

Perhaps the best way to learn to live in the present is to allow your observer self into your consciousness. The observer self is that nonjudgmental part of you who acts as a witness to the events of your life. She can look at how you feel and act and know that particular actions and feelings are not your total self. The observer self is a mirror in which you can look at your own behaviors and actions without judgment.

If you have spent many years in guilt and shame, you may not believe this aspect of yourself exists. But it does, and you can develop it.

Developing your observer self is different from dissociating from your body and feelings. You do not step outside of yourself to avoid facing yourself. You do not use the defense mechanism of abandoning yourself because it's too painful to be present. Rather your observer self provides you with a quiet place from which to view your own behavior with reflection and acceptance.

Allowing your observer self to be with you on a daily basis will enable you to notice, for example, that you tend to wear your most sexually revealing clothes to NA meetings, or that when you put on makeup in a certain way men make sexual remarks to you, or that you are using sex to get power, or that you are having sex with a partner who does not really satisfy your needs. Your observer self does not judge these actions, but simply brings them to your attention so that you can choose how to work on them.

A Daily Inventory

Your observer self helps you to stay in the present. Staying in the present in relation to your sexuality and noticing what you are doing can be real work; but it is work that pays off in untold dividends as you become able to choose your sexual behavior rather than simply acting out unconscious patterns.

Taking a daily inventory can help this process. Writing things down in a journal can be especially helpful, because it allows you to review your progress. For example, each night before you go to bed you might ask yourself the following questions: Did I feel sexual today? How did I express this? You will soon find that it gets easier to recognize your feelings and to focus on their place in your life.

Another discovery that may emerge is the realization that you are a combination of the thoughts and feelings and experiences that have accumulated throughout your life. You may discover that you still react like a child or adolescent in some situations. As you observe yourself, you may begin to recognize the inner child, the critical self, the shamed self, the romantic self, the workaday self, the mature adult self—all the different parts of yourself. You can begin to question the attitudes and beliefs that control the different aspects of yourself. Then you can begin to consciously choose which stance you will take in any given circumstance.

Partner selection involves choices. Understanding the influence of our past relationships is the first step. Seeing how and where they continue to affect us is the second. Realizing that we have choices about who to select in the present and future is part of the awakening experience.

PART THREE

THE POWER OF CHOICE: ONGOING RECOVERY

The transition between early and ongoing recovery is marked by a feeling of reconnection with your inner self, that wise and nonjudgmental part of yourself from whom you have been estranged for so long. As you move into ongoing recovery, a stage that you will explore for the rest of your life, this connection with your inner self allows you to tackle deeper issues that you were too fragile to handle earlier.

As you delve deeper, you will become aware of how your feelings of guilt, shame, and responsibility for your own abuse have restricted your sexual energy and left you drained and immobilized, avoidant or compulsive, unable to choose the forms of sexual experience that resonate with your inner self.

In ongoing recovery you will move away from feeling guilt and toward healing the pain of childhood sexual issues and dissolving your shame. When you are able to let go of these negative and destructive feelings, you will discover your core of power.

Building a foundation of honesty is an essential element in early recovery. As you continue to build on this foundation in ongoing recovery, you will begin the major task of reclaiming your sense of empowerment. This will allow you to create a healthy, fulfilling sexual life.

Chapter 8

Choosing a New Sexual Life

One does not look to the oppressor to change
the conditions. We who feel hurt or wronged
must bring about change, and men of vision
will become our allies.

—Jean Baker Miller

One is not born a woman, one becomes one.
—Simone de Beauvoir, *The Second Sex*

The journey of sexual recovery is developmental. You must walk down the path of early recovery before you can turn the corner into ongoing recovery. Yet each woman creates her own unique version of that path, tackling these stages in her own way, doing inner work or taking outer actions as the need arises and issues present themselves.

The process of sexual awakening and recovering takes the form of an upward spiral (see Figure 7). As you pass through one stage, and then another and another, you will revisit the same issues but on higher levels of understanding and work. Where first you needed the most basic definitions, now you also see the subtleties. Life seems to present the same issues over and over again. But when you are working on your recovery you will see these issues with a new sense of depth and complexity. Progress means moving to another level of self-exploration, not "fixing" yourself or getting rid of a particular issue once and for all.

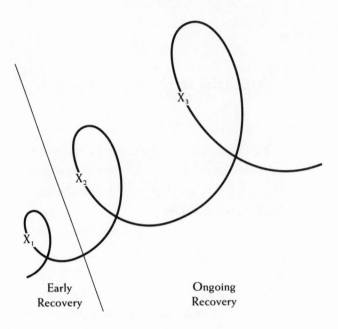

Early
Recovery

Ongoing
Recovery

X = Issues of Sexual Abuse

X_1 = Person learns that sexual abuse occurs on a continuum that includes but is not limited to coercive sex; there is some physical discomfort, but no explicit memories are experienced.

X_2 = Memories return; physical reactions like nausea—along with anxiety—may occur when discussing sexual history.

X_3 = Person able to acknowledge sexual abuse: past experiences and feelings become more separated from those of the present.

NOTE: This is a hypothetical case, an example. No one else's feelings and experiences are quite like your own. How issues of sexual abuse—past or present—are addressed in recovery varies widely with individual circumstances and according to the opportunities for change, resources, and support that are available to the person.

Figure 7. The Upward Spiral of Recovery from Sexual Abuse

The Twelve-Step motto Progress, Not Perfection describes the process of sexual recovery precisely. Your goal in sexual recovery is not to become a perfect lover but to become increasingly aware of the role sexuality plays in your life. You want to grow in your ability to recognize your sexual feelings and act on them. In that process you will come to accept yourself as human: sometimes you close down when you want to be open; sometimes you make inappropriate sexual demands on those you love; sometimes you miss opportunities to express caring through sexual touch. But as you move up the spiral to greater understanding, you will also begin to notice the times you are truly there for yourself and your partner; the times you treat your body and the bodies of those you love with respect and love; the times you simply love yourself for being you.

Sexual recovery is not a calm ocean that you sail over like a stately ocean liner. You will still have your ups and downs. But in recovery, as opposed to addiction, you have hope. You know that you can change your sexual patterns, because you already have. The hopelessness of addiction is no longer your constant state of being. And as you gain hope, you also begin to gain personal power.

The Power to Change

Women often find it difficult—or even terrifying—to confront the issue of their own personal power. Society tells us that women are not supposed to have power; it's the prerogative of men. This social disapproval does not encourage women to strive for power. In fact, a powerful woman is often perceived as unfeminine, a bitch, or a shrew, or in other equally unpalatable terms. This misperception is based on a complete misunderstanding of the meaning of personal power. If we are to be truly empowered as women, we must first attempt to understand power.

Men and Money

Men, as a group, have more power than women, particularly economic power. They earn more money, they have access to a greater variety of jobs, and they are the entrenched leaders. Society measures power in terms of money, status, prestige, and the capacity to command people and resources, and women simply have fewer of these elements than men do.

The statistics are staggering. The salaries of women are still only 63 percent as large as the salaries men make. Over 75 percent of the poor in the United States are single women and their children. Even though women are becoming more visible in highly paid white-collar positions, we continue to be clustered in the six lowest-paid occupations: retail sales; secretarial, clerical, and domestic work; food service; and the service industry. Men without high school degrees make more on the average than women who have graduated from college. Women who divorce find that their standard of living plummets by an average of 70 percent, while that of their former husbands rises by 42 percent.

This lack of economic power leads women to stay in marriages that no longer fulfill them sexually or emotionally, or to stay with men who are violent and abusive. These women know that even educated, middle-class single mothers find it difficult to afford day care while they work. Clearly, then, our economic options mold and influence our sexual relationship decisions in a way that doesn't happen for men.

The Courage to Act

In our society, power has often meant power over: the ability to control others. Historically, that power has been supported and buttressed by physical might and violence.

As women have become more aware of their need for empowerment in contemporary society, they have also turned away from the traditional forms of power over—hierarchy, authority, physical force, and violence. Instead, many women have sought out new definitions of power that match their values.

Jean Baker Miller, M.D., is one of those who is seeking a new and more appropriate definition of power:

> My own working definition of power is the capacity to produce a change—that is, to move anything from point A or state A to point B or state B. This can include even moving one's own thoughts or emotions, sometimes a very powerful act. It can also include acting to create movement in an interpersonal field as well as acting in larger realms such as economic, social, or political arenas.*

When we define power in male terms—in terms of physical strength and the ability to dominate—we don't have it. In our focus on male power, however, we have missed the reality of women's experience. We need to look at our own lives to see the ways in which we manifest powers that are uniquely our own. I agree with Dr. Miller's suggestion that "The first step [toward empowerment] is indeed being together and talking together, clarifying and checking out with each other, and giving support as much as we can; then comes action for ourselves and our children."

Recovery is about wanting to change. Sexual recovery is about self-empowerment. Both involve the decision to explore and identify choices, to become aware of your options. As you gain in awareness and expand your capacity to meet your own needs, you can start to enlarge your capacity to act rather than react. You increase your personal power as you increase your capacity to produce change.

In 1974, researcher Shere Hite published the first compilation of women's responses to a sexual questionnaire, *Sexual Honesty By Women for Women*. For the first time women had a chance to report on what they wanted and what worked for them sexually. Since then, Hite has

---

*Jean Baker Miller, "Women and Power,*Work in Progress #1* (Wellesley, MA: Stone Center Working Papers Series, 1982), 2.

published two more books of self-reports by women. Other women, including Lonnie Barbach and Betty Dodson, have conducted workshops and written books on masturbation and orgasm. Betty Whipple first reported on the G-spot and female ejaculation.

Women in some major cities across the country have opened stores for women that sell sex toys and erotica. In fact, women have started to write their own erotica, including the bestseller *Ladies' Own Erotica* by the Kensington Ladies' Erotica Society. Women overall are becoming more willing to be sexual, more willing to assert their sexual needs and desires, and more willing to leave relationships that don't meet their needs.

Learned Helplessness

In discussing early recovery we explored the impact of socialization on your sexual identity. The very fact that we needed to discuss and explain empowerment points out how society actually teaches women to be helpless. This learned helplessness prepares women to accept as their due a life of underachievement, underemployment, and personal and sexual disappointment.

As girls we are rewarded—subtly and not so subtly—for becoming helpless and depending on others to meet our needs. We learn to look to others to make decisions, to protect us, and to determine the directions our lives will take. Sexually, we learn to depend on others to decide where we're going on a date, to ask us to marry them, to bring us to orgasm. This pattern is infantilizing, and it can render us incapable of knowing how to meet our basic daily needs. Moreover, it prevents us from developing the repertoire of balanced responses that evolves and is enriched by making choices, changing our minds, and refusing to adopt someone else's truth or voice as our own.

Veronica is an example of a woman whose learned helplessness seemed to serve her well. Its destructive effect became apparent only after she was forced to live on her own for the first time. Veronica's journey to empowerment didn't begin until midlife. When her alcoholic husband moved out, she lived alone in the house they had shared. The small tasks of daily living, which she had always left to her husband, suddenly piled up on her. Taken alone, each was trivial. But together they were overwhelming.

"Here I am, living alone for the first time in my life, and I'm sure I can handle it. I work in a lab, handling viruses. I'm extremely competent in my work—I have to be. Well, the first thing that happens is I get a flat tire. I don't know how to fix a flat tire; my husband always did that. I opened up the trunk to look for a spare, and it wasn't there. I knew it was supposed to be there somewhere, and I absolutely panicked. Finally some young guy stopped to help me and he found it easily—under the car, neatly hidden out of sight. Well, I was grateful for his help but I felt really stupid. I mean, this was my own car!

"A couple of weeks later I needed to mow the lawn. Fine. I get the lawnmower, and then I realize that I don't know how to start the damn thing. Do you just pull that string, or do you have to push a button first? I was really afraid it would blow up on me if I did the wrong thing. I stood there looking at it for so long that my neighbor finally offered to start it up for me.

"Now I'm feeling less and less competent. One night the lights go off, the TV goes off, everything's off. I look down the street and see that everybody else's lights are on, so it must be a fuse. A fuse! Where's the fuse box? Can you get electrocuted touching those things? I finally just got paralyzed with the whole idea and went to bed.

"Then I got sick. I was so sick I couldn't get out of bed. I wanted to call the doctor, but the phone was in the kitchen and my husband wasn't there to make the call. I just lay there and sobbed. It felt like I was going to die just because I didn't have a phone in the bedroom.

"That did it. It was like hitting bottom again. I looked at my life. I looked at how I had depended on my husband for everything. I couldn't fix a flat and I couldn't save my own life. I was never encouraged to do things for myself. Why should I bother learning? There would always be a man to do it for me.

"When I was growing up with my brothers, I could have learned to be handy around the house right along with them, but I didn't. I was a girl. I was encouraged to need and ask for help as my natural due. It had just never occurred to me to do things for myself. I guess it's kind of like my brothers not being able to boil water or do a load of laundry.

"And I'm still rewarded for not knowing how to do stuff, on some level. It's easier to ask a man for help than it is to learn how to do something yourself. And it's totally socially acceptable. No one will ridicule me for not figuring it out and doing it myself. In fact, the man will feel flattered and needed. He'll jump to do the job."

This series of experiences really made Veronica think about all the ways she had learned to be helpless. When she thought about it, she realized she was just as helpless about her personal finances and her insurance as she was about mechanical devices. And in her sexual encounters, she assumed that her partners would buy condoms and be disease-free. As she grew in recovery, however, she knew that she could not continue this way. Even though she was an adult woman, she had to relearn how to take care of herself.

The Legacy of Abuse

Learned helplessness is compounded by childhood abuse. Women who were victimized as children learn that they are unable and unentitled to protect themselves physically and emotionally. They grow up thinking that emotional, physical, and sexual abuse are normal, and they become accustomed to the idea that they are not valued, cherished, or protected. As a consequence they have few expectations from adult life.

Women who have been victimized in this way have little understanding of how to create the conditions that would move them out of the victim role. They perceive life as happening to them, and the world as a frightening place where they are at the mercy of events that are out of their control. Sexually, they play out this learned helplessness by expecting someone else to initiate sex, to give them an orgasm, and to know how to satisfy them.

Alcoholic and chemically dependent women who have been through Twelve-Step groups know that one of the first acts in achieving sobriety is to acknowledge their powerlessness over the objects of their addiction. But, paradoxically, at the same time they also first recognize their own personal power: the power to make choices, including the choice not to return to addictive behavior. In letting go of the areas in which they are truly powerless, they make room for the areas in which they have true power. This is also true of sexual empowerment.

Sexual empowerment means freeing yourself from your learned helplessness in the area of sex. It means moving away from identifying yourself as a victim. As you get in touch with your childhood abuse, with your guilt over past behavior, with your shame of being who you are, you can recognize and acknowledge your powerlessness over the external circumstances that created those situations. Acknowledging your powerlessness—as overwhelming, painful, and difficult as that may be—will free you to take power and be responsible for creating your life now, the way you want it to be.

Theresa found the idea of sexual power complex and disconcerting. "I've been struggling with this issue for months in therapy. Deep down I felt like I was responsible for my mother's boyfriend molesting me. Maybe I could have made him stop, or said 'no' more forcefully. . . .

"I like to think of myself as in charge of my life. It was simply too painful to feel like I didn't have the power to protect myself. Somehow it felt better to think I was responsible than to acknowledge that I was truly powerless over his actions.

"I've slowly come to acknowledge that I did everything I knew to try to protect myself, and none of it worked. He was bigger and more powerful. I was a child and he was an adult. That realization freed me up to learn how to better protect myself now. As long as I kept thinking I was responsible for my childhood abuse, I kept being victimized as an adult. Once I let go and accepted my powerlessness, I started being more powerful. I stopped acting like a victim and started taking responsibility for my life—including my sexual relationships."

When Theresa accepted her powerlessness, she was able to forgive herself for her past, both for events she was powerless to prevent and for those in which she didn't exercise the power she did have. Like Theresa, as you forgive yourself, you can begin to take responsibility for where you are now. You can make amends where appropriate and learn to respond consciously as things happen. You can accept that you have some choices, even if they are narrow ones, and that you can exercise them. You can accept your power to respond differently to events over which you may have no control.

Sexual Assets

When you begin to reclaim your personal power, it is essential to look at how you used your sexuality to get your drug of choice. You may have done this consciously, as Theresa did with her drug dealer boyfriend. You may have done it unconsciously, allowing men to buy you drinks in bars. Or you may have allowed men to take you out and spend money on you, hoping they would fall in love with you and support you financially through marriage.

Women, lacking economic power and drawing on learned helplessness, almost naturally turn to their sexuality as a form of currency. Most women were introduced to drugs and alcohol by their boyfriends. In contrast to men, who generally go out and buy their drugs and alcohol with their own money (or steal money to buy drugs), many women continue to get alcohol and drugs through boyfriends, lovers, and husbands well after they become adults.

Here are some of the ways women trade their sexuality for chemicals:

- Many women date men or women simply because they know they'll be taken to parties where there will be drugs and alcohol, or to restaurants where they can drink.
- Many women date people they don't really care about in order to get their drug of choice.
- Some women become groupies to wealthy or famous people or to dealers.
- Many women stay married to men they don't really love or respect so they can continue drinking and using while being economically supported.
- Some women directly sell their sexual favors for money to buy alcohol and drugs.

All of these are acts of prostitution: using one's sexual self to get something. More often than we like to admit, we exchange our sexuality—the one commodity all women own—for our drug of choice. The most common form of prostitution that chemically dependent and codependent women engage in is staying with partners they don't love for the sake of economic support.

Nancy, a recovering alcoholic, was married to Dan for twelve years. After one year of sobriety she divorced Dan and got custody of the children, two boys and a girl. They look a lot like her—small-boned with dark good looks. Nancy is charming and effusive, with a ready smile, but the deep sadness of her dark eyes attests to years of stress.

"I got married at the end of graduate school, partly because of family pressure, partly to keep up with my younger sister who'd gotten married the summer before, and partly—I think—because I'd never been on my own. My parents had paid my way through school, including apartments, and I knew I couldn't support myself in the same style my family had provided.

"Dan, my husband, was a few years older than me, already established as a lawyer and ready to settle down with a wife and family. He was just the kind of man my family wanted for me—he was just like them, upper-middle-class WASP all the way. He had a good job, he was successful, he liked going to good restaurants, he dressed well, he'd buy me a safe and quiet house in the suburbs. It all seemed perfect.

"Of course, what no one knew was that I'd been drinking heavily since my freshman year in college. I was in a sorority, and drinking was a perfectly socially acceptable party activity. But I'd been having blackouts since the beginning. Being married was ideal for me in terms of drinking. I felt safe; I could drink at home from the cocktail hour on without worrying about what would happen. Even though I continued to have blackouts, I thought everyone who drank forgot things.

"The real problem was that within a month of getting married, I knew I'd made a mistake. Dan and I just weren't compatible sexually, and as a result we fought about everything. The only thing we had going for us was that we liked the same social activities.

"So there I was in the suburbs of Chicago drinking wine at lunch and then drinking from the cocktail hour until bedtime. I knew I was unhappy, but I wasn't able to face being divorced and drunk. Then, of course, without planning it, I got pregnant. And more than once. Dan and I had three children in less than four years.

"Having those babies to look after pretty much destroyed any possibility that I'd leave the marriage. Sure, I knew I wasn't really there for my children, especially at night. I put them to bed as early as I could, completely dependent upon Dan to handle nighttime trauma and requests from the children. I knew if we were divorced and something happened, I would not be in any shape to function. I was too high to deal with any problems by seven o'clock at night. I was afraid. I knew that as long as I was drinking like that, I couldn't count on myself to respond in a crisis.

"Dan never expressed any unhappiness with the marriage. I was attractive, well-dressed, socially adept, and other people thought I was a good mother. Our kids did well in school, were in Boy Scouts and Brownies, Girl Scouts—the whole bit—and excelled at lots of school sports. We entertained extensively and went sailing with other couples. I looked good on the outside and was the kind of wife that Dan wanted. I helped him have the kind of life he wanted to live. Everything was taken care of on the home front, leaving him free to concentrate on his law practice.

"But inside, things weren't so great. Our relationship continued to deteriorate, and our drunken fights got really mean and vindictive. I knew I wasn't happy and was just staying with him because I was afraid that without him I couldn't take care of the children. I constantly threatened to leave, but never once followed through.

"Finally, I 'hit my bottom,' called up AA, and went to a meeting. I got a sponsor and stayed sober with only one slip. But I knew that I needed to leave the marriage; I'd never really been there emotionally— even at the beginning. I told Dan that they suggested in AA not to make any big changes during the first year, but that once the year was up I was going out the door. I knew then that I could take care of the kids myself, even if it was hard. I wasn't drunk any more at night; now I could be responsible.

"Luckily I had some help from my parents, and I got half the assets in the settlement. I look back now and see how many years I stayed in a marriage because I couldn't stop drinking. I wonder how women without financial resources ever leave. I wonder how many of them are still with men and husbands they don't love. I'm not proud of what I did. I used Dan and I used myself. He got the right kind of wife and I got to drink without facing the consequences. It may not have been prostitution in the traditional sense, but it was prostitution just the same."

Nancy had to work to put her life back together. She needed to learn to parent alone and to meet her own needs directly and without alcohol. At first she was bitter that her graduate degree in art history netted her only offers for secretarial positions, but she kept trying.

Nancy learned to feel compassion for herself during those years. She had exchanged her ability to be a "good" wife for the freedom to be able to drink. In recovery, she began to take pride in her ability to learn new skills, and she took a variety of jobs to figure out what she really enjoyed. Over time she accepted her past and forgave herself. After several years of sobriety she took a job in a battered women's shelter and returned to school for course work in alcoholism counseling.

Nancy knew it was difficult and scary to live an honest life. She knew how long it took her to make a move and she was especially understanding with the women who came to the shelter. So many of them kept returning to their abusive husbands, but some of them chose not to. Nancy's insight and encouragement were tremendously helpful both to the women and to herself. She knew about the struggles and the trade-offs that had to be worked through in order to live honestly.

The path of growth, the upward spiral, is always a path that requires choosing on a daily basis. Growing in the ability to choose recovery is a conscious path of self-empowerment. It is never easy or quick. Taking a step at a time, and allowing others to support those steps of growth, produces its own reward in a sense of well being and a growing hope of the possibility of expansion.

Chapter 9

Choosing
Personal Power

Of what have I ever been afraid? To question or to speak as I
believed could have meant pain, or death. But we all hurt in
so many different ways, all the time, and the pain will either
change or end. . . . And I began to recognize a source of
power within myself that comes from the knowledge that,
while it is most desirable not to be afraid, learning to put fear
into a perspective gives me great strength. . . . My silences
had not protected me. Your silence will not protect you.
                                    —Audre Lorde, *Sister Outsider*

We keep ourselves from being able to use our personal power in many
ways, but three are most common: by feeling guilty for our past behavior, by taking responsibility for childhood abuse, and by identifying
with our core of shame. When you choose to make changes in these areas, you will be taking a positive step on the journey to empowerment.

Moving Through Guilt

Guilt is about behavior. We feel guilty when we feel that we have violated our own values, when we feel we have done something that goes

against who we think we are or should be. Guilt also accompanies feelings of regret and remorse about something we have done. Most often we feel guilty in regard to something we think we have done to someone, so guilt is also about our behavior with other people and our thoughts and feelings about other people. When we feel guilty we cannot live in the present, because we are stuck on something we regret having done in the past.

It is very common for women in recovery to be burdened with a sense of guilt related to sexual issues. We live in a society that tends to blame the victims rather than the aggressors. Since women and children are most often victimized, we internalize the blame and feel guilty for experiences that we did not cause. Women who are chemically dependent have an added burden. Women addicts are viewed as worse than male addicts, so they internalize that stigma and subsequently feel guilty for being chemically dependent and guilty for the sexual events that occurred during that time.

Recovering women typically experience guilt about the following sexual experiences: their violation of their own sexual values; the expression of sexuality around their children; rape or other aggressive acts of sexual violation that occurred while they were drinking or using.

The Sexual Sellout

Once you have charted your sexual/chemical lifeline and filled out the relationship chart, you will have the opportunity to name accurately your past sexual experiences. When you first realized your unconscious participation in destructive behaviors, you may have felt guilty. Now, in ongoing recovery, you can begin to forgive yourself for the sexual patterns you were caught in and begin to change them.

The first step toward change is to stop living in guilt. You will need to decide to relinquish the hold the past has over you and start living in the present. This means taking responsibility for the consequences of your actions, even those you engaged in while actively drinking or using. You will need to make amends and acknowledge behavior that hurt others and behavior that hurt yourself.

For example, you may have picked poor partners or engaged in sexual activities when you didn't want to. You may have done things while intoxicated that you wouldn't have done sober, like Jackie, who kissed her colleague on the dance floor in front of the entire office. Your task is not to become obsessed about these incidents, beating yourself up for them time and again, but to forgive yourself and move on, knowing that now you can and are ready to make wiser choices.

You may also be dealing with guilt over having exchanged some form of your sexuality—your attractiveness, your ability to be a good wife, your willingness to be sexual—for alcohol, drugs, or money. In ongoing recovery you will need to take responsibility, as Nancy did, for learning to develop other avenues to money and personal power, including making sure you have the education and job skills necessary to support yourself and your children.

The "Bad" Mother

Alcoholic mothers are especially stigmatized by a society that places the welfare of children almost exclusively in the hands of women. The words we associate with alcoholism—irresponsible, loud, aggressive, promiscuous, erratic, violent, emotionally unavailable—are the very opposite of the words we associate with motherhood—responsible, quiet, tender, chaste, consistent, steady, and accessible. Thus "alcoholic mother" almost seems like a contradiction in terms.

Chemically dependent mothers in recovery need to understand the effects their drinking had on their children. In early recovery, the guilt mothers experience about the parenting they did while actively drinking often causes them to deny that drinking affected their parenting at all. I've heard women say, "My babies weren't affected by my drinking—they were too young to know," "I did everything a good mother does and I never drank in front of them," and "My daughter came first; I took care of her the same as any mother would." None of these statements are completely accurate. Children are inevitably affected by their parents' drinking, no matter how hard the parents may try to be "perfect."

In ongoing recovery, these same mothers are better equipped to move out of denial and honestly look at the effects of their parenting. Empowerment about mothering means moving out of guilt and taking responsibility for what happened in the past, as well as what is happening now. Women who don't resolve their guilt often overcompensate in recovery, striving to be perfect mothers.

There's only one problem: to be a perfect mother you have to have perfect children. Your children will be under tremendous pressure to behave well and to have only positive feelings so that they will reflect well on your mothering. They won't be allowed to be human, to express their full range of feelings and behavior.

This is a no-win situation both for the woman and for the children: The children will always fail, because, as human beings, they can never be perfect. The mother, who must also fail in the attempt to be perfect, continues along the downward spiral of guilt and failure.

To break out of this pattern, you first need to accept and forgive yourself for the quality of your parenting while you were drinking or using. You must stop seeing yourself as the "bad mother" and your children as helpless victims. Instead you will need to see that the entire family is a casualty of alcohol or drug use and now needs to be restored.

Once you forgive yourself and accept that your past was not what you would now choose, you are free to move forward to become the kind of parent you want to be. You can take responsibility for your actions in the past and present and begin to nourish your children's growth.

Most alcoholic or chemically dependent mothers also grew up in dysfunctional or chemically dependent homes. Thus you probably had no good role models for good parenting. You may lack skills in setting consistent limits, disciplining without violence, and discriminating between your children's needs and your own needs. You may have little knowledge of normal child development and have unrealistic expectations of appropriate child behavior.

Parenting is a difficult responsibility, and many women raised in dysfunctional families feel inadequate to the task. These women can find assistance and education in parenting classes, which are now available in many areas. These classes teach techniques of consistent limit setting, active listening and communicating, alternatives to physical discipline and verbal threats, and the importance of establishing clear boundaries between parent and child. Such classes can be extremely helpful in changing your parenting patterns. Usually they are sponsored at little or no cost by schools, family service agencies, YWCAs, and Jewish Community Centers. I also recommend the book *Children: The Challenge* (see appendix C) for learning more effective parenting skills.

In your quest to improve your parenting, you may work so hard to make up to your children for your past neglect that your own recovery needs become secondary. If you are a working single mother, you may find that you spend all your time working and trying to meet your children's emotional and physical needs. But a good mother is also one who takes care of herself. By taking care of yourself—getting exercise, eating well, getting enough sleep, spending time alone, and taking time for outings with adult friends—you model for your children healthy self-care.

It is especially important that you build a network of other recovering mothers. You need to have a safe place to discuss how the issues of recovery and mothering come together, and a place where you can express your concerns and feelings about your mothering responsibilities.

Being a responsible parent also means taking some responsibility for your children's recovery process. If they are grown, this may not be realistic. But if they still live with you at home, you will need to provide them with information about alcoholism and how it has affected you and the family.

Your children may need to be in a counseling group for children of alcoholics or take part in individual or family therapy. Strange as it may seem, children can have a tough time adjusting to your sobriety, and they may resent your attempts to resume the parental role. They may be very angry at what they perceive as your neglect and abandonment, and they may need a safe place to work through these feelings.

Check with women's treatment programs in your area for counseling groups for children whose mothers are in recovery. If these centers don't have them, they can usually refer you to an individual counselor experienced in working with children from alcoholic homes.

You may have guilt about your sexual behavior while drinking. Your children may have heard you called sexual names, seen you nude while drunk, or seen you passed out in the bathroom. They may have observed you in sexual encounters or acting sexual with a stranger. You may even have inappropriately expressed your sexuality toward your children, violating sexual boundaries or being sexually suggestive. If you have guilt about any of these sexual areas and your parenting, it is important to get counseling for you and your children.

After you have been in recovery for a while, you may discover that one or more of your children has been molested or been the victim of incest. A very high percentage of sexually abused children come from chemically dependent families, and it is extremely important that you not be in denial about that possibility with your children.

If you discover evidence of sexual abuse of your children, you must identify the abuser and make certain that he (or she) no longer has access to your children. This may be especially difficult if the abuser is a family member; but it is absolutely essential that your children know that you will protect them and that you will put their needs first. Although you were incapable of protecting them while you were drinking, you can protect them now. You need to take an active stand on their behalf so you can start a healing process together.

Don't let your guilt about your child's sexual abuse immobilize you. Studies have indicated that children recover much faster from sexual abuse if they are allowed to "say no" to the abuser in some form. "Saying no" may include making a report to Children's Protective Services. It may mean confronting the abuser directly. It may mean refusing to visit a family member's home. It will certainly include getting counseling for sexual abuse victims and their families.

Dealing with the sexual abuse of your children can bring up stored memories of your own sexual abuse, if you were abused as a child. You will need to work through your feelings about your own past as you deal with your guilt about your children's abuse.

Healing is nearly always possible. If children are offered safe opportunities to tell the truth about their experiences, and if we are willing to learn how to parent in a more responsible fashion, then families can heal. Just as there are many different forms of neglect and abuse, so are there varied pathways to healing. Therapy and process groups can help break the chains that keep your family confined to the past.

Rape: The Blameless Victim

Rape is an ever-present possibility in women's lives. Most women are all too aware of this, and to some degree it limits how we live our daily lives. We are all concerned about our physical safety, we all have places where we do not go alone, times we will not go outside, and situations we're careful to avoid. Each of us is constantly vigilant in a way that no man has to be. Just because we are women, we are targets for physical assault and sexual violation. Few women can protect themselves so completely that they can disavow or completely ignore the risks attached to their gender.

Rape is not a sexual crime. It is a crime of violence, power, and aggression. The instrument of assault, however, is sexual—the penis. In prisons, where women are not part of the power hierarchy, men rape each other as a form of dominance, terrorization, and ownership. It works on other men, and it works on women: we are terrorized by what may happen to us, and we are careful to avoid dangerous circumstances.

We used to believe that most women were raped by strangers, men who jumped out of the bushes. Now we know that 75 percent of women know their rapists, that so-called date rape is common, and that rape in marriage is prevalent. Women are raped by co-workers, acquaintances, friends, dates, lovers, ex-lovers, husbands, and ex-husbands.

Until the latter half of the 1970s it was not a crime in the United States for a man to force sexual intercourse on his wife. (It is now a crime in only eleven of our fifty states.) Sexual intercourse in marriage was seen as the husband's right, regardless of the wife's wishes. Thus, marriage carried with it the right of forcible coitus. Even in a 1988 study, 87 percent of seventh- to ninth-grade boys and 79 percent of girls said rape was okay if a couple were married.

Date rape has been accurately named only recently. Some 30 percent of first-year college women reported an attempt at forcible intercourse in 1990, and 60 percent of college men say they would attempt intercourse by force "given the right circumstances." In the study mentioned above, 24 percent of seventh- to ninth-grade boys and 16 percent of the girls said it was acceptable for a man to force a woman to have sex with him if he had spent money on her.

Every six minutes in the United States, another woman is raped; and 44 percent of all women report having been the victim of a rape or attempted rape during their lifetime. As a recovering woman, your chances of having been raped are even higher than those of the non–chemically dependent woman. Almost 60 percent of alcoholic women report having been raped. If you have been a victim of incest or other childhood sexual abuse, the risk of being raped is still greater.

Society tends to blame the victim for the crime, and this is even worse for the alcoholic victim of rape. All women get the message that they "asked for it" by dressing provocatively, acting seductively, or being in the wrong place at the wrong time. This message is even stronger for the woman who has been drinking.

Society as a whole blames the sexual aggression of men on the drunken woman. If you have been raped while you were drinking, you probably blame yourself even more than you would if you had not been drinking. It is important to remind yourself that no circumstance justifies rape. Nothing about you—how you were dressed, how much you had to drink, or what you "didn't do to prevent it," has anything to do with rape. Rape is an expression of power—the angry, reckless power of a man in a rage. The rapist is responsible for committing an act of sexual violence on his victim; the woman is not responsible for that act.

Healing Sexual Abuse

Your sexuality does not exist in isolation from the rest of you. It is an expression of your emotional, physical, and spiritual selves. Thus your feelings about your sexual past have a powerful effect on you.

The feelings of sexual guilt, shame, and self-loathing you may have covered up with alcohol, drugs, or other addictions begin to surface during recovery to affect your current sex life. Chief among these is childhood sexual abuse.

Sexual abuse during childhood isn't limited to specific acts of fondling and penetration. It occurs across a continuum from invasion of sexual privacy to comments about your body, being kissed in a way that felt uncomfortable, being touched in sexual areas, and being encouraged to have sex you didn't want. The continuum moves from psychological incest to covert incest to overt incest. Figure 8 shows this continuum.

You may have been sexually mistreated in a variety of ways that you didn't initially identify as sexual abuse. Yet those instances can greatly affect your current sexual feelings and experiences. Four common patterns of unhealthy sexuality emerge in dysfunctional and alcoholic homes:

1. Sexuality is totally repressed. Family members show little or no affection and rarely touch, and the no-talk rule is strictly enforced.

2. Sexuality is expressed only when the parent is drunk or otherwise intoxicated. Then the parent may be lewd, inappropriately suggestive, or sloppily affectionate.

Psychological Incest	Covert Incest	Overt Incest
1. Blurring of generational lines	1. Inadvertent touch	1. French kissing
2. Closed system	2. Household voyeurism	2. Exhibitionism
3. Enmeshment/disengagement	3. Physical punishment while naked	3. Fondling
4. Telling child inappropriate secrets	4. Sexual hugs	4. Fellatio
5. Disrespect of privacy needs	5. Ridicule of developing bodies	5. Cunnilingus
6. Emotional abuse	6. Lewd reading/video watching with child	6. Penetration

Figure 8. Incest Continuum*

*Adapted from Sue Evans and Susan Schaefer, "Incest and Chemically Dependent Women: Treatment Implications," in Eli Coleman, ed., *Chemical Dependency and Intimacy Dysfunctions* (New York: Haworth Press, 1988), 150.

3. Sexuality is coupled with both drinking and violence. The only time a child sees her parent being sexual is after an argument or fight.

4. Sexuality is overly open. Everything is oversexualized and the children are raised in a seductive environment.

Let's look at these patterns more closely.

Repressed Sexuality

In the cold and inexpressive home, affection and sexuality are missing. Neither parent need be actively drinking or using for this atmosphere to exist. In the chemically dependent home, this state exists because one of the parents is so focused on the drug of choice that no energy or interest is left over for sex. If the father is an alcoholic, he may have lost the ability to have an erection. If the mother is an alcoholic, she may be experiencing loss of desire, difficulty lubricating, or inability to have an orgasm. In either case the other parent is probably extremely angry, resentful, and lacking in tenderness and trust. Parents caught up in this dynamic don't provide good role models of loving, sexual adults.

Children in this situation may grow up with no sexual teaching in the home. They learn everything they know about sex from school and their peers. Because they have few positive images of sexuality, they may grow up to exhibit one of two extremes: (1) difficulty with sexual expression, making them cold, distant, fearful, or nonsexual, or (2) sexual rebellion, leading to dangerous sexual encounters.

Sexuality and Intoxication

When a parent expresses sexuality only after drinking, then sex is no longer the expression of a loving, respectful relationship. Sex seems to be a nest of "bad" impulses that only alcohol can release, and then with disastrous results.

Children may come upon their parents nude when the parents are drunk; parents may engage in intercourse with the bedroom door wide open; or they may bring partners home and be sexually aggressive—as a seductive prelude to the act itself—in front of the children. Sexual expression then becomes a series of humiliating, shameful incidents.

Sexuality and Violence

In homes in which sexuality is associated with violence, alcohol and drugs are frequently, though not always, part of the equation. Parents may argue over their sexual behavior with others while drinking. They may be sexually aggressive or seductive, be rebuffed, then explode in verbal or physical violence. They may drink, fight, and then be sexual.

In any case, children begin to associate violence with sexuality. As adults, these children may become so fearful of sexual expression that they avoid it at all costs, or they may repeat the family patterns and become enmeshed in violent sexual episodes.

Hypersexuality

The hypersexual home has no appropriate sexual boundaries. A seductive feeling pervades the atmosphere of the home, and everything becomes focused around bodies and sex.

For example, the mother may think nothing of answering the door in her slip; parents may habitually burst in on their teenagers in the shower; the father may routinely make suggestive remarks about his adolescent daughter's developing body; parents may ask invasive questions about their teenagers' dating life.

Children in these homes grow up without boundaries. Everything is allowed, all the time. The mother and daughter in such a family may even sleep with the same man on consecutive nights. Adults raised in hypersexual homes have great difficulty setting limits in all aspects of their lives.

The Shocking Statistics

Unhealthy sexual functioning in dysfunctional families often results in incest—sexual touching by a trusted family member or parental figure. Daughters from alcoholic homes are particularly vulnerable to experiencing incest before they reach puberty.

The new awareness of incest and childhood sexual abuse is largely the result of the women's movement. As women talked to each other in consciousness-raising groups in the early 1970s, sexual assault emerged as an overriding concern. It became clear that women's needs related to sexual assault were not being recognized. The first rape speak-out was held in 1971, and thousands of rape crisis centers, organized by women, sprang up all across the United States.

Within this new context of freedom to talk about sexual assault, women began to come forward with their long-buried stories of incest, and books began to be published on the subject (see appendixes C and D).

In 1977 Diana Russell completed the first random survey of women about their experiences of sexual violation. She found that in a random sample of 930 women, 38 percent reported having been sexually violated by an adult before the age of eighteen; 16 percent reported having been sexually molested by a relative before the age of eighteen. This study shocked authorities and brought the awareness of incest and other sexual abuse of children out of the closet. Earlier studies had placed the incidence of childhood sexual abuse at from 3 percent to 5 percent.

The rates of sexual violation among chemically dependent women are even higher. My own research of a matched sample of alcoholic and nonalcoholic women found that 50 percent of nonalcoholic women reported childhood sexual abuse, compared to 74 percent of alcoholic women.* Clearly, not all of those women were raised in alcoholic

---

*Stephanie Covington and Janet Kohen, "Women, Alcohol, and Sexuality," *Advances in Alcohol and Substance Abuse*, vol. 4, no. 1, Fall 1984.

homes. Girls are at high risk for being sexually abused whether or not they grow up in alcoholic homes.

Surviving Blame and Guilt

Women in recovery deal with the effects of childhood sexual abuse in various ways. Many of them first retrieve their memories of abuse after they enter recovery. Others will have covered their memories with alcohol and drugs but remain aware of them.

As we have seen, the term *incest* covers a spectrum of behaviors from inappropriate emotional bonding to penetration. Incest creates victims; yet I want to talk about these women as *survivors*. This emphasizes the fact that healing is possible.

Whatever form of incest you may have experienced, you were not responsible for its occurrence. A child is *never* responsible for the sexual intrusions of an adult. It is always the adult's responsibility to set and keep sexual boundaries.

As a child, however, you didn't know that, so you may feel responsible for the harm that was done to you. You feel that you should have stopped it, or could have stopped it, and that somehow it was all your fault. Your guilt about being molested may be even greater if you experienced sexual pleasure, appreciated the attention and affection you received, or were especially close to and fond of the offender. This is natural, but it doesn't make you responsible.

In early recovery your attention is on exploring the layers of denial about your addiction, on forming an identity as a recovering person, and on maintaining sobriety. If you become aware of childhood sexual abuse during this period, it is best to note its relationship to your present recovery but not to explore it in depth. You can read books about the healing process, gaining some insight into what that process might mean for you, with an eye toward in-depth healing work during ongoing recovery. A number of excellent books on this subject are listed in the appendixes.

Many incest survivors find that both group process and individual therapy are helpful. Group work with other incest survivors allows you to get to know and identify with other women who have been through similar experiences. You will be able to feel at a much deeper level that you are not alone, that you are not crazy, and that your reactions and feelings are shared by others.

Incest groups should be and usually are led by skilled, licensed therapists who have extensive experience working with women abused as children. Groups may last from twelve to twenty weeks (although not all groups are time limited) and consist of five to eight women. It is affirming to bond with other women who have had similar experiences. The release from isolation, secrecy, and shame can be liberating.

Individual therapy is particularly good for understanding your present relationship to your family, for exploring the effect incest is having on your present relationships, and for making the changes in your life that your incest experiences have prevented you from making. Long-term individual therapy can also recreate the parent-child relationship in a healthy way and be a corrective experience to your abusive past.

In individual therapy it is absolutely essential that the therapist establish and maintain appropriate boundaries. If for any reason you feel that the therapist is violating boundaries and creating inappropriate intimacy, even in the smallest way, terminate your work there and find another therapist. Rape crisis centers and women's treatment programs may have referrals to therapists who are experienced at working with incest survivors and careful about maintaining boundaries.

Recently, various Twelve-Step programs for incest survivors have started across the country (see appendix E for resources). Twelve-Step programs hold meetings that enable incest survivors to break out of the victim role and the nightmare of terror, guilt, and confusion. Original perpetrators of incest or rape, or victims who later became initiators, do not attend meetings. In some locations there are women-only meetings.

Some women find Twelve-Step incest meetings to be a helpful adjunct to a process group and/or individual therapy. If there are no meetings in your area, you can start one. Write to the addresses listed in appendix E for start-up literature.

During ongoing recovery you have the opportunity to look at past experiences that stand in the way of your own awakening and expansion. If your incest experiences do not become part of a healing process, they can become the source of unmanageable emotions that threaten your recovery. Although it takes a great deal of courage to peel away denial about abusive experiences in order to face and heal the pain without relying on chemicals to dull the pain, it is always worth the effort. The kinds of growth you can experience from such healing are phenomenal. For the first time in your life, you may find yourself able to be in healthy, loving relationships that support you as much as you support them.

Your Sexual Rights

Incest survivors often gravitate toward one of two extreme sexual lifestyles. They may become sexually isolated, withdrawn, and avoidant, leading a nonsexual life; or they may become sexually active in a self-destructive way.

Incest survivors experience adult forms of sexual contact at an early age and learn little about sexually appropriate behavior. They often grow up sexualizing their contacts with adults and authority figures, leading to further exploitation. It is common for women who were sexually abused by a family member to experience later abuse by another authority figure and to experience rape. Many incest survivors report having felt uncertain as teenagers about the appropriate progression of sexual contact in dating, which resulted in a reputation for being sexually "loose."

As we saw earlier, lack of sexual desire is a common complaint of incest survivors, along with a variety of other problems related to arousal. Many women go numb at a certain point in experiencing sexual excitement; others disconnect or dissociate from their bodies and find themselves unable to feel; and some experience flashbacks or sudden images of the abusive situation. All of these experiences interfere with sexual pleasure and may make sex an anxiety-provoking and painful encounter.

The physical sexual repercussions of incest are often serious: inability to lubricate, inability to come to orgasm, painful intercourse, vaginal spasms. This is the body's way of saying that sex is not safe. Your body's memories of incest may override your emotional desires, making it impossible for you to engage in sex.

Incest survivors learned to put the sexual needs of another ahead of their own. They learned that their own needs were not important, and that to secure the love of another it was important to have sex. As adults, most survivors place primary importance on their partner's experience and remain out of touch with their own needs and desires. It is not uncommon for survivors to identify their own pleasure with pleasing their partner. To obtain pleasure, however, we need to focus primarily on our own experience during sex.

Incest survivors have been conditioned by their negative childhood sexual experiences to associate sex with helplessness, disgust, pain, anger, loss of control, shame, guilt, and hate. Therefore, it is often extremely difficult for the survivor to experience adult sexuality with any degree of pleasure and abandonment. She may find it almost impossible to surrender to positive feelings during sex, since current positive feelings are being blocked by negative feelings from the past.

The sexual problems that result from incest do not go away by themselves. However, healing can occur, and incest survivors can make positive changes in the sexual areas of their lives. Survivors can move out of old, self-defeating patterns that reinforce unsatisfying sexual experiences and move into experiencing the kinds of sexual lives that they want.

Each of us has rights concerning our sexuality. Wendy Maltz and Beverly Holman, in their book *Incest and Sexuality*, developed a "Sexual

Bill of Rights" from the advice of survivors, and this is a good starting point for learning new skills and behaviors. In my workshops I often ask participants to create their own sexual bill of rights, and I would ask you to do the same. Some of your rights might include the right to say yes, the right to say no, the right to feel safe, the right to safe sex, the right to experiment, the right to choose your sex partner, the right to talk about sex, and the right to have limits.

Go through your list of sexual rights and note each that is not now an integral part of your sexual life. Ask yourself why you don't feel you have that right. Explore why you are afraid to have that right. Visualize yourself having that right, and see what you would have to do to create it for yourself.

Ongoing recovery is a good time to work in individual or group therapy on incest issues. If you want to heal from incest you must maintain your recovery so that you can remain conscious and responsible for your sexual choices.

Therapy is a safe place for you to retrieve your memories of what actually happened to you and to work on believing that it did happen. In therapy you will have a chance to break your denial and silence and learn to tell your story. This can help you resolve your self-blame and accept that the abuse wasn't your fault.

You will probably be filled with the leftover unexpressed feelings that result from abuse—guilt, shame, pain, humiliation, anger, and rage. You may even feel overwhelmed by them. But it is important to express them and work through them. As you grieve and mourn the loss of your childhood, you will learn to reparent your inner child, who still lives within you. Finally, you will learn to resolve the issue and take responsibility for creating new and healthier patterns of sexual relating.

Even if incest has powerfully affected your ability to experience sexual pleasure, the healing available to you is just as powerful. As a survivor you learned to deal with the most abusive situation possible in childhood. In adulthood, with time, energy, and patience, you can also heal from that experience. Reclaiming your sexuality from an abusive past is possible. You have the right to positive, healthy sexuality.

Overcoming Shame

Shame is the feeling that "There is something wrong with me, with who I am as a person. I can't ever change it, it's who I am." Shame, then, is a no-win situation. We feel that we are no good at our very core. This feeling is so horrifying, so burdensome, that we become secretive about our shame. We don't want anyone to know how bad we are.

As solid and impervious as this shame may feel, you can effect its eventual disintegration. One of the first steps in dissolving this core of shame is to share your secrets, to look into your past, to explore all the painful circumstances and bring them out into the open.

Sources of Shame

Women have many sources of shame to draw from. In our society men are valued more highly than women, so simply being a woman can be the beginning of shame. Men's "rational" thinking is valued above women's more circular, complex, intuitive thinking, which is labeled "irrational." Men's hard, muscular, small-hipped bodies are valued over women's rounder, softer forms, so high-fashion models look like twelve-year-old boys with flat busts, small hips, and no bellies.

Men's tendency to emotional detachment and distancing, which is part of their own socialization, is called independence and is valued as the norm. In fact, independence is not even a human reality: we are all interdependent.

If you are not white, not middle class, not successful, or not heterosexual, you will have another layer of shame to contend with. Children of color absorb all these shaming experiences and labor under their constricting and restricting influence. Audre Lorde, in *Sister Outsider*, describes one such shaming childhood encounter:

> The AA subway train to Harlem. I clutch my mother's sleeve, her arms full of shopping bags, Christmas-heavy. The wet smell of winter clothes, the train's lurching. My mother spots an almost seat, pushes my little snowsuited body down. On one side of me

a man reading a paper. On the other, a woman in a fur hat staring at me. Her mouth twitches as she stares and then her gaze drops down, pulling mine with it. Her leather-gloved hand plucks at the line where my new blue snowpants and her sleek fur coat meet. She jerks her coat closer to her. I look. I do not see whatever terrible thing she is seeing on the seat between us—probably a roach. But she has communicated her horror to me. It must be something very bad from the way she's looking, so I pull my snowsuit closer to me away from it, too. When I look up the woman is still staring at me, her nose holes and eyes huge. And suddenly I realize there is nothing crawling up the seat between us; it is me she doesn't want her coat to touch.

Poor women receive similar messages. "My mother struggled to support us," says one woman. "She made $4.50 an hour, cleaning other people's houses, and she did the best she could. But we grew up thinking there was something wrong with her, and with us, because we weren't rich."

Women who know when they are young that they are emotionally and erotically drawn to other women know intuitively that in this society they must hide that knowledge. Lesbians know without a hint of discussion that they must keep their feelings secret because the way they are—in fact, who they are—is just not acceptable.

Women who grew up in dysfunctional families were made to feel ashamed by their parents, both intentionally, as a form of control, and unintentionally, out of their own shame-based childhoods. Such parents don't reassure their child that she is okay though her behavior is upsetting. Instead the child herself is branded as a failure.

So as women—as chemically dependent women, abused women, women from dysfunctional families, women of color, poor women, lesbian women—we have experienced humiliation, ridicule, disparagement, abandonment, or simply self-hate. We have learned to feel that there is something irrevocably wrong about who we are, something that cannot be fixed. And around this core of shame we have formed our identities.

Shame now exists independently in our psyches, and we carry those feelings with us wherever we go. These shameful feelings can be triggered by internal or external experiences.

The Power Drain

Ongoing recovery is about empowerment, the ability to feel power and take action. Healing your sense of shame is basic to your empowerment.

Shame immobilizes you and drains away your power. You feel that you have no energy, no hope, no sense of the possibility of movement. And this shame becomes a vicious circle. The more shameful you feel, the more you are robbed of your initiative. You don't move out into the world as much, and therefore you have fewer positive, affirming experiences.

Taking a long, hard look at the source of shame in your life is the first step toward becoming assertive. You will certainly find that you have no control over many things. For some, sources of shame in our society include race, ethnicity, cultural orientation, education, income, and sexual preference. Yet these are just part of the variety of ways of being that gives life its rich complexity. If you are in touch with your wise inner self, you will know that there is no shame—or glory—attached to any of it. You simply are who you are, and that is the way it is.

Moving away from being influenced by your shaming experiences is a long-term process. There is no easy cure or quick fix. Therapy can help you restore a healthy process of dealing with life rather than acting from shame, but effecting such change takes time.

During this process of dissolving your core of shame you will need to examine some of the subtler aspects of your behavior. In the process, you may reexperience deep feelings of shame that you have typically controlled with compulsive behavior, including alcohol and drug abuse. As you work with those feelings and learn new patterns of behavior, you may find yourself feeling extremely vulnerable. This is a time in your life when you will need extensive support, from both your therapist and your extended family and friends.

You can begin to move into a more healthy way of being by creating a sense of personal sexual dignity, empowering yourself to act on your sexuality in your own behalf without violating or coercing others, and becoming accountable for your sexual self and your recovery. Working with the issues that have kept you from empowerment and responsibility—learned helplessness, guilt, sexual abuse, and shame—will enable you to experience intimacy with yourself and with those you love.

Sarah and Danielle are both struggling in their own ways to gain empowerment and take responsibility for themselves. Sarah is working hard to learn more about herself, her needs, and her motivations, but she is still far from choosing personal empowerment. She recognizes her pill addiction, she sees and understands her enmeshment with her mother, and she is aware that she has recreated in her two marriages the dynamics of her own dysfunctional family of origin. Yet she cannot move forward; she is stuck.

Sarah is stuck because she is paralyzed by fear. She is afraid to take risks, afraid of change, afraid to displease others and risk being abandoned. Her fear keeps her from understanding that she has choices. She views all change as loss, without understanding that some changes can be losses but still not be negative. She's unable to make the leap from her own place of fear to a pathway of changes and unknowns. Sarah is searching for courage to act in the face of fear, rather than waiting for fear to subside. Fear often doesn't disappear. The key is to realize it need not prevent decision making and action.

Sarah heard and internalized her family's message that instructed, "If you are afraid, then don't. Negative feeling must be avoided." This message continues to exert a powerful influence on her, despite the very real progress she has made. She still tends to choose known pain over unknown change.

Sarah is also stuck being overly critical of Scott and blaming him for their relationship problems. She projects the cause of their unhappiness completely onto him and sees herself as free of blame, almost a victim. Because Scott refuses to be in marital therapy, she relieves herself of responsibility for causing any part of their problems. This abdication of personal power—even the way that Sarah has done it is tinged with self-righteous anger and hypervigilence— is Sarah's major roadblock. She will be able to progress in her recovery only if she moves forward in spite of her fear and trusts the momentum to carry her. It is an act of faith.

Danielle is beginning to relax her focus on "having it all" and to understand that money, clothes, physical appearance, and possessions are not the ultimate markers of happiness and success. Her role models when she was growing up were women in magazines. Now Danielle realizes these are not the best choices—they appear two-dimensional, unrealistic, and empty. As she begins to relinquish her concentration on externals, she ventures inside to find and meet the unknown, inner Danielle.

It has been important for Danielle to be in a group with a variety of types of women from whom she has felt disconnected in the past. Over the months she has begun to see the powerlessness and victimization of some of these women, and instead of feeling smug she feels for their pain and struggles. She feels empathetic when she hears a sexual abuse survivor talk about fear and anxiety, or a lesbian discuss the pain of hiding a loving relationship from family and co-workers.

Because of her parents' work with migrant laborers, Danielle is socially conscious in many ways and supportive of the individual struggles of the women in the group; yet she does not personally identify with their powerlessness. She muses, "I'm not black, lesbian, or abused; I've never been afraid to touch myself; and my mom's never tried to restrict or control me like Sarah's did." But she too lacks the power of choice. Her realization is made more difficult because she appears so perfect. She has accepted society's ideal of woman, one that discourages an emotional life. She sees with some pain that she has become, to some degree, the two-dimensional woman she so admired: plastic, synthetic, manufactured, a commodity.

When she looks over the events of her life, it is clear that sex with so many men didn't work. She was acting out the role of a fun-loving, free young woman. But she was disconnected from her feelings; she was actually reacting to society's messages like a puppet who moves when certain strings are pulled. Her behavior was an expression not of inner desire but of the expectations she had built into a repertoire. She lived to conform to a societal image of what she should be. So no matter how many men she slept with, how many times she climaxed, or how proficient a partner she felt she was, her inner longing remained untouched.

Gradually, Danielle understood how she had used alcohol to feel like a member of her peer group and to fulfill her duty as a woman. It helped her to see how the alcohol separated her from her inner self, dulling and anesthetizing her feelings, and how it separated her from the pain of longing. She thought the alcohol somehow took care of the problems her feelings caused. Now she knows alcohol only worsened her predicament. Her drinking limited the choices she could make and disabled her capacity to know what she felt about anything or anyone.

With this new awareness, Danielle realizes the depths of her struggle and the strength of her resolve to change. Gaining personal power means seeing what has been externally imposed and understanding that we have choices and the capacity to make changes. There are choices that expand the self, just as there are those that do not.

Danielle's computer-oriented mind translates this into an equation: choice = power = expansion = integration. Danielle has found a beginning, a possibility of expanding her emotional side and integrating her inner and outer lives. She's genuinely excited about getting to know the new three-dimensional Danielle, a woman of many choices and quiet power. She is no longer content to wait to be realized; she is actively becoming.

PART FOUR

AWAKENING
TO INTIMACY

Experiencing authentic intimacy is one of the most hope-filled and ex-
hilarating aspects of being human. But I am continually brought back to
the need for trust, the kind of trust between individuals that produces
equality, mutuality, and reciprocity. Intimacy can occur only between
peers. Developing these dynamics between yourself and others is a lifelong task.

Awakening to intimacy and awakening to your sexuality are inter-
related. Both are dimensions of the ongoing process of recovery. In recovery we begin to understand what we have longed for, what we really
want in our lives. It gives us the opportunity to create change and to integrate sexuality and spirituality in our intimate relationships. This next
level of awakening poses an exciting challenge for all of us, no matter
where we are on this path.

Chapter 10

Discovering Self-Intimacy

When one is a stranger to oneself then one is estranged from others too. If one is out of touch with oneself, then one cannot touch others. How often in a large city, shaking hands with my friends, I have felt the wilderness stretching between us. Both of us were wandering in arid wastes, having lost the springs that nourished us—or having found them dry. Only when one is connected to one's own core is one connected to others, I am beginning to discover. And for me, the core, the inner spring, can best be refound through solitude. . . . Solitude alone is not the answer to this; it is only a step toward it, a mechanical aid, like the "room of one's own" demanded for women, before they could make their place in the world. The problem is not entirely in finding the room of one's own, the time alone, difficult and necessary as this is. The problem is more how to still the soul in the midst of its activities. In fact, the problem is how to feed the soul.

—Anne Morrow Lindbergh, *Gift from the Sea*

What Is Intimacy?

Why do we have so little understanding of what it means to be intimate? I think it is because there is such a tremendous taboo in this culture against knowing ourselves. Most of us have spent far more time thinking about the content of our jobs than we have spent thinking about and exploring who we are. As children we were cautioned not to be "selfish and self-centered," which usually referred to our attempts to understand ourselves and our motivations. But as we attempt to move toward establishing real intimacy in our lives, it becomes clear that unless we know ourselves—unless we're intimate with ourselves—we are unable to be intimate with others.

The strongest model of intimacy we carry within us is our parents' relationship. For the vast majority of recovering women this is a dismal model at best. Most of us have so little real experience of intimacy that the word itself is baffling or surrounded by fear and mistrust. I would like to share with you three definitions that I think will help you get a feeling for what we will be talking about in this chapter:

- Intimacy means that what is happening on the inside is congruent with what can be seen on the outside.

- Intimacy is the spontaneous expression of feeling in an atmosphere of little or no personal threat.

- Intimacy is me teaching you about me.

These definitions may be different from what you have conceived of as intimacy. *Intimacy* is a worn-out word in our society. Sometimes we use it as a catch word. We say, "I'm having an intimate relationship with someone," which society understands as, "We're having sex." But it's not the same thing. Not even close.

We live in a society that confuses and mixes together love, sex, and intimacy. Often when we're looking for one, we go out and get another. When you're looking for intimacy you may end up in a sexual encounter; the fact that it is sexual does not make it intimate. Conversely, you may be very intimate with someone with whom you are not sexual at all.

Recovering women must also contend with the damaging effects of the addictive process. Addiction prevents intimacy; it destroys even the possibility of intimacy. An addictive relationship with anything or anyone is a relationship that is out of balance. The object of addiction—alcohol, drugs, food, a person—becomes the focal point of a woman's life. In essence, it becomes the only love object—that which the addict loves, trusts, and cares about. Even if the love object is a human being, as with codependence or sexual addiction, the objectification of that person renders intimacy impossible.

With mood-altering substances such as alcohol or drugs, there is also a change in how we experience feelings. Substance abuse limits our capacity to be intimate, because intimacy is about feelings. Addiction interrupts the process of intimacy. It interferes with the ability to experience deep connection with others; our perceptions become distorted, our behavior becomes defensive, our feelings become altered.

Intimacy is complex. There are different ways of experiencing and expressing it. Emotional intimacy involves sharing our feelings; intellectual intimacy involves sharing our thoughts; physical intimacy involves sharing our bodies. Emotional intimacy does not always accompany physical intimacy. You may have a deeply intimate emotional connection to someone you have never embraced.

Being intimate with yourself does not mean being narcissistic, obsessing endlessly about yourself and your own wants and needs. It does not mean you have to focus on yourself to the exclusion of others. It simply means knowing who you are, being in touch with your feelings as they occur, and knowing why you react to events and situations as you do.

It comes down to the ancient philosophical advice, "Know thyself." Knowing yourself begins with knowing your feelings and then goes progressively deeper as you learn to know your mind, your spirit, and your sexual self. The inner journey is often difficult but ultimately richly rewarding. As you learn to know yourself on different levels, you discover what a wonderfully complex being you really are.

Know Your Feelings

Feelings are feelings. They are okay just as they are. You do not have to judge them or deny them or act upon them; it is enough to feel and observe them.

Chemically dependent women are generally accustomed to acting out feelings without really being aware of them, and that acting out often has a compulsive quality. But as you allow yourself simply to feel your feelings, whether of sadness, anger, joy, or loss, you will lose your need to act impulsively from them. Simply being with your feelings, noting them, and allowing them to exist within you can free you to be able to choose how to express them.

You may have compressed your feelings into one feeling state—anger, hurt, fear, or anxiety—and this state may have become your constant way of being. You may have lost your ability to feel a wide range of feelings, or to discriminate between feelings. Ask yourself what dominant feeling you are experiencing. Are you angry or hurt? Disappointed, maybe frustrated? Fearful, or perhaps anticipatory? Some of your feelings might include irritation, delight, distress, abhorrence, heartache, satisfaction, dread, intolerance, excitement, and so on.

There are literally hundreds of words that describe the many different feelings and shades of feelings. Claudia Black, in *It Will Never Happen to Me* (see appendix C), makes a list of various feelings we all have and provides an exercise for rating the expression they were allowed in our families. If you are having trouble identifying your feelings, this is a good place to start.

Many recovering women have a lifetime of stored up, unexpressed feelings lying buried underneath today's feeling. You may have repressed your feelings from the fear of being overwhelmed and engulfed by their intensity and strength. This is not unusual; children from dysfunctional families receive both direct and indirect messages not to identify and express feelings. In recovery, however, access to feelings is more immediate. Without the dampening down effect of the addiction, unexpressed feelings may come rushing to the surface.

It is important to know that your inner self will not allow you to feel more than you are able to handle. Creating a safe environment in which to process your feelings and trusting in the wisdom of your psyche can help you deal with the fear of being overwhelmed. Let your feelings wash over you, like waves over the shore. Like waves, they will ebb and flow, returning you to your calm center. The center is yours to claim as a harbor to which you can always return. It is the source of wisdom, power, and peace. It is the self.

There is great value in being connected to old feelings in order to dissipate them. When you allow old feelings to dissolve, what you feel relates to today. The only way to be truly in the present is first to feel the past and then to let it go.

Know Your Body

When you are disconnected and estranged from your body you are missing a valuable source of self-knowledge and self-understanding. Your body is a repository of knowledge about yourself. How and what your body feels can tell you a great deal about what's going on with you. Often, feelings you don't express emotionally find expression through your body. Headaches, stomachaches, backaches, muscle tension, hypertension, and breathing disorders may all be signals that some feeling needs your attention.

Because we express our sexuality with our bodies, knowing our bodies precedes a full knowledge of who we are as expressive sexual beings. In early recovery, you learn the importance of accepting your body and your genitals, and an awareness gradually develops of your own sexual responses as separate from a partner's. In ongoing recovery you begin to assert your body's needs in relation to the needs of others.

Now you can build on your knowledge of your own body and its responses and begin to explore some areas of your sexuality that may have lain dormant. You may enjoy nonsexual activities, such as dancing and exercise, that make your body feel good and allow you to enjoy being in your body more. You may expand your ability to touch others and yourself with greater variety, and become more flexible in your sexual responses and behaviors.

The Emotional Body

The idea that the body and emotions are intimately connected is not a new one, but today we are even more aware of the subtle interaction between the two. Whether you are feeling happy, sad, fearful, vibrant, exhausted, frustrated, angry, or forgiving, your body contains the feeling. Your unexpressed feelings stay in your body until you express them. If you suffer from chronic headaches, backaches, stomachaches, muscle tension, or other such complaints, you are very likely carrying around feelings that need to be appropriately expressed. Holding these emotions for a long enough time can actually result in physical disease or degeneration.

Many times women do not know what they are feeling. Paying loving attention to our bodies is an important avenue to identifying these feelings. Veronica, for example, who would fall asleep drunk with her alcoholic husband after sex, but never had an orgasm, later realized that the headache she always woke up with was caused not only by the alcohol but also by the sexual tension she had been storing up and not releasing. Often pain is the only way our bodies can tell us that something is wrong.

Bodywork—Swedish or Asian massage, acupressure, or other techniques—is a powerful way to bring back past childhood memories and feelings, and provides another way to uncover your past. Energetic, joyful physical activity, such as dance, or slow, thoughtful physical activity, such as yoga, can also release emotions in surprising ways. One woman relates, "Every time I would do a particular yoga pose, I would feel very, very sad and begin to cry. To this day I don't know why that pose brought on that response, but it did serve to release that sadness and bring it to my attention so I could work on it."

You may discover that you have been holding your breath without realizing it. This can manifest as hyperventilating, faintness, chest pains, and headaches. You may be doing this in response to anxieties rooted in either the past or the future. As you learn to live in the present, you will become aware of your breath patterns. If you are feeling anxious or depressed, taking time out to breathe quietly and slowly is a good way to bring yourself back to the present.

Learning to stay in the present takes practice and attention, but it is rewarding. The more you try to do it, the more you will be able to do it. At first you may be able to be present only for a second or two, then a minute or two. Soon you will begin to notice that, perhaps for several hours, you have been lost in a dream of the past or future. This is the dawning of a new self-awareness.

When you begin to awaken to the moment in this way, you are well into your journey of awakening to your sexuality. The inner work you have done is able to manifest itself in your actions and interactions. You begin to feel yourself present in the steps you take. Now, as your inner and outer journeys merge, you take hold of the power of choice that is ongoing recovery.

Know Your Mind

Western culture has traditionally considered thinking a male province, and women's thought processes historically have been devalued and downgraded. Many philosophers have emphatically pronounced women to be irrational and incapable of sustained, focused thinking.

Women's thinking can be characterized as different from men's, but it is not less than men's. Throughout the centuries women's thinking has developed in a different direction. Women tend to think in complex, circular patterns rather than in a linear progression. Our problem solving takes in many variables and has different ends. Our moral judgments tend to be less rule-bound and more situational. Our so-called women's intuition is an expression of our unconscious empathy and emotional connection.

Because our minds have been devalued both by society and by our dysfunctional families, many women have not explored either how they think or what they think. Becoming familiar with your thinking—how your mind works, what triggers a thought process, how you solve problems, what prevents you from thinking clearly about an issue—can be very exciting. Simply giving yourself permission to explore your intellectual capacities may be a new experience.

Alcohol and drugs make it very difficult to think clearly. If you are recovering from chemical dependence, you will find yourself thinking more clearly. As your recovery progresses you will find that you are more able to concentrate, and you will be less forgetful and more present to your own thoughts.

Recovering your thinking self can be one of the most satisfying experiences of sobriety. You may find yourself taking on new intellectual challenges, going back to school, or learning new skills—all as a result of honoring your mind and its capabilities.

As you reclaim your thinking you will also begin to clarify your thoughts on sex. You may begin to see how your sexual thinking affects your choices in the area of sexuality. You may observe when you lapse into fantasy regarding possible sexual interactions. Sarah told her group, "Last night I really felt like having sex. But I said to myself, 'I'm sure Scott isn't feeling sexual, so why bother?' And then suddenly I realized that this entire situation was inside my own head. I had no idea what Scott was feeling." Like Sarah, in ongoing recovery you will become more and more aware of your sexual thoughts and how they affect your actions.

Know Your Spirit

A fundamental part of knowing yourself is knowing your spiritual self, investigating that part of who you are that connects you to the universe. Whether you think of this spiritual aspect as God or Goddess, Higher Power, or pure spirit is something you decide for yourself. It is important that you become intimately familiar with that yearning and movement for transcendental connection. It is a powerful energy source and the momentum behind your life force. It also acts as a kind of receiving zone for those connective energies directed toward you by another with whom you are in a relationship.

Women find their spiritual connection in infinite ways. You may find yours in nature, in meditation, or in prayer. You may set time aside for devotional reading or silence. Whatever form your spiritual quest takes, it is vital that you respect your need for spiritual sustenance.

It can be difficult to respect your spiritual needs in a society that appears so focused on the material and external. Knowing yourself spiritually is not simply knowing what you believe; it also includes recognizing and validating your spiritual longings by taking the time out of your busy life to fulfill those needs. As you search for wholeness, for harmony, for connection to something greater than your ego, you will come to know who you are, to better understand what it means to be human and embody the divine.

Mimi's playful, healing relationship with Sheila eventually ended. The two women had different priorities: Mimi was interested in a long-term, committed relationship, while Sheila was very involved with raising her children from a heterosexual marriage and building her career. They agreed not to have contact for a period after they ended their relationship, allowing for the relationship to change. Later they were able to reconnect and build a solid friendship.

A few months later Mimi met Lynn, a sculptor, at the home of a mutual friend. They seemed to connect on a deep level, despite their dissimilar careers and interests, and they gradually developed an intimate relationship.

Mimi has been able to retain the best parts of who she was with Sheila in her new relationship with Lynn. Mimi had been worried that the playful, very pleasurable aspects of her sexuality were due to Sheila; but she was pleased to find that she had awakened long-dormant parts of herself in that relationship.

Over her years with Lynn, Mimi has experienced the ebb and flow of sexual desire, which is common in long-term relationships. But their basic foundation of trust, a constant element in their relationship, has allowed the two women to develop a capacity for widening connection that they both appreciate and periodically marvel at—and each experiences an expansion of self. Both describe this as a growth-promoting relationship.

Their sense of safety allows them to experiment and explore their sexual selves. Mimi and Lynn feel not only connected to each other but more connected with others and to the universe. Together they have learned that sexuality is indeed not separate from spirituality. The urge to unite and merge sexually with another being is closely related to the desire to merge with all Being.

Ecstasy, which we tend to connect with physical pleasure, was considered by the ancients to be a merging with the divine, truly heaven on earth. In ongoing recovery you will learn to honor the sexual part of yourself as an irreplaceable and integral aspect of the sacredness of your being.

Know Your Sexuality

In ongoing recovery you will form or solidify a sexual identity that integrates your inner and outer journeys. Your identity should be true to your inner self and needs, and it should feel authentic in the outer world. Creating this sexual identity is a complex and gradual process. As time passes and your needs change, your sexual identity will reflect this change. You may change regarding the kinds of sexual behavior you enjoy and the types of people you are attracted to, and you may even find yourself becoming attracted to another gender.

Although our society socializes us to be exclusively heterosexual, sexual identity is not fixed. It is fluid and exists across a continuum from exclusively heterosexual to exclusively homosexual. Understanding this will free you to be able to explore your sexual identity without having to categorize yourself into a rigid definition that may not fit your experience or feelings.

Kinsey's Sexual Identity Scale

The earliest research on the actual sexual experiences of Americans was done by Alfred Kinsey and his associates in the 1940s. Kinsey developed a seven-point scale to describe the range of sexuality that was experienced by the people he interviewed. He did this after face-to-face interviews with some ten thousand people about their sexual fantasies, experiences, and behaviors. He then described these on the following scale:

0 — exclusively heterosexual behavior
1 — primarily heterosexual, but incidents of homosexual behavior
2 — primarily heterosexual, but more than incidental homosexual behavior
3 — equal amounts of heterosexual and homosexual behavior (bisexual)
4 — primarily homosexual, but more than incidental heterosexual behavior
5 — primarily homosexual, but incidents of heterosexual behavior
6 — exclusively homosexual behavior

Kinsey found that most people fell somewhere between 1 and 5 on the scale and that they fell at different points on it at different times in their lives. Most human beings, it seemed, were born with the capacity to respond erotically to both sexes. Many people in the United States were scandalized by Kinsey's results, but his research proved to be indisputable.

Kinsey and his colleagues discovered some other interesting material in their research. For example, they found that 80 percent of all men had had some adult sexual experiences with other men. Although women were less likely to have had sexual experiences with other women as adults, over half reported some experience. Women, on the other hand, were more likely to have close emotional attachments to other women than were men to other men.

Our sexual socialization seems to account for these differences. It is often much harder for men to be deeply emotionally attached to each other than it is for them to be sexual with each other. Men who find it acceptable to be sexual with male hustlers would never kiss another man or cry with another man. There is little taboo, however, against women being deeply attached to each other. Women friends often feel emotionally closer to each other than they do to their husbands, but do not consider being sexual with each other.

Your Place on the Scale

No one really knows how a particular sexual identity develops. The only facts we're clear about is that all sexual identities are normal, that they fall along a continuum, and that they can change and develop over time.

You can use the following four factors to determine your particular place along the scale at any specific time. I suggest you answer these questions three times: once for when you were actively drinking or using; once for today; and once for your ideal future—where you'd like to be. These three sets of answers will give you some idea of how your sexual identity has developed and the direction you'd like to move in. Start with where you are today.

1. *Fantasies:* Who are your fantasies about? Do your fantasies include both men and women? Do you fantasize about particular acts with

either men or women? If you have fantasies about only one sex or the other, you would fall at either end of the scale.

2. *Eroticism:* What feels erotic to you? Do you find women's bodies erotic? Do you find men's bodies erotic? Do you find particular characteristics of men or women erotic? Are the lingerie ads in women's magazines erotic to you? Are the jockey shorts ads erotic? What excites you about both men and women? Mark your place on the scale somewhere between 0 and 6.

3. *Emotional attachments:* Where do your strongest emotional attachments lie? Are you equally attached to both men and women? Who are your emotional bonds and connections with? Select a spot on the scale that accurately reflects your emotional attachments.

4. *Sexual behavior:* What is your sexual experience? Do you have sexual activity with both men and women? With whom have you had sexual activity? Choose a number from 0 to 6 that represents the variety of your sexual experiences.

Add up the numbers you have chosen for each of these four factors and divide by four. The number will tell you where you tend to fall on Kinsey's Sexual Identity Scale. As most people fall somewhere between 1 and 5, only a small percentage of people are exclusively heterosexual or homosexual on all four of these factors.

Now answer the questions again. This time try to re-create your experiences while you were drinking or using, and see how your sexual identity has shifted with recovery. Now answer the questions again with an eye toward the future.

When Danielle did this exercise, she was surprised to find that she had fantasies about women. She had always considered herself to be exclusively heterosexual and had even felt sorry for women living what she saw as a difficult lesbian life-style; but as she reviewed her answers to these questions, she realized that she had automatically excluded women from her sexual activity. She decided in the future to pay more attention to her sexual desires and to be more open to new erotic experiences and emotional connections.

Accepting Yourself

In my study of recovering alcoholic women, I asked them what their sexual identities had been before drinking became a problem, during their active alcoholism, and after sobriety. Before their drinking became a problem, 74 percent reported that they had been heterosexual, 20 percent bisexual, and 6 percent lesbian. While they were actively drinking, 57 percent reported they were heterosexual, 37 percent bisexual, and 6 percent lesbian. After sobriety, 66 percent reported they were heterosexual, 17 percent bisexual, and 17 percent lesbian.

These self-reports show that many women allow themselves to have a variety of sexual relationships when they are drinking. Evidently, drinking gave them the freedom to explore their erotic attraction to women.

After they became sober, some of the women who had identified as bisexual started identifying as heterosexual, but most began to identify as lesbians. The emphasis on honesty in early recovery often propels us to look at who we are and who we want to be with sexually, allowing women to recognize that their bisexual behavior during drinking may be more truly expressed by adopting a lesbian identity.

Recovery means learning to accept who you are in every area of life: emotional, physical, spiritual, and intellectual. This acceptance is especially difficult in the area of sexuality, but it can be achieved. Recovery also means breaking though denial, whether it's denial of your feelings for women or denial of your self-hatred for having those feelings. Learning to be sexual sober while working through issues of sexual identity and self-acceptance requires a supportive environment and a network of other women who are dealing with similar issues.

Chapter 11

Creating
Intimacy with Others

To love deeply in one direction makes us more
loving in all others.

—Madame Swetchine

Love from one being to another can only be
that two solitudes come nearer, recognize and
protect and comfort each other.

—Han Suyin

Discovering and inhabiting your own interior sexual landscape is just
the beginning of the journey toward intimacy. No matter where you fall
on the sexual identity scale, you will have to work through various challenges and stages in order to have a fulfilling sexual life. Taking this journey a step at a time will make recovery more manageable and fulfilling.
As you learn and grow in each new phase, you will find that you have
more light for the next step.

Creating Intimate Friendships

Women often find themselves concentrating on their sexual relationships to the detriment of their friendships. This is particularly true of

women in sexual recovery, who have a heightened awareness of sexual issues. In friendship—a close relationship without sex—we can experience intimacy without the complicating factor of sexuality. The qualities we develop and deepen in friendship are the same ones that can make our sexual relationships meaningful.

The joys of being friends with other women are many. Throughout history women have been each other's supports. In meetings at the river to wash clothes or in each other's homes for a quilting bee, in writers' and artists' groups or businesswomen's networks, women have always come together through their life events to support and nourish each other. Often as the maintainers and nurturers of men and children, we have had only each other to look to for recognition, information, understanding, and companionship.

Taking the time to nurture and maintain our friendships is not easy, but it is essential to our sustenance and nourishment. Having a friend who has known you and supported you over time, no matter how frequently or infrequently you see one another, helps to remind you of the reality of your experiences, the continuity of your life, and your value and presence in someone else's life.

Equality, Mutuality, and Reciprocity

True intimacy is based on mutuality and equality. Equality means that neither friend has more power than the other. The dominant/subordinate quality that characterizes so many of our interactions has no place in a true friendship.

When there is a lack of equality in a relationship, one person has more power than the other. Commonly the one with less power learns more about the dominant partner than vice versa, because she needs to know more to survive. In our society the poor know more about the middle-class, who, in turn, study the rich; people of color know more about whites, and women know more about men. To be truly intimate, friends must work though any social inequities that may seem to exist between them.

The lack of social equality between men and women often makes friendship difficult. Yet many women are striving to create intimate friendships that do not include sex. As women and men break out of their traditional roles, they are finding that they have much to give to and receive from each other. Creating friendships with men can become a new and challenging experience.

In mutual relationships, we experience reciprocity—a reciprocal interest in giving and receiving. We each have a mutual desire to create and maintain the relationship. There's a mutual intentionality about the friendship between us. We both find the friendship important and value it in a similar manner. In a mutual friendship, we express similar degrees of vulnerability and ability to trust. We both put energy into being together and listening to and supporting each other. No noticeable imbalance or wide disparity exists between how much each of us works to maintain the relationship.

In a close friendship, we act as mirrors for each other. If I see you doing something, I can ask myself without judgment, "Do I do that? Is there some part of me that has the capacity to do that?" We become more empathic as we see ourselves mirrored in each other. On the other hand, we also learn about ourselves from seeing the reactions our own behavior stimulates. We say, "What in me created that kind of behavior in the other?" An intimate friend can help you to realize when some response was not provoked by anything you did but was about something entirely different and separate from you. Also, the same friend might be able to help you understand how something you've said or done— which you regarded as innocuous—has had a tremendous effect. The mirroring of an intimate friendship allows us to know ourselves better.

In friendship you can allow yourself to be seen and heard and to really see and hear another person. You can allow yourself to be influenced by and to influence someone else. You are willing to both act upon and be acted upon. In an intimate friendship you integrate the interaction of your inner and outer lives. You can share your inner self—thoughts, feelings, desires, needs—with those you are close to (the outer). Thus your inner and outer lives meet and become whole, which is an essential experience to your recovery.

You may find that you have some difficulty creating intimate friendships with other women. We have been taught to compete with each other for men, to judge each other on the basis of our appearance and clothes, and to compare our children and their accomplishments. But since the women's movement began, we have realized more and more that we need each other. We do not have to live in this world in isolation from other women, focusing on our families for our only support.

The rewards of friendships that endure over time are great. Our friends see us change and grow, and they can provide us with an understanding that comes only with years of intimacy. Abiding friends have been with us through numerous ups and downs, family struggles, job changes, and years of raising children. They can provide us with continuity of intimacy in a time when sexual relationships may be difficult to sustain.

Within any particular friendship there will be an ebb and flow to the pattern of intimacy, times in both your lives in which you're close and times you're more remote. Nonetheless, staying connected to friends over distance and time can provide you with strong and enduring bonds of intimacy that can sustain you through the most difficult trials.

Creating Sexual Intimacy

Being intimate in a sexual relationship is not that different from being intimate in friendship, but it includes an important added dimension: the sexual expression of your erotic potential. Good sex, however, is not enough for lasting intimacy. No matter how in love you think you are, a love relationship, like all friendships, needs equality, mutuality, and reciprocity to succeed.

Being inside an intimate relationship is like being inside a warm home whose walls expand to encompass your growth. Within this relationship you are free to express your vulnerability, to experience being truly seen and heard, and to become empathic in both understanding and response. You and your partner act as mirrors for each other, reflecting each other's moods and thoughts and actions. An intimate relationship can enable you to see yourself in a completely new way.

Intimacy takes place on a deep level. You are letting another person into a special place, letting yourself be seen and known. Becoming intimate with someone you are sexual with can be a frightening experience; and becoming sexual with someone you are intimate with can be equally frightening.

The vulnerability and openness of the relationship may feel deeply threatening. You may feel unsafe and respond by withdrawing or erecting barriers between yourself and your sexual partner. You may distance yourself sexually, objectifying your sexual actions by thinking of sex as an activity rather than as a deep sharing of your innermost self. Or you may allow yourself to share intimately while you're being sexual, but avoid vulnerability in your daily life.

You may find a certain level of intimacy comfortable in your sexual relationships, but panic when that relationship begins to grow and deepen. This often happens when the intimacy of sexual relations touches early childhood wounds. You may begin to react by repeating destructive early childhood family patterns; you may begin to sabotage the relationship or test it to the breaking point. You may act out your fear of intimacy, expressing in outrageous behavior the message, "I don't know how to trust—how to trust you, or me, or us."

If you were sexually abused as a child, you may have a particularly difficult time maintaining intimacy in sexual relationships. You will have to give yourself time to regain the capacity for trust and closeness that still lives within you.

It is commonly said of alcoholics that they have severe problems expressing intimacy. But for women alcoholics the fear of intimacy is actually a well-grounded fear of emotional, physical, and sexual abuse. We know that women and girls from alcoholic backgrounds are most likely to experience violence, abuse, and violation from those with whom they are intimate—their friends, lovers, and families. It is natural for alcoholic women to fear intimacy; most have grown up in situations in which their boundaries were violated by those who said "I love you."

Joyce was in her mid-forties when she entered therapy. She had been in recovery from alcoholism for two years, as had her husband, Howard. They had been married for twenty years and had two boys, both in their late teens. For the last ten years of marriage Joyce and Howard had not been sexual.

The first time I met Joyce she seemed burdened. She was neatly dressed, but her shoulders sagged and even her hair seemed limp. Yet she was ready to talk and her story came tumbling out of her mouth. "My husband has an erectile problem, we haven't had sex for ten years, I'm in recovery, and I'm living my life really fully. But this piece is missing and I don't know if I want to remain married knowing we're never going to have sex again." They no longer touched; they were distant friends living in the same house but never connecting.

I wondered how I could be of help to this woman if her husband would not participate in therapy. Clearly, after ten years, Howard didn't feel good enough about himself to risk being vulnerable. Even if his erectile dysfunction were not based on a physical problem, his performance anxiety and fears after such a long time would be enough to create problems. I decided we would aim not toward sexual performance but toward building trust. I would treat the sexual problem as a relationship issue and try to help this couple develop a feeling of closeness and intimacy.

I began by taking Joyce's sex history, including her family's attitude toward sexuality, her childhood experiences, and her adult experiences.

Periodically she would tell Howard what was going on in therapy. He felt that her attempts to get his sexual history were intrusive. He felt very protective about his own sexual experience and was very threatened and intimidated by his wife being in therapy. Many times he poohpoohed it, saying, "No one has any business knowing about our sex life." He was not an active and willing participant in this process. Finally Joyce had to piece together her husband's history from what he had told her over time.

Eventually I asked her to list all the sensual activities she wanted to experience with her husband. Then she listed them again in the order of things that would be easiest to ask for. Each activity was to remain discrete: they were never to proceed further. For example, if he gave her a back rub he was to confine his touching to her back only. In addition, only positive feedback could be given.

Then it was time to try the list on Howard. She started with the least difficult, asking him to give her a back rub. His initial response to the back rub was, "This is ridiculous, what's the big deal about this?" Joyce replied, "This is something I really want to do." So he rubbed her back, she said it felt good, and he just sort of grumbled.

The next week she had him rub her back again, but now with body oil. This time when she said it felt good he said, "Oh, well, this does feel better." I was encouraged. This was the first clue I had that Howard had feeling or sensation in his body and that he could admit to her that somehow it felt better to touch her body with oil. So Howard did feel, and what he was feeling could be accessed more easily than I had initially thought.

Several weeks later she took a shower with him. It only lasted a minute, but they did it. Then they took a bath together, and eventually they enjoyed a bubble bath, with music and candles. Throughout this process Howard never had an erection. But as they went through the list of activities something more important began to happen: they found themselves having spontaneous moments of connection, separate from the exercises. Sometimes, while they were watching television, he would reach out and hold her hand. When they went to bed he would cuddle up close. When he said good-bye in the morning there was a different quality to the hug and kiss. Joyce began to feel differently about Howard, more connected. At times she was very touched and moved by his spontaneous expressions of affection. The quality of their connection had begun to improve.

Even though their activities were externally focused, what they were working on was internal change. Joyce realized that she had been missing not only physical contact but some kind of closeness and intimacy. And this was now returning to their relationship.

The last thing on her list was oral sex. Joyce had tried oral sex with a lover before she married Howard, but they had never experienced it together. To Joyce's surprise, Howard was amenable to the idea and even a little excited about it. Joyce had an orgasm, and Howard was absolutely delighted. He got a great deal of pleasure out of giving her pleasure. As a result, something really changed for him. It was a very powerful moment. Somehow this man, who had not been sexually active for ten years, had brought his wife to a point of real pleasure, and he was very moved by that experience.

Soon after that, Joyce terminated therapy. Howard periodically initiated physical contact with her, and she felt grateful for the changes in their relationship. About six months later she called me on the phone. She was laughing. "You're not going to believe what happened. Howard just called me and said he was on his way home and he had made his own list of things he wanted to experience with me!"

To this day I don't know whether or not Howard and Joyce ever got back into having intercourse. Heterosexuality is very focused on sexual performance culminating in the act of intercourse, yet this couple was able to reconnect and have a satisfying relationship without it.

The Risk of Sexual Intimacy

Learning to be intimate in a sexual relationship may take time. It will certainly require that you take risks, and inevitably you will make mistakes.

As you learn to develop satisfying relationships, you may find yourself becoming intimate with a sexual partner who can't match you in an equal, mutual, reciprocal relationship. You may put your trust in people who eventually disappoint you. These mistakes will not be as devastating if you have developed a strong, grounded sense of intimacy with yourself and supportive friends.

Making poor choices along the way does not have to stop you from trying again and learning from the experience. You don't have to internalize feelings of failure about poor choices, and you don't have to tell yourself you just can't be intimate. In *The Courage to Heal*, Ellen Bass and Laura Davis have developed a set of questions to help women determine whether their sexual relationships have the capacity for intimacy. Ask yourself the following questions about your sexual partner before you take the risks true intimacy involves:

- Do I respect this person?

- Does this person respect me?

- Is this a person I can communicate with?

- Do we work through conflicts well?

- Do we both compromise?

- Is there give and take?

- Can I be honest? Can I show my real feelings?

- Do we both take responsibility for the relationship's successes and problems?

- Could I talk to this person about the effect child sexual abuse is having on our relationship?

- Is there room for me to grow and change in this relationship?

- Am I able to reach my own goals within this relationship?

- Is this person supportive of the kind of changes I am trying to make?

- Is this person willing to help me?

If you answer these questions affirmatively and decide that your current sexual partner is someone with whom you'd like to become more intimate, you'll need to realize that doing so is a process that takes time. If you have had little experience of true intimacy, your tendency may be to plunge into intimate sexual relationships prematurely, to mistake codependence for intimacy, or to avoid being both intimate and sexual with the same person.

In order to develop an intimate sexual relationship gradually, you will need to learn how to take calculated risks. That means taking a sexual or emotional risk that is appropriate to how vulnerable it makes you feel in that stage of the relationship. Begin with small risks that don't have enormous consequences if they don't work out. If they do work out, you can move on to bigger risks. All the way along you should continually reassess the relationship and what is happening to you. And keep checking to make sure you're being honest with yourself, both emotionally and sexually.

You'll know you're in trouble if you start hiding your feelings, including your sexual feelings, from your partner. It is essential to be able to express your feelings, and to be able to trust your partner to honor them rather than denigrate them. Ask yourself whether the relationship still feels equal, mutual, and reciprocal; whether you and your partner are giving and receiving at similar levels; and whether the relationship has gotten out of balance in any area.

Look at your level of trust. Is it growing? Or are you distancing and withdrawing? If the relationship continues to develop and deepen, then you can take greater risks that require more vulnerability. In so doing you will create a conscious relationship instead of one driven by unfulfilled childhood needs.

The Social Challenge of Intimacy

It takes a great deal of effort to create intimacy with yourself and with others, and there is the added challenge of doing this within a society that does not provide an environment conducive to intimacy. No one can ignore for long the real life situations in which we all have to live and work and create relationships.

Heterosexual Relationships

Even though our culture is supportive of heterosexuality, women who identify as primarily heterosexual often have problems with men in relationships. Much of this is directly related to the difference in women's and men's socialization. Men are socialized to express only a narrow range of feelings. "Being a man" means you don't express feelings of confusion, weakness, fear, vulnerability, tenderness, compassion, and sensuality. To do so is to be called a "sissy" and be ostracized as you are growing up.

So most men develop powerful denial systems that allow them to block out certain feelings—the ones women now find they miss in a man. The qualities that men have learned to embody—aggression, competition, independence, control, decisiveness—are of limited value in forming and maintaining intimate relationships. As we begin to recognize the limits of our own socialization, relationships with men become more problematic and less satisfying. One of my clients who was recently widowed found herself with mixed emotions. Although she grieved for the loss of her husband, she also felt some relief. "Everybody always remarked on how well we got along. We never fought. But the reason we got along so well was that I did everything he wanted, like the good little wife. Now I feel like I have a chance to get myself back."

Women in heterosexual couples often come to therapy complaining about the inability of their partners to be intimate. This is often a reflection of gender differences. Men, it seems, are most comfortable with what is termed "side-to-side" intimacy, such as with colleagues at work, and "back-to-back" intimacy, as in team sports. But women are looking for eye-to-eye, face-to-face intimacy. This is what we are most comfortable with. It may be necessary for both partners in a couple to realize that there are varieties of intimacy and to try to share the variety with which each partner feels most comfortable.

Because men often have a hard time talking about their feelings, they depend on women for the emotional aspect of a relationship. But women tend to feel cheated when they end up providing a kind of sharing and intimacy that they don't receive. Men have little experience in revealing themselves or being sensual without being sexual. Women often have to teach their partners how to share themselves on a deep emotional level. In fact, this is a continuing problem for Sarah and Scott.

Men's socialization in the area of explicit sexual behavior creates another sort of problem. Men are socialized to be in charge sexually, to be aggressive, to make the moves and risk rejection. They work hard to learn how to perform sexually, and they feel as if they are responsible for making sex happen. This goal-oriented drive to ejaculation and orgasm, and an accompanying lack of attention to "foreplay," often leaves women angry and frustrated.

As you work to become able to ask for what you want sexually, you may find that men are turned off by your increased assertiveness. A man may find it harder to get an erection in the presence of a sexually assertive woman; he may also find it impossible to be passive and let a woman make love to him. Many men have great difficulty allowing themselves to receive and be receptive. You may find that just as you are struggling to change and grow sexually, men are having just as much trouble changing themselves.

Men, however, often feel that they are not choosing to change, but that change is being thrust on them by the women they are with. Sometimes they react with panic, unable to imagine how to do things differently; sometimes they react with defensiveness, hostility, or anger, feeling they're being punished for doing what was required of them.

It is also becoming more and more difficult for women to meet men, to find men they want to be sexual with, and to establish ongoing, satisfying, intimate sexual relationships with them. After working so hard to break out of our own inauthentic sexual behavior to experience who we really are, we don't want to go back to performing a sexual role.

Yet it becomes harder and harder to find a nontraditional man as we get older.

Women in recovery from alcohol or drugs may find establishing an intimate relationship even more difficult, because they want to be with men who don't drink. In self-help meetings a larger percentage of men than women tend to be married—wives tend to stay with alcoholic husbands, while men tend to leave alcoholic wives. Bars are no longer available as places to socialize; and parties are dominated both by alcohol and by couples.

Alternatives to marriage are still not well defined or entirely socially acceptable. We are living in a period of transition in regard to successful forms of relationships. All this leaves heterosexual women feeling that they have nothing solid to hold on to in terms of the kinds of relationships they want. At this particular moment in history, women are moving beyond traditional sex roles. This search for a wider variety of sexual behavior is fraught with difficulty for the traditional heterosexual model of relationship.

As Theresa continues to work in therapy, she has begun to see that Jeff isn't perfect. She wants him to be more communicative, to share his feelings, but he resists. He is glad that Theresa is no longer chemically dependent, but he's a little confused by the changes in their relationship.

Although Jeff loves Theresa and has stayed with her through some very difficult years of usage and early recovery, her former emotional unavailability and the fact that she made few demands on him was unconsciously just what he wanted. The chaos of her life, contrasted with his reliability and dependability, made him feel powerful and in control. In recovery, however, she wants a more flexible, spontaneous, generous partner.

Theresa is beginning to know herself as a sexual person in her own right and has some sexual needs and desires of her own. She wants to be held and touched; she wants affection without sex. She also wants Jeff to focus on her sexual pleasure without so much concern for his own. She is beginning to experience him as selfish and unassertive.

Theresa is also becoming uncomfortable with Jeff's increasing use of pornographic material when he masturbates, and she feels very fearful and angry when she sees how women are generally portrayed in men's magazines. The subservience of and violence against women is intolerable: it feels like a re-creation of her childhood. Theresa and Jeff have some hard work to do as their relationship moves into a new stage.

Lesbian Relationships

If you identify as being primarily lesbian, you will have to deal with a different set of issues. Lesbian women do not complain primarily about relationship problems in communicating, tenderness, or performance. The greatest problems seem to stem from living in a culture that is unsupportive of the lesbian identity.

Our society's tremendous bias toward heterosexuality, and corresponding negativity toward homosexual identity, is a given. Despite this, at least 10 percent of all women identify as lesbians as adults and over 50 percent report having some homoerotic experience as adults.

Alcoholic women report having a wider variety of sexual experiences and a wider variety of sexual partners than do nonalcoholic women. In early recovery many women begin to confront questions of sexual identity; they come to those questions socialized like everyone else in our society, with a negative attitude toward identifying as lesbians.

Many women used alcohol and drugs as a mediator between sexual behavior or desire and self-acceptance. Without the numbing effect of chemicals, recovering women encounter their past sexual histories and current sexual desires directly. These encounters can be painful and difficult. Some women may have used alcohol and drugs to anesthetize their feelings for women; others may have been able to be sexual with men only when high or drunk, separating themselves from their lack of desire for men.

In an early recovery group, Bernice described her sexual attraction to women. Although she had known since high school that she wanted to be erotically involved with women, she had not acted upon those feelings yet. She had used drinking as a way to feel "normal," that is, heterosexual, and as a way to continue going out with men.

"I knew I was attracted to women when I was in high school. I always wanted to hang out with other girls. I found guys boring; they just didn't hold my interest. In the eleventh grade I knew I was in love with my best friend, Sherry. I thought she was perfect, beautiful, and intelligent, and we shared almost everything. I would get so close to telling her, but I always stopped myself. I knew she really liked boys, and the last thing I wanted was for her to reject me. I knew if I told her I'd lose her as a friend too.

"I wanted to be with her, so I started dating guys. But I had to get drunk to do it. I had my first sexual experience in a blackout. I really only knew it happened because the next morning my underpants were gone, and there was blood on my jeans. I kept that up for years—dating men, getting smashed to have sex, and spending all my other time with women."

Some women, such as Mimi, use alcohol and drugs to help overcome their fear and confusion about their desires for women and to allow them to move through their negative feelings in order to be sexual with other women. Mimi recalls her senior year in college:

"I'd go to women's bars and stand around and look. And drink . . . and drink . . . and drink. One night I was pretty high when somebody asked me to dance. Suddenly on the dance floor, moving to the music, I could feel how turned on I was. I ended up making love to a woman I'd just met that night. From then on I'd drink to get high and then I would be able to be sexual, sometimes with a total stranger. When I was drinking, thoughts of what my mother would think just faded away."

The Struggle for Safety

Whether you are a woman struggling to create a satisfying relationship with a man or a lesbian struggling to create a satisfying relationship with a woman, you need to have a safe place in which to explore your sexual feelings and needs. Individual therapy and groups for women who are investigating their sexuality can be particularly helpful during this time. Family and friends can rarely supply that space, because they usually have an investment in a particular outcome.

Sometimes being bisexual can be the most difficult identity of all. The support of the lesbian community is often not available to bisexual women. They may not be perceived as trustworthy, based on their decision not to relate exclusively to women. And the heterosexual community sometimes has a hard time relating to bisexual women, whom they perceive as breaking norms and as ambivalent about their sexual identity.

If you are heterosexual you may find yourself in a group that supports being sexual only within a traditional, long-term, committed relationship such as marriage. A heterosexual who is sexual and not in a traditional relationship also needs to be supported by her peers and support group facilitators to see various sexual options as healthy.

If you are a lesbian you may find yourself in an AA group, a process group, or an aftercare group that sees your homosexual experience as a problem that your drinking created or as a phase you're merely passing through. If that is the case, you will need to find another group that is more knowledgeable about the diversity of normal sexual identity. In recovery some women may identify as heterosexual even after having had sexual experiences with women while they were drinking. But that should not be viewed as the only healthy option. You may also identify as lesbian or bisexual.

The rewards of intimacy are great but not easily obtained, as you can see from the challenges and risks that we have confronted. But I do have an increasing sense of hope for women as we all struggle to move toward more fulfilling intimate and sexual relationships.

Chapter 12

Spiritual Intimacy

What I love about sex is that it is never completed. You
think it is finished and you realize that you never get there. I
think of a prism . . . .

—Anica Vesel Mander

In any relation . . . that touches the deepest levels, [there is]
a chance . . . to participate in the fateful experience of life's
august suprapersonal powers. . . . This is especially true in
the sex act itself, in which personalities of the participants
are momentarily suspended in an experience they share
with all but the most primitive forms of life. Intercourse is
not primarily an experience of personal love, as women try
to make it, but of the gods, which yet happens through the
union of the two. The love comes before as a preparation,
or after, as a result. But the love is then changed. The partner is no longer felt to be limited to the familiar conscious
personality, but has become also the gateway to the infinite
mystery of life.

—Eleanor Bertine, *Human Relationships*

The journey of sexual awakening has led us to explore the richness of
women's sexuality in its many aspects: emotional, physical, mental, and
now spiritual. We have seen that the act of sex is not the ultimate goal of
sexuality, but is one important facet in a complex expression of our
whole being. We have seen how continuing recovery can enable us to

experience intimate relationships. We often describe the totality of such relationships as love.

Passionate love is what brings us together. It's that longing for union with another, a bridge to end our separation, a longing for connection. When intimacy and healthy sexual expression merge in one relationship, you will make a profound connection.

Falling in Love

You may be propelled into becoming intimately and sexually connected to another by the experience of "falling in love." In such a relationship you idealize your potential partner, seeing in him or her someone who can meet all your needs, who has the qualities you want, and who will be able to love you as you have always wanted to be loved.

At the same time you experience a longing to merge with your loved one, to become one in body and spirit. Both idealizing the love object and longing for merger are essential to the experience of falling in love. These experiences provide the energy that creates the level of intimacy in the heightened emotional and sexual connection. With them you feel energized, excited, euphoric—on top of the world.

Once you become connected to another person sexually and emotionally, you begin to know who that person really is. Then the idealized image begins to fade away. The only way to keep the idealized image is to stay in the fantasy or go into denial.

Now comes a more mature choice. Ask yourself, "Is this someone I want to maintain a connection with? Is this someone I want to build a relationship with?" If you can honestly answer yes, then you can begin taking some calculated risks and begin to build the kind of intimate love relationship that will sustain and nurture you, deepening your relationship in evolutionary stages.

In seeking deep connection, you may find yourself sidetracked into two other paths that women often mistake for sexual intimacy: love addiction and codependence.

Love Addiction

Women who are addicted to love feel that they cannot live without those euphoric feelings they have in the idealization stage. If you are addicted to love, you will find yourself beginning to back away from the relationship when the idealization starts to fade. Instead of choosing to build an intimate sexual relationship, you will go looking for someone else to fall in love with, and you will abandon this relationship too as the initial euphoria fades into the work and choice making demanded by authentic connection.

You will go from relationship to relationship, seeking those magical moments, in an addictive search for the high of being in love. Unfortunately, such a search will leave you feeling empty, because real intimacy never has time to develop. The feelings of "falling in love" may be the impetus to join intimacy with sexuality, but they aren't the basis for the profound sharing upon which authentic intimate sexual relationships are based.

Codependence

The other mistake so common to women is to create codependent relationships rather than conscious ones, losing themselves in their desire to merge. If you are codependent you will put your partner at the center of your life and sacrifice your autonomy of self to a life of "we."

Your essential identity becomes connected to being part of a couple. How you feel about yourself becomes a reflection of how your partner feels about you. In this process you sacrifice true intimacy for a life of caretaking, placing someone else's needs in a primary place, often to the exclusion of your own.

The sad fact is that our socialization as women tells us that caretaking is intimacy. But using caretaking to meet your intimacy needs will actually prevent you from creating intimacy. As a caretaker you focus exclusively on your partner's needs, while your own get lost in the distortion of mistaking "care for" for "connection with."

In an intimate relationship each person asks for what she or he needs. In so doing, both become aware of their own needs and of their vulnerability in asking. Both partners share the inner process and allow themselves to be seen. Both take the risk of being told no, as well as being told yes.

Codependents anticipate and automatically fulfill the needs of their partners, cutting off the process of asking and being vulnerable. At the same time the codependent's own needs are ignored; a choice has been made to be invulnerable to the partner and not to expect her or him to give to you.

There is something wonderful about having another person tell you what she or he needs and wants from you, and being able to say in return, "Yes, I can give you that." But in a codependent relationship, that process is not allowed to happen from either side. The risk taking of intimacy and vulnerability is sacrificed for the security of caretaking. The result is a stagnant relationship and a self closed off from the give-and-take dynamic true intimacy demands.

Conscious Love and Commitment

The experience of falling in love can be the prelude to spiritual experience. In conscious love you choose to be with each other, to build a relationship together. Choice is crucial to conscious love: the power and capacity to choose is fundamental to being human, and exercising that ability is basic to your recovery. In addiction you lost your ability to choose and experienced constriction, powerlessness, and loss of freedom. In recovery, you experience the power, freedom, and expansion that being able to choose will give you.

In choosing conscious love you also choose mature dependence. You allow yourself truly to connect with and depend on your partner, but you retain your autonomy of self. You choose a partner who values your recovery and who also chooses to engage in the process with you.

Choosing to be together and build an intimate sexual relationship is commonly called commitment. Commitment is not about the length of time you've been together; we all know couples who have stayed together, without respect or mutuality, for forty years. Commitment is about choosing to be there; to be intimate, open, and vulnerable; to do your best to be available to the other person. Commitment will allow you to feel safe and secure, knowing that the other has also chosen to be open, available, and vulnerable.

Commitment creates an atmosphere of trust that allows for vulnerability. The value of healthy, intimate sexual relationships is in their power to heal and change us. They empower us and cause us to grow.

Because we are living in a particularly challenging time of transition in regard to commitment in intimate sexual relationships, many women feel adrift, bereft of certainty about what form of commitment is viable. You may view your commitment to work as both liberating and exciting, for example, but see possible commitment to a partner as limiting and restricting. You may long to fall back on lifelong vows that are unrelated to your changing needs and wants. You may reach middle age longing for the stability that a twenty-year relationship can bring, concerned about the seven-year average of current marriages. You may find yourself anticipating three or four more intimate sexual relationships before you die, and find yourself longing for the kind of connection that lasts until death parts you from your loved one. In a world whose values are changing so quickly, many women are struggling with these issues.

Still, the work is to be done in the present moment. Being committed means that you have promised to engage in a process with your partner. The key is your willingness to be present with each other through the changes in your lives. You can learn to move into relationships gradually, both emotionally and physically.

It's possible for a couple in a long-term relationship to lose intimacy but to regain it anew. Some couples who have been together for years in a dysfunctional relationship may need to start their relationship all over again. They may need to relearn such basic elements of intimacy as how to hold hands, how to sit close on the sofa, how to experience physical intimacy. Slowly, bit by bit, the levels of emotional and physical intimacy and connection can deepen.

Theresa's relationship with Jeff is an example of commitment and the capacity to stay together through the process of recovery. Theresa is now in her second year of recovery, and both of them describe their sexual relationship as very satisfying.

Theresa has awakened to herself as a sexual person and has learned to be aware of her own state of desire. She is able to experience her sexual feelings separate from Jeff and knows what she prefers in terms of a sexual activity. She has learned that the affection between them is important and that the emotional content of their connection directly affects their physical experience.

She no longer has flashbacks, although she still actively fears and dislikes a number of men. She appreciates many aspects of Jeff's personality and frequently tells him of her appreciation. She shares her feelings—not just her sexual feelings—more openly, and so does Jeff.

Theresa and Jeff struggle every day with communication issues and differences in desire: Jeff wants sex more often than Theresa; Theresa still has very mixed feelings about Jeff's masturbation; she wants Jeff to be more spontaneous and outgoing, and she has growing concerns about his workaholism. They are both pleased with the fact that they can raise these issues without threatening the stability of the relationship.

In general, Theresa and Jeff are expressing their caring through touch and affection that doesn't always lead to sex. For Theresa the sexual relationship is now not just the physical aspect but also the emotional connection. She experiences this as an integration, a deepening of their relationship.

There is more tenderness in their lovemaking. Theresa doesn't "dress up" for Jeff any more, and they hardly ever use toys or do scenes. As their relationship settles into this new phase, Jeff finds that he has far less desire to use pornography when he masturbates.

Sex feels different now. The passion is still there, but it is no longer such a driving force. It seems to come from a deeper place. "We laugh more," says Theresa. "Sometimes when we are making love I feel as though I'm dissolving into Jeff, not losing myself but becoming deeply connected."

No Boundaries

The bond created in a committed, intimate sexual relationship can be an intensely healing experience. Your childhood wounds can be transformed as you love one another. The "healing power of love" may sound like a cliché, but it is a deep spiritual truth. When we engage with another at a deep level, we tap into our interconnection with all of life and become restored to our divine selves.

In sexual experience with an intimate partner, we may go beyond expressing our deep emotional involvement and erotic attraction; we may also touch each other's souls and express our spiritual affinity. In the act of sexual union with another, we can experience the wonderful loss of self that is akin to the mystical. It is not an accident that we have called our intimate partners "soul mates."

The loss of a sense of the spiritual possibilities of sexuality is expressed in our culture by an increasing emphasis on its external aspects. We are inundated by sexual images in advertising, on television, and in the movies. We are told that sex sells. Products such as cars are called "sexy," and attractive women grace ads for tractors, tools, automobiles, and fax machines.

As we see sexuality used as a commodity in our culture, we fall prey to the same kind of thinking. Sex becomes an "it" that we "do" with one another, rather than the expression of caring and loving. We lose touch with the mystery behind sexual contact and focus on techniques and skills.

Rather than honoring the extraordinary awareness—the expanded consciousness—that can come with sexual experience, we reduce sexuality to an ego-centered experience, to an external event. Yet our inner selves cry out for recognition of the spiritual potential of "being" with another. On some deep level we know that sexual experience can be the occasion for direct contact with spirit, but this is seldom mentioned or talked about, even in books about sex.

Sexual experience is one way for us to stay in the moment and fully experience the "now." In being sexual we often meld with the other, losing the boundary of skin to skin, and exist in timelessness where all consciousness originates. In the intimate sexual embrace we may discover that we are not really distinct from the other but that we are both part of a unitary consciousness. Sometimes sexual experience can even be our introduction to the authentic spiritual dimension of our natures.

Chemically dependent women in recovery often have more familiarity with their spiritual needs and desires than most Americans. While they once drowned their spiritual thirst for wholeness in "spirits," they now seek through prayer and meditation to improve their conscious contact with a higher power. In that seeking, sexual experiences can also become a source of contact with the Infinite.

The widening, expansive qualities of Mimi's and Lynn's relationship create the possibility of transcendent experience. Mimi shares the following story:

"Before I got sober I had no inkling that sexuality and spirituality might be connected. If you'd asked me a question about their relationship, I'd have thought you were crazy. My parents were as repressed about spirituality as they were about sexuality, and my academic training certainly didn't encourage me to open up to such intangible ideas.

"It was AA and the concept of trusting in a Higher Power that introduced me to a regular spiritual practice. First I started praying, although I was uncomfortable with it. Then I added some time spent in silence each day. Later I began to read a variety of spiritual material, and some of it struck a deep chord within me.

"After I'd been sober about five years, and my relationship with Lynn felt really comfortable, I felt like I wanted to develop a fuller spiritual life. On the spur of the moment I signed up for a week-long intensive meditation retreat with women in the desert. I'd never done anything like that before, and I was really nervous about what was going to happen.

"Well, that experience was amazing. We meditated for hours each day, sometimes in silence, sometimes walking, sometimes listening to teachings. We were in a beautiful place, where nature was still unspoiled. It felt like there were few distractions between us and our spiritual selves. While meditating, every now and then I could literally feel the energy move up my spine to the top of my head, where it felt like a crown of fire. Other times it seemed like my body disappeared and I was a being of pure energy. Once in a while my body would start to vibrate spontaneously, as if it simply couldn't hold all the energy that was there.

"Later, similar experiences began to happen in bed. Ever since I'd been sober, my sexual experiences had been changing and deepening. I kept increasing my capacity to be intimate, and my relationships reflected that. Not only had sex gotten better as I learned to be in my body and stay in the moment, but somehow sex started being very similar to other spiritual experiences I was having. In sex I began to experience a different level of consciousness—something more than physical.

"I noticed that during sex sometimes it felt like my physical self melted and I was energy vibrating at the same rate as Lynn's—merging with her.

"I was never able to control when I would have that kind of sexual experience. It seemed to just happen to me, or to us. I think the occurrence was related to my ability to let go and be there. To simply be with what was happening without an expectation or goal. As soon as I wanted to have spiritual experiences in sex, they went away.

"Now I have few expectations. Of course I hope that I'll continue to have these sorts of experiences—both in sex and in meditation—but I've let go of them as goals. I'm sexual because I enjoy touching Lynn's body and being touched by her. Bonding with her feels great. And if sometimes we touch on another level of consciousness together, that's just an added dimension."

The Continuing Journey of Sexual Recovery

Recovery is about expansion. It's about awakening to all that's possible in life. It's about integrating your inner life and your outer life, so that what's happening on the inside—your values, your beliefs, and your feelings—are being represented in your outer life, which is your actions with other people in the world. If your inner and outer lives are consistent, coherent, and congruent, you will experience integrity.

Our sexuality and our spirituality are connected; they are not separate things. We sometimes feel, and rightly so, that we have been trained to give up our sexuality in order to be more spiritual. Patriarchal religion says we must put our sexuality aside in order somehow to be redeemed.

But this is not true: sexuality and spirituality are interconnected. They are both about the life force that is within us. When we try to live out of the only sexual model we are given in society—the whore in bed and the virgin at the breakfast table—we make ourselves sexually and spiritually sick, because it asks us to split off parts of ourselves that should be together.

Passionate love is what brings us together. It's that longing for union with another, a bridge between people, a bridge between body and soul. Passionate love promises to end our separation and fulfill our longing for ecstatic experience—the very lifeblood of spirituality.

In our essence we are energy—rates of vibration. Our essential nature is not as physical beings. In every sexual encounter, the union of two energies creates a third energy, a new energy. And this is where we have to begin to be sexually responsible, this is the creative aspect of our sexuality. What kind of energy are we creating in our sexual connections? What kind of energy are we creating in our recovery? Recovery involves taking responsibility for the kind of energy that we put out into the universe.

One of the most profound human experiences is to be intimate with another human being. To know and be known, to see and be seen, to understand and be understood—this is intimacy. It is especially satisfying to be able to love each other throughout the evolution of that intimacy, and to integrate and express that love and intimacy in a sexual way—and then perhaps to have that rare moment when it feels as if your experience of joining with another had been touched by the divine.

The Sexual Response Cycle

Female Sexual Response Cycle

For most women, our lack of information about our own bodies extends to the sexual response cycle. In my recovery groups for women, only one out of every eight women reports having received her primary sex education from her mother, and even then most of the information imparted was about menstruation and reproduction. Very rarely does a woman report having been told what would actually happen to her body during a sexual encounter.

Some women report having learned about the female sexual response cycle along with reproduction in sex education class, and some women report learning from friends. But most women have never talked about what really happens to their bodies during sexual arousal and experience. Women, unlike men, don't do a lot of comparing with each other about their sexual experiences.

Lack of knowledge for women about our bodies and how they work is compounded by alcohol use in families of origin. The no-talk rule of alcoholic families is almost always extended to sex, so growing up with an alcoholic parent often doubles the "normal" lack of sexual knowledge for women.

Misinformation about women's sexuality is only now being corrected. The first real observational data about women's actual sexual experience was published by Masters and Johnson in 1966. Their research finally laid to rest the myth of the vaginal orgasm as well as supplying information about various forms of female sexual experience.

Masters and Johnson found that women basically experienced the same sexual response cycle whether they were touching themselves, using a vibrator, or having sex with a partner. In all cases, the clitoris was the center of sexual pleasure, and some stimulation of the clitoris—either indirect or direct—was required for orgasm to occur. In the 1970s, Shere Hite published the first self-reports of women about their sexual experiences. Of the women who responded to the Hite questionnaire, only 30 percent reported being able to achieve orgasm through vaginal penetration alone. Most women needed additional direct clitoral stimulation to achieve orgasm.

The First Stage: Excitement

The first stage in the sexual response cycle is arousal or excitement. As women move from desire to actually being touched, the response of the body is heightened. Some women can experience the excitement phase without being touched. Wanting another, reading sexually explicit literature, or fantasizing may all bring on the bodily sensations of the excitement phase.

As women become excited, the clitoris and its surrounding tissues fill with blood, and the clitoris becomes erect, retracting under its hood. At the same time, the vagina lubricates and expands. In its nonexcited stage the vagina has a very small opening, about the size of a pencil, but as a woman becomes more and more excited the vagina opens up and balloons out.

The uterus also becomes engorged with blood, enlarges, and rises from its resting position. The color of the outer and inner lips, clitoris, and vaginal walls deepens and becomes darker, duskier, or rosier. Blood pressure rises, the heart rate increases, and breathing becomes faster. All of the tissues surrounding and supporting the clitoris fill with blood and become swollen. The breasts and nipples become swollen, and the nipples become erect. Sometimes the entire body exhibits a rosy flush and the woman feels sensations of warmth and flushing. The excitement stage in women may last from a few minutes to several hours. Generally speaking, it lasts much longer in women than in men; that is, women take longer to go from initial arousal to plateau to orgasm than men do.

The Second Stage: Plateau

The plateau stage is to the period between initial arousal and orgasm. As a woman becomes more excited, the clitoris becomes more erect, the clitoral shaft becomes quite hard, the clitoral legs—which extend inside the body along the vagina—continue to engorge and become rigid, and the clitoral hood enlarges. The clitoris withdraws under the clitoral hood and the Bartholin's gland within the vagina secretes mucous.

The vagina continues to lubricate and gets very wet. Lubrication may moisten the inner lips. Sexual tension increases; breathing becomes rapid, muscles rigidify, and the woman may break into a sweat.

The Third Stage: Orgasm

Orgasm occurs when rhythmic muscle contractions begin; these contractions may be barely noticeable or they may be very powerful. The clitoris shortens dramatically and the inner lips tuck in, covering it. All the muscles surrounding the clitoris contract involuntarily, as do the vagina and the uterus. The contractions generally occur at .8-second intervals and can often be felt in the vagina, clitoris, uterus, and anus.

All orgasms are physiologically similar and are created by stimulation of the clitoris. The source of stimulation may vary. Orgasms may also vary in intensity and duration and certainly in the amount of time required to produce them, but physiologically what happens is the same. They occur because of stimulation of the clitoris—direct stimulation of the glans or indirect stimulation of the hood and inner lips, the shaft, or the clitoral legs that lie internally along the sides of the vagina.

However, the contractions of the orgasm occur throughout the pelvic platform and are not felt primarily in the clitoris.

For years, reports of female ejaculation were dismissed by scientists and sexual researchers alike, but in the 1980s the possibility of female ejaculation became more accepted. Female ejaculation occurs when a few teaspoons to one cup of a clear, odorless fluid is released from the vagina during orgasm. In the past, many women were embarrassed by this phenomenon, thinking that they were urinating.

But recent studies of the female sexual response cycle show that ejaculation can occur in some women. Release of the fluid seems to be more common in women when the G-spot is stimulated. In addition, the fluid release can be self-inhibited; that is, some women report that they can stop themselves from ejaculating if they try. Perhaps more women would report experiencing ejaculation if they didn't hold themselves back because of fear of urination.

The G-spot was named after Dr. Ernst Grafenberg, who wrote about it in 1950. However, little information was available about this additional source of female pleasure until the 1980s. The spot feels like a small lump that swells when it is stimulated. It is located toward the upper front wall of the vagina about halfway back between the pubic bone and cervix. Although it is difficult to reach by a woman herself when she is lying flat, it can be reached easily by a partner's fingers, by a dildo, or by special attachments made for some vibrators (and sometimes by a penis when the woman is in the female superior position). Some women report that their orgasms feel deeper and more pleasurable when accompanied by stimulation of the G-spot. Other women report the orgasmic expulsion of fluid, the "female ejaculation," after G-spot stimulation.

In women there is no refractory period, that is, no time that has to pass between one orgasm and continued stimulation to the next orgasm. Women may be able to have multiple orgasms if they choose to be stimulated again. After the completion of one orgasm, they can resume stimulation and become orgasmic a second or third time if they so desire. Often the glans of the clitoris is too sensitive to be touched, but the shaft and the inner lips may be receptive. Sometimes immediate restimulation may feel uncomfortable or painful, or having one orgasm may be sufficiently satisfying and fulfilling. Women often have felt shame about their ability or inability to ejaculate or to have multiple orgasms. There is a great deal of variation among women, and the same woman's experiences may vary radically over the course of her life.

The Fourth Phase: Resolution

Resolution occurs when stimulation ceases—both after orgasm and after plateau without orgasm. If orgasm does not occur, resolution may take place over a number of hours. With orgasm, resolution usually takes a half hour or so. In resolution, the body returns to its unexcited state. Engorgement recedes, the glans, shaft, hood, and legs of the clitoris return to normal, and the vaginal walls collapse again to form a small opening. The uterus returns to its resting state and the color changes fade.

Variations in the Cycle

The Female Response Cycle chart shows various courses the sexual response pattern may take in a particular woman. In experience C, the woman is touching herself. As you can see, the time from desire through sexual excitement to plateau is fairly short, and orgasm is more intense. This is typical of the masturbation experience whether by hand, by using other forms of pressure such as water, or by using a vibrator.

When women masturbate, they can provide themselves with instant and perfect feedback. In masturbation women can touch themselves wherever they need to, with appropriate pressure as long as they need it. If something isn't working, they can immediately change to something better. Most women come to orgasm more quickly and more intensely when stimulating themselves than they do in partner sex, although the subjective experience may be less intense.

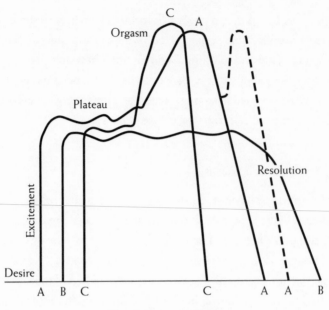

Female Response Cycle

In experience A, the woman is having partner sex. She becomes excited to plateau, then falls back to the excitement phase, then reaches plateau again, falls back to the excitement phase, reaches plateau, then has an orgasm. Experience A is not at all atypical of women's sexuality. The dotted line indicates the possibility of having multiple orgasms, that is, more than one orgasm during the same sexual encounter. As mentioned previously, there is no particular period of time a woman must wait from having one orgasm until she can have the next. For men, there is a period of time (refractory period) after the first ejaculation during which it is physically difficult to get an erection and ejaculate again. This period lengthens with a man's age and may vary from a few minutes in a teenager to several days for a man in his seventies.

Women generally take much longer to achieve orgasm than men do to achieve ejaculation. It is not unusual for women to get excited to the plateau stage, then get less excited, more excited, and so on until they reach orgasm. For example, a woman's partner may suck her breasts and stroke her inner thighs until she gets very excited, then switch to stroking around the vaginal opening, which may be less exciting, then stroke along her inner lips, which may be very exciting, then penetrate the vagina, which may be less exciting, and finally stroke along the clitoral shaft, which causes orgasm.

Most orgasmic female sexual experiences tend to be less linear than the male experience. Rarely is there a direct line from desire through excitement to orgasm for women. Women's experience tends to lack the physiological inevitability that often characterizes male sexuality.

In experience B, the woman is having partner sex without orgasm. She gets excited, reaches plateau, then falls back to the excitement stage again without coming to orgasm. In this case, resolution takes several hours, because there are no orgasmic muscle spasms to empty the pelvic area of blood congestion and swelling.

This experience also is not unusual for women. Some women find themselves unable to come to orgasm at all and repeatedly experience Pattern B. Some women find themselves experiencing Pattern B only in certain circumstances, such as having sex when the children are still up, with particular partners, or with certain sexual techniques such as missionary position intercourse. Some women find themselves able to experience orgasm only when self-stimulated and not with a partner.

All of the above sexual experiences may occur in the life of any one woman. None is atypical or unusual. As women become more sexually experienced, they may shift from more instances of one experience to more instances of another, but it is not uncommon for women to continue to have a variety of sexual experiences throughout their lives. It is highly unlikely that a woman will have only one of the experiences described above.

Sexual Problems in Alcoholic Women

Most experts report that approximately 50 percent of all Americans will report problems of sexual functioning during their lifetimes. That figure is even higher for alcoholics—both men and women. In my study of alcoholic women, only 55 percent of the recovering alcoholic women reported that they were satisfied with their sexual responsiveness at least half of the time, as compared to 84 percent of the nonalcoholic women. Clearly, difficulties with sexuality for alcoholic women extend beyond active drinking into sobriety.

Physiological Problems During Drinking Phase

The physiological effects of alcohol have a significant impact on women during their drinking phase. Alcoholic women experience more gynecological problems than do nonalcoholic women. They experience more vaginitis and painful vaginal discharges. They experience more hormonal disruptions from the effects of alcohol and they have more liver damage, which affects sexual functioning.

In addition, alcohol has a depressant effect on sexual arousal as well as on other physiological mechanisms, creating lowered sexual desire. Alcohol dries up the mucous membranes and inhibits vaginal lubrication, making penetration less comfortable and sometimes even painful. Alcohol retards pelvic congestion, making swelling less likely to occur. With inhibited lubrication and retarded swelling, excitement to orgasm will take longer and require more pressure, if it occurs at all. Alcohol also deadens sensory input, and with less sensitivity to touch, women require more stimulation to get the same effect.

In sobriety, although these physiological factors are no longer operative, alcoholic women's sexual difficulties often continue. In my own studies of recovering women, I found that 39 percent reported lack of sexual interest, 43 percent reported lack of sexual arousal or pleasure, 36 percent reported lack of lubrication, 51 percent reported lack of orgasm, 20 percent reported painful intercourse, and 10 percent reported vaginal muscle spasms that prevented penetration.

Lack of arousal and lack of lubrication usually go together. During menopause the ability to lubricate naturally decreases. If you enter recovery during menopause, you may be mistakenly attributing lack of lubrication to lack of arousal. Most women experience a fairly pronounced difference in the amount of vaginal lubrication during menopause, even if they continue to get as aroused as before menopause.

Lack of Lubrication During Recovery

For heterosexual women, lack of lubrication associated with lack of arousal can often be attributed to the differences in the sexual response cycles between men and women. Arousal leading to erection is fairly direct and quick with men. Although the time from desire to full erection in men lengthens as they age, the time still remains significantly less than that for women.

Some men report full erections after three to eight seconds of stimulation of their scrotum and penis, while women often report full lubrication after twenty minutes of varied stimulation. Men often report having erections from such indirect stimulation as looking at erotic pictures or watching others in erotic situations. Women, on the other hand, require more direct stimulation and more time to lubricate fully.

Unfortunately for us as women, sexual coupling has been defined and discussed primarily by men. The terms of the discourse have been set by men, and the language of sexuality is one largely dominated by men's needs. The caressing, stroking, touching, sucking, biting, and teasing that women require to become excited have been relegated to the term *foreplay*, which is seen as less important than penetration. The "fore" suggests that everything that precedes penetration and ejaculation is simply setting the stage for the "real sex act." It may be for men. For them, the important part of sex may occur only after erection. For us, however, that's not the case.

Our ability to feel sexual pleasure and our ability to achieve orgasm is directly affected by the amount of touching and caressing that we receive. Without a lot of touching, by mouth or by hand, without prolonged tactile stimulation, we don't get aroused, and the lubrication and swelling phase gets bypassed.

For women, lack of lubrication and swelling is analogous to lack of erection in men. Although society has taken the view that lack of female lubrication is not significant and is easily solved by using lubricant, we know that it is significant. If we haven't lubricated, we're not aroused (this may not be true for women who have reached menopause). Without arousal, sexual activity is not pleasurable, and penetration may even be painful. Without arousal, orgasm is impossible.

If you are not in menopause and are experiencing a lack of lubrication, the only answer is not to run down to the drugstore and buy a lubricant. The first step is to see whether you are getting the sexual caresses that you find arousing. As recovering women, we may find that we don't really know what sorts of stimulation we find most exciting. We may have depended on alcohol to get us through quickly fumbled caresses to penetration and ejaculation to passing out.

The easiest way to find out what kind of touch turns you on is to touch yourself. Touching yourself can give you the confidence to begin asking for the kind of touch you would like to receive from someone else. Only through experimentation and asking for a variety of touches can we learn what's pleasurable for us. Some of us like to have our breasts cupped and squeezed; others prefer the nipples only to be sucked. Some of us like to be licked from inner thighs to belly button; others find that licking turns them off. Some of us like being lightly bitten on the ass; others don't want anyone's teeth near them. These are just a few examples of the kinds of caresses that women find exciting. Examples in the hundreds could be cited. But the fact is that each of us finds different forms of touch exciting. In addition, what is exciting to us may vary according to the stage of our menstrual cycle, how much desire we feel before we start touching, and the particular partner we're with.

Learning what we want during sex and asking for it can seem almost impossible for women. We have been raised to wait for men to let us know what they want. We've been trained to find our pleasure in giving others pleasure. Although taking care of another's sexual needs does provide satisfaction, if it's a one-sided interaction it breeds resentment and undermines relationships. Exploring what we want and what turns us on, and being explicit about it with our partner(s), creates a truly mutually satisfying sexual experience.

The key is mutuality, and mutuality is impossible when you don't know or say what you want. If we say out loud what we need, then we give our partner the opportunity to please us. We give our relationship a better chance of survival and we experience sexual pleasure. Sexuality is perhaps the hardest area of our lives in which to assert ourselves. But it's also an area in which self-assertion pays off in almost immediate dividends.

Don't settle for continued sexual experience without lubrication. Explore your own sexual history, when you were turned on and why; examine your present sexual relationships to see if you're getting the kind of touch that you want; and finally, touch your own body to learn about your sexual reactions and desires.

Lack of Orgasm During Recovery

Over 50 percent of the recovering women that I interviewed experienced lack of orgasm. Lack of desire and lack of orgasm continue to be the two most common sexual difficulties that all women report, whether in recovery or not. In the past, lack of orgasm in women was seen as a psychological problem; women who didn't have orgasms were called frigid and assumed to be in flight from their own femininity.

Now, after the work of Masters and Johnson, we know that lack of orgasm is primarily a problem of lack of adequate stimulation. Any woman who has a clitoris can have an orgasm, but orgasm cannot occur without full arousal and clitoral stimulation. The kind of clitoral stimulation necessary for orgasm is rarely achieved with just penetration.

And the missionary position, which is so common to white Western-
ers, is the coital position least likely to provide the clitoral stimulation
necessary.

Women report that the easiest way for them to achieve orgasm is
by self stimulation with a vibrator. The vibrator provides constant,
even stimulation. It doesn't get tired or sore. When you use it yourself,
you can maneuver it into any position and use it with any degree of
pressure.

Next after vibrators comes manual masturbation. Women report
touching themselves with their hands, using water as in shower sprays
and hot-tub jets, and rubbing against pillows.

In partner sex, women report greatest ease in coming to orgasm
when their partner stimulates them manually or orally. The most difficult way for women to come to orgasm is through vaginal penetration
without direct clitoral stimulation. Some coital positions provide more
clitoral stimulation than others. Positions with the woman on top, guid-
ing the penis and directing the angle of insertion, can provide more contact with the clitoris. Side-by-side positions can also provide more
clitoral stimulation.

If you have never had an orgasm and would like to experience orgasms, learning to masturbate with a vibrator is the easiest way to start.
Once you are able to experience orgasms through the use of a vibrator,
you may have to practice some more to learn how to have orgasms by
hand. And after learning how to have orgasms by self-stimulation, you
may need practice to learn to have orgasms with a partner.

It is not at all uncommon for women to be able to stimulate themselves to orgasm but remain unable to have orgasms with a partner. If
you don't have orgasms with your partner, but do with yourself, the
quickest way to teach your partner what works for you is to put your
partner's hand over yours while you masturbate. Then your partner can
directly feel what works for you.

The clitoral stimulation needed for orgasm can be applied by your
partner's hand or mouth. Some women prefer manual stimulation, while

others find the sensitivity and wetness of the mouth and tongue more exciting. Many women find stimulation along the shaft of the clitoris, above the clitoris, and along the vaginal lips most exciting. After they are excited, many women find direct stimulation to the glans of the clitoris to be too intense and almost painful. Some women like to have their breasts touched or sucked while they're being otherwise stimulated; others find the added touch distracting.

For women the most difficult way to come to orgasm is via penis-vagina intercourse without additional clitoral stimulation. The average coital encounter consists of sixteen thrusts, and most books define premature ejaculation as occurring after only two or three thrusts. Clearly, female anatomy is not designed to achieve orgasm through penile thrusting alone.

If it's important to you and/or to your partner that you achieve orgasm through intercourse alone, there are techniques that can make orgasm more likely. Thorough arousal and then manual or oral stimulation to the plateau stage before penetration will help. The female-on-top and side-by-side positions are helpful; if using the missionary position, thrusting and removing the penis and rubbing it over the vaginal lips to the clitoris can be effective. In any case, 70 percent of women report their inability to experience orgasm with intercourse alone, although vaginal penetration may be very exciting and pleasurable and part of achieving orgasm.

You may find that you can experience orgasm in some situations but not others, or with a particular partner but not another. Such experiences are not at all unusual. Many women report that they can have orgasms only at home in their own beds with the door closed. Other women report that orgasms come most easily for them in a slightly dangerous situation, such as in the back of a car parked on a side street.

Each of us has particular cues toward greater excitement. For some of us, safety and security provide the atmosphere that allows us to reach abandonment. For others, danger heightens arousal and sharpens sensation. Each of us is unique in terms of what situations are conducive to orgasm. Don't criticize yourself if your exciting situations don't match those of your partner. Generally speaking, men are more excited by the idea of having sexual encounters in semipublic or other slightly dangerous surroundings. Women often need the safety and security of privacy to let go.

If you are having trouble achieving orgasm with your current partner but have had orgasms with previous partners, you and your partner may need to experiment with various positions and techniques. Sometimes we become rigid in how we think we ought to achieve orgasm. Clearly, once we know we can achieve orgasm in a particular way, it may be hard to try new ways in which we're not assured of success.

As recovering women, we're probably all familiar with our propensities toward rigid behavior. If, after experimentation, you still can't achieve orgasm with your current partner, you may want to masturbate in your partner's arms. If you find this frightening or embarrassing, try it at first in the dark or use the "spoons" position, freeing your hands but keeping full body contact.

You may want to use the vibrator and have your partner use the vibrator on you. Each of these possibilities allows you to achieve orgasm within the context of partner sex. Most partners will be quite turned on and feel much closer sharing such an intimate act with you. Allowing yourself to have an orgasm in a way that works for you will prevent you from building up resentments and casting yourself in the victim role.

Helen Singer Kaplan has called the "myth of the mutual orgasm" the most destructive heterosexual sexual myth now current in American society.* She points out that simultaneous orgasm is made almost impossible by the differing rates in the sexual response cycles of men and women and by their differences in anatomy. Many become erect with little direct tactile stimulation, and they ejaculate with very few penile thrusts. Women take much more time to get excited and require clitoral stimulation, not penile thrusts, for orgasm. It's very difficult to get the

---

*Helen Singer Kaplan, *The New Sex Therapy* (New York: Brunner/Mazel, 1981), 124.

two together, and it's really too bad that doing so is seen as an ideal in our culture.

If you are trying to achieve simultaneous orgasm, you would be far better off reveling in the pleasure that you do have rather than creating additional frustration. A noted researcher C. A. Tripp says, "In fantasy, simultaneous orgasm may be an ideal achievement. But in practice it is so disappointing that experienced partners, especially if they are well matched, try to avoid it. A vicarious participation in a partner's reactions is part of the enjoyment of sex—and since a person's awareness of everything external is at a minimum during his [sic] own climax, simultaneous orgasm blinds both partners to each other at precisely the wrong moment.*

Male Sexual Response Cycle

The sexual cycle in males is completely analogous to the female cycle. It is composed of the excitement, plateau, orgasmic, and resolution phases, all of which occur in the same order and are produced by similar biological reflexes.

The First Phase: Excitement

In the male excitement phase, a vascular reflex causes the genital organs to become engorged with blood; this is similar to the engorgement of the pelvic structures in the female. The male experiences the engorgement as penile erection, which often occurs within three to eight seconds after direct stimulation, particularly in younger men. Males report, however, that they often have erections without any direct stimulation. Men are very easily stimulated by visual and other sensory stimuli, and arousal leading to erection is fairly direct and quick. Although the time from desire to full erection in men lengthens as they age, the time is still significantly less than that for full lubrication and engorgement in women.

---

*C. A. Tripp, *Homosexual Matrix* (McGraw-Hill, 1975), 98.

In young men, especially, erection may occur so easily as to be embarrassing. Men commonly report having erections from looking at erotic pictures, from touching a desirable woman, from watching others in erotic situations, and sometimes even from smelling a particular perfume.

In addition to penile erection, the scrotal sac thickens, flattens, and becomes elevated; the nipples become erect and the testicles elevate and increase in size. Other reactions reported in the description of the female excitement phase also occur: blood pressure rises, heart rate increases, and breathing becomes faster.

The Second Phase: Plateau

As male excitement increases to the plateau phase, the penis becomes further engorged and increases in circumference. The testicles enlarge by 50 to 100 percent and become fully elevated and rotated. Often the corona of the penis gets a purple flush, and the Cowper's gland secretes a mucous discharge. The skin becomes flushed, muscle tension increases, and hyperventilation occurs.

The Third Phase: Orgasm

In orgasm, contractions generally occur at .8-second intervals for three to four contractions, then slow down for two to four more contractions. Contractions occur in the penile urethra, the vas deferens, the seminal vesicles, the ejaculatory duct, and the prostate. Ejaculation occurs.

The Fourth Phase: Resolution

The resolution phase is characterized by loss of the penile erection and by a refractory period during which it is physically difficult for another orgasm and ejaculation to occur. Some males have a sweating reaction during the contractions of orgasm; they may continue to hyperventilate, and the heartbeat may reach 150 to 180 beats per minute.

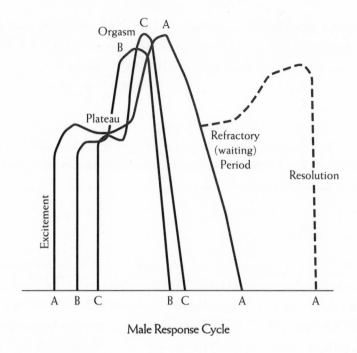

Male Response Cycle

Variations in the Cycle

The Male Response Cycle chart shows the various experiences a man may have during the course of his sexual life. In experience C, the man is masturbating to orgasm. The line from the beginning of arousal to plateau is very steep, the plateau phase is short, and orgasm and ejaculation occur with a greater degree of physiological intensity than during partner sex.

In experience A, the man is having partner sex, with a second orgasm and ejaculation occurring after a refractory period. In this case the man is young, and the refractory period lasts less than an hour. After the refractory period ceases and before the resolution phase is complete, the man regains his erection and has another orgasm with ejaculation.

In experience B, the man is having partner sex with premature ejaculation. In this case, ejaculation occurs after a very short period of excitement and almost no plateau phase. Premature ejaculation is not as common a problem for alcoholic men during their active drinking as is retarded ejaculation. The various physiological effects of alcohol combine to make orgasm and ejaculation more difficult to achieve. However, during sobriety, premature ejaculation may again become a common sexual problem.

The most common difficulties experienced by men in sobriety—loss of sexual desire and erectile difficulties—are not represented on this chart. In both of these cases, erection is not achieved and penile penetration is either difficult or not possible.

Sexual Problems in Alcoholic Men

Both alcoholic and nonalcoholic men experience erectile dysfunction (impotence) with intoxication. As the alcohol level in the blood increases, males report decreased tumescence, increased latency to orgasm (retarded ejaculation), and subjective reports of decreased arousal and decreased orgasmic pleasure and intensity. All of these physiological reactions are similar to those experienced by women. Men also report decreased sexual interest and desire as their alcoholism progresses, probably for the physiological reasons outlined above.

Like women, men do not automatically regain their full sexual functioning during early sobriety. After a year of sobriety, at least 50 percent of men can expect to have their ability to experience an erection restored and their tendency to retarded ejaculation ameliorated. The restoration of sexual functioning is more likely if the men talk about sexual problems and get sexual counseling, both of which can help decrease their performance anxiety. Again, it is important to reiterate that sexual behavior is learned behavior. The anxiety created by erectile dysfunction during chronic alcoholism can easily carry over into sobriety, further impairing the sexual self-image.

The sexual socialization of men connects their ability to achieve an erection with power, potency, and virility. Masculine identity may be severely threatened when men are unable to attain erection consistently.

Attaining an erection for men is analogous to lubricating in women, yet there is no similar stigma attached to women for lack of lubrication. In fact, lack of lubrication is viewed by the society as a minor problem that can be resolved with a tube of lubricant from the drugstore. This is yet one more example of the destructive effects of the sexual socialization that men receive.

Appendix B

Women and AIDS

In the 1980s AIDS (Acquired Immune Deficiency Syndrome) became a major health issue that affected the sexuality and sexual expression of everyone in this country. In a book about women's sexuality and chemical dependence, it is especially important that we address the issue of AIDS and its transmission. Probably few of us are unaware of AIDS and its impact; however, it is doubtful that many of us know particular information about women and our vulnerability to AIDS.

As women in recovery we may be especially concerned about HIV (human immunodeficiency virus) infection and its symptoms and progress. However, it still remains very difficult to get solid information about AIDS and women. In working on this section, I called a number of the traditional AIDS organizations, seeking information about the differences between HIV infection in men and in women. Invariably, I was told that there was little information about the disease in women, that women were not part of the early AZT trials, and that no long-term studies of HIV infection in women had been undertaken.

Just as the medical profession has not viewed women as possible victims of HIV infection, we ourselves may be in denial about our vulnerability. We may identify the disease with male homosexuality, with having a very large number of sexual partners, or with anal intercourse, and deny looking at our own sexual and IV drug-using behaviors that may have put us at risk. In 1990, only 10 percent of those known to have AIDS were women, but that figure should not lull us into complacency about our vulnerability. The startling prediction is that in 1991 AIDS will be the fifth leading cause of death among all women of childbearing age in the United States. Currently the rate of infection is 2.5 times faster among women than men.

The following appendix summarizes what we know about women and AIDS, not in an attempt to create more fear but in an attempt to educate and dispel denial. Only when we know fully about HIV infection and how to avoid its transmission can we empower ourselves to make responsible sexual decisions.

Until 1986 over 50 percent of women diagnosed with AIDS became HIV positive by sharing needles with someone who was HIV positive. However, that percentage is dropping rapidly as more and more women become infected by engaging in unprotected heterosexual sex with infected partners. One-third of the women who now have AIDS became HIV positive from having unsafe sex with male partners, and that proportion is expected to increase to over half in the next few years. Ten percent of women contracted AIDS from receiving blood transfusions before 1985, when the blood supply began to be screened, and the rest contracted AIDS from unknown sources. Only two cases of lesbian transmission of AIDS have been reported at this time.

Of the women who have been diagnosed with AIDS so far, 50 percent are African-American, 23 percent are Latina, and 26 percent are white. A small number are Asian, Native American, and from other backgrounds. After sharing needles, the most common form of HIV transmission for women is long-term monogamous sex with an infected partner. In studies of couples with one infected partner, women were more likely to become infected after having unsafe sex with men than vice versa. It seems that the virus is more easily transmitted from men to women through vaginal intercourse than from women to men.

As women recovering from alcoholism and drug addiction, we are likely to have engaged in sexual behaviors that put us at risk for HIV infection. We often have engaged in unsafe sex with partners who might have been HIV positive, and we may have shared needles with IV drug users who might have been HIV positive. These are the two primary ways that women are exposed to possible HIV infection.

As women in recovery from chemical dependence, we cannot afford to be complacent about possible HIV infection. Although women still represent only 10 percent of diagnosed AIDS cases, the rate of infection in women is growing at a faster rate than that of any other group.

What Is AIDS?

In 1978 a number of young, white gay men were diagnosed with Karposi's Sarcoma, a very rare cancer that was usually seen only in older men of Mediterranean or African descent. Over a period of two years, more and more cases were diagnosed of similarly fatal infections, including pneumocystis carinii pneumonia (PCP), in young, previously healthy men.

At first medical practitioners thought that the disease was related to the homosexuality of their initial patients, but in 1980 they began seeing the same condition among intravenous (IV) drug abusers who were primarily heterosexual. And soon they recognized the same symptoms in those who had received blood transfusions, recent Haitian immigrants, female sexual partners of infected men, and newborn babies of infected women.

In 1981 the Centers for Disease Control (CDC) in Atlanta, a federal agency, set up a task force to study the disease and to track its spread. In 1983 the disease was identified and named AIDS. The A in AIDS stands for Acquired, meaning that AIDS is a transmitted rather than a genetic disease. The I and D stand for Immune Deficiency, meaning that the immune system is attacked, leaving it deficient and vulnerable to various opportunistic infections. The S stands for Syndrome, meaning that HIV infection isn't a particular disease in and of itself; rather it's a syndrome of different infections to which the body becomes vulnerable as its immune system is broken down.

In 1984 a virus (now called HIV) was identified as the primary source of AIDS infection. The virus was found to remain latent for long periods of time; that is, the time between becoming infected with HIV and showing symptoms of AIDS-related infections might be years. During that time, people could feel and look healthy and not know that they were infected, yet be infectious and pass the infection on to others. Research showed that the virus exists in bodily fluids and is transmitted by the direct exchange of semen, blood, and vaginal secretions.

Having HIV infection or being HIV positive cannot be confirmed directly. However, over the six to twelve weeks after a person becomes infected, his or her body usually develops antibodies to the infection. Tests for the presence of the antibodies were developed, and people who had engaged in unsafe sex or the sharing of needles were encouraged to be tested. These tests only confirm exposure to HIV. They do not tell you when or if you will develop AIDS.

After the discovery of HIV, media attention on the disease often contributed to both widespread hysteria and individual denial. The following factors seemed to contribute to this phenomenon:

- Many people became HIV positive long before we knew the virus existed and before we knew that not exchanging bodily fluids (semen and blood) could prevent its transmission.

- Because there is a long period of latency between infection and the onset of AIDS, there is no way to make a visual judgment about whether someone is HIV positive. Most people are infectious for years without having any symptoms and don't know themselves that they are HIV positive.

- Because there is a lag between infection and the production of HIV antibodies in most people (thought to be six to twelve weeks), a negative HIV test may be inaccurate, creating a false sense of security.

- Many people associate HIV infection with being gay or being an IV drug user rather than with particular behavior—exchanging bodily fluids with an infected person.

The result of hysteria combined with denial has often been that people have become needlessly worried about contracting AIDS from casual contact but at the same time have continued to have unprotected sex. The following section will give you information about various ways in which HIV infection is transmitted.

How Is AIDS Transmitted?

HIV is a relatively fragile virus and cannot exist outside the body for an extended period of time. It cannot be transmitted casually; you can be infected only by receiving blood, semen, or vaginal secretions into your own bodily fluids. The easiest form of transmission is through the exchange of blood. Most hemophiliacs in the United States are infected now, because they received so many blood transfusions before we knew the virus was transmitted via blood. In 1985, all blood banks started screening their blood supplies and destroying blood that contained the virus. There is now practically no chance that you can contract the virus from a blood transfusion administered in the United States.

Intravenous drug users become infected by sharing needles that have been used by an infected person. The needle contains a residue of blood from the previous user. Thus, the virus is introduced from the bloodstream of the infected person directly into the bloodstream of the uninfected person. In some areas, IV drug users do not show a high rate of infection. That's because they don't generally share needles. In other areas, which are known for their shooting galleries, IV drug users show a very high rate of HIV infection.

The second easiest way to contract HIV infection is by engaging in unprotected anal intercourse. Because the rectal tissues are easily torn, semen deposited in the rectum enters the bloodstream directly. That's why gay men were the earliest victims of the AIDS virus. They often engage in anal intercourse—a form of sex that transmits the virus most readily. Unfortunately, the fear of AIDS became attached to gay men rather than to unprotected anal intercourse, which can be engaged in by heterosexuals also.

The virus can also be transmitted via semen through unprotected vaginal intercourse. The vaginal walls seem to be more sturdy and less permeable than the walls of the rectum, making this form of transmission more difficult than through anal intercourse. Yet it still is a major form of HIV infection and is expected to become the primary form of transmission for women in the next few years. Infection by the virus is more likely to occur if there is any kind of break in the skin on the penis, such as an open sore or lesion, or if there is any trauma to the vagina that creates tiny tears in the vaginal walls.

Another way the virus can be transmitted is through vaginal intercourse from an infected woman to her partner. The virus is contained in vaginal secretions and menstrual blood and can be absorbed through the penile opening, although this form of transmission is more difficult than transmission from the male to the female.

The virus can also be transmitted by an infected pregnant woman to her unborn infant or to the infant during birth. Some cases have also been reported of transmission from an infected mother to her infant via nursing.

A very small number of cases of transmission have been reported in the following circumstances: (1) oral sex that involved swallowing semen of an infected partner, (2) oral sex that involved ingesting vaginal secretions and blood of an infected partner, and (3) needle pricks received by health-care workers from needles that had been used on infected patients. No cases of transmission of the virus have been reported by family members, caretakers, or health-care workers who haven't received needle pricks.

The good news about the virus is that it is very fragile and easily destroyed. It can't live outside of the body, so it isn't transmitted via the air, through food, or on toilet seats or utensils. It can't pass through condoms and it's easily destroyed by 5 percent nonoxynol-9, a common ingredient of spermicides and some sexual lubricants. It can't live upon contact with a mild solution of bleach, so rinsing needles with bleach destroys the virus.

How Can I Avoid Getting Infected?

First, let's look at three ways that you *can't* avoid getting infected.

- You can't avoid AIDS by only being sexual with men who look strong and healthy. There is a long period, perhaps lasting up to twelve years, between HIV infection and the first visible symptoms of AIDS. During that time, the HIV-infected person often doesn't know he has AIDS, although he can still transmit it to you.

- You can't avoid AIDS by only being sexual with heterosexual men who do not use IV drugs. Many heterosexual men have had sexual contacts with other men who were infected but have never thought of themselves as homosexual. Some of them have shared needles with friends but have never considered themselves IV drug users. Some have had unprotected sex with prostitutes who were infected; this is especially common in men who were in the armed services between 1975 and 1985.

- You can't avoid AIDS by reducing the number of your sex partners. Unfortunately, you can become HIV positive by having one unprotected sexual encounter with one infected partner. Reducing the number of partners may not rule out the one who is infected.

- You can't avoid AIDS by being monogamous with a long-term partner. That partner may have become infected years before he met you. Or he may have become infected during one unprotected one-night stand. Repeated unprotected sexual contact with an infected person increases the likelihood that you will become infected. In fact, in New York, wives of needle-sharing IV drug users make up the single largest group of women infected.

However, you can avoid contracting AIDS by consistently and properly using a condom and foam containing 5 percent nonoxynol-9. The virus cannot travel through latex condoms. If you are sexual with a man who is infected and he uses a condom correctly and you use spermicidal foam, you greatly decrease your chances of becoming HIV positive.

Unfortunately, using condoms and foam is not an absolute guarantee that you won't become HIV positive. Condoms sometimes break or leak. Sometimes foam is not an effective barrier. But when both are used together, they provide the greatest protection short of total abstinence.

There are only two guarantees to complete safety from possible HIV infection. One is to have no sex at all. The other is to engage in sexual practices that involve no contact with the bodily fluids of another person.

Using a Condom

For condoms to work effectively, they have to be used consistently and properly. Only one time of not using a condom with an infected partner can result in your becoming HIV positive. And the more times you are exposed to the semen of an infected partner, the more likely it is that you will become HIV positive. Condoms deteriorate as they age, so have a supply of relatively new ones at hand. Don't depend upon a condom your partner has been carrying around in his billfold for eons. Condoms also deteriorate when exposed to sunlight, so don't leave them lying on the windowsill next to the bed.

If the condom breaks or comes off during sex, having used a 5 percent nonoxynol-9 foam will further protect you from possible infection. Although the spermicidal jelly used with a diaphragm is effective as a contraceptive, it is not effective against HIV infection. A diaphragm with jelly blocks sperm from entering the cervix, but it does not protect the vaginal walls. HIV infection is transmitted through the vaginal walls, so you will need to use foam that covers the insides of the vaginal walls and destroys the HIV-infected semen before it can be absorbed by the vagina.

As an added protection, some people use condoms that already contain nonoxynol-9 in their tips. Brands that contain nonoxynol-9 include Manform Plus, Prime with nonoxynol-9, and Trojan Plus. Some people place a dab of nonoxynol-9 spermicidal jelly in the tip of their favorite condom. Using a nonoxynol-9 lubricated condom may prevent infection from condom leaks, breaks, or spillage.

It is extremely important that you not use oil or petroleum-based lubricants when using a condom. Oil and petroleum-based lubricants attack latex and cause it to dissolve and break. So don't use baby oil, cold cream, Vaseline, vegetable oil, mineral oil, Crisco, Nivea lotion, hand cream, Albolene, or massage oil when using a condom. Don't put any such oils on the condom or in or around the vagina or anus/rectum.

When using a lubricant, choose a water-soluble one such as K-Y jelly, Astroglide, Probe, ForPlay, Slippery Stuff, Joy Jelly, Slip, Lubafax, Ramses, Lubraceptic, Delfen, or Anal Lube. Most of these lubricants are tasteless and odorless, and some contain nonoxynol-9. They vary in consistency and texture and can be purchased at most drugstores. Since they are water soluble, they easily wash off. If they dry or become sticky during use, their slipperiness can be revived with a little saliva, water, or vaginal secretions. Some people keep a spray bottle of water by the bedside for lubrication emergencies.

Condoms should be put on an erect or partially erect penis. If placed on a penis before erection, the condom may slip off as the erection hardens. Open the condom package carefully so that you don't gouge it with your nails. Never open the package with your teeth. The Gold Circle Coin Type condom is an especially easy one to open.

With your thumb and forefinger, gently press any air out of the receptacle tip at the closed end. Air bubbles can cause tears. If adding nonoxynol-9 lubricant, squeeze a little dab into the receptacle tip. Often, lubricant gets rid of possible air bubbles in the condom as well as increasing sensation. Unroll the condom onto the erect penis, leaving about half an inch free at the tip to catch the ejaculate. If your partner is uncircumcised, the foreskin should be pulled back before covering the head with the condom.

Make sure the condom covers the entire erect penis. If the condom is not tight, your partner should hold it at the base of the penis as he inserts it so that it doesn't come off. Certain sexual positions may tend to cause the condom to slip. During vaginal intercourse with the woman on top, the condom may be lifted off by the vaginal lips. Simply holding the condom at the base of the penis can prevent that. Condoms may also come off if the penis becomes soft or if the vagina or rectum is very tight. Again, holding the condom at the base of the penis will solve the problem. If slipping is a problem, Mentor condoms come with an interior safety seal and Huggers are tapered to fit more snugly.

Put the condom on before you begin sex play. If you wait until you're ready for penetration, it may be too late. Drops of semen may ooze from the uncovered penis, and even one drop is enough to cause infection.

After ejaculation, make sure your partner holds the condom around the base to avoid spilling the contents or losing it inside you. Have your partner withdraw gently and immediately throw the condom away. Don't ever use a condom a second time.

If you use sex toys, be sure to clean them before using them again, and don't use a toy on your partner and then on yourself. Wash it in between. In addition to soap and water, the following kill HIV: hydrogen peroxide, ordinary rubbing alcohol, diluted household bleach (one part bleach to ten parts water), and ForPlay Adult Toy Cleanser. If you use a dildo, be sure to cover it with a condom too. And throw the condom away before using the dildo again.

Remember, condoms don't work in the drawer or in your purse. They only protect you from possible HIV infection if they're put on the erect penis before sex play, used properly during penetration, and removed carefully from the rectum or vagina. If, when your partner withdraws, he finds that the condom has split, broken, or come off, immediately retrieve the condom and throw it away, and insert additional spermicidal foam containing five percent or more of nonoxynol-9. Absolutely do not douche! Douching can cause microscopic vaginal or rectal tears that make infection more likely.

Using Vaginal Foam

Using vaginal foam with at least 5 percent nonoxynol-9 along with condoms makes it much less likely that you will become infected with the AIDS virus. Using vaginal foam alone, or condoms alone, is less effective than using both. Vaginal foam is more effective than a sponge, cream, gel, or jelly because it expands to fill the entire vagina, covering the insides of the vaginal walls and protecting them from infected ejaculate. Foam with 5 percent or more nonoxynol-9 has been found in laboratory tests to kill the human immunodeficiency virus upon contact. Be sure to insert the foam with the applicator before you engage in sex. If you decide to engage in penetration again later, insert another full applicator. Foam can be purchased at a drugstore without a prescription. Two of the common brands are Delfen and Emko.

Taking Responsibility for Safer Sex

As a woman in recovery, you are learning how to take responsibility for your own health. In order to take responsibility for not becoming HIV positive, you will need to learn how to buy and use condoms, lubricants, and vaginal foam. None of these products require a doctor's prescription, and all can be purchased at your local drugstore.

Sometimes it is very difficult for women, especially if they live in small towns, to purchase such "sexual" items at a local drugstore. You may feel that purchasing these items on your own means that you are a sexually aggressive "slut." Unfortunately, if you don't have these items on hand you may end up in a sexual encounter in which you get infected with the AIDS virus. The mail order houses at the end of appendix C sell condoms and lubricants also.

Just as women have had to take primary responsibility for contraception, they will probably have to take primary responsibility for safe sex. It seems unlikely at this time that men will insist upon the use of condoms and vaginal foam. Even men in recovery may be in denial about having taken part in high-risk activities during their active using and drinking.

As we said earlier, it is important that you learn how to put condoms on an erect penis. Practice putting them on dildos, zucchini, or cucumbers. Some women have even learned to put on condoms with their mouths. Most men find condom use much more erotic if the woman incorporates it in her repertoire of sexual play.

Purchase a variety of condoms in various sizes and colors. Take them out and blow them up and stretch them. (Just don't use them after doing that!) Become familiar and confident with using them; it will make it much easier to ask your partner to use a condom.

Women generally report that it is extremely difficult for them to ask new sexual partners to use condoms, as well as to remain consistent in insisting that regular partners always use condoms. Since the 1970s, women have learned to take sole responsibility for contraception. They take pills, get IUDs, and insert diaphragms, sponges, gels, and foams. Men have gotten out of the habit of taking any responsibility for contraception and subsequently for using condoms at all. In addition, curing sexually transmitted diseases has become easier with the advent of antibiotics, so using condoms to avoid disease has become fairly rare.

In this sexual climate, men are often quite reluctant to start taking responsibility for possible HIV infection. They may use a variety of excuses and even threats to avoid having to use condoms. They may complain about how it decreases their pleasure. They may insist it causes them to lose their erection. They may intimate that you don't trust them or that you think they're bisexual (clearly a slur on their manhood). They may even say that they don't want to be sexual if they have to use condoms.

Although it is extremely difficult for women to hear such reactions and remain firm with their intentions to use condoms, it is absolutely essential that women become their own constant and assertive caretakers. It is very clear that men will not take care of women in this regard. Unless we learn to assert our own needs for sexual safety and health, those needs will not get met. We must learn to take responsibility for our own well-being.

Should I Get Tested?

Once women in recovery begin to look honestly at their past sexual histories, many realize that they may be HIV positive. While chemically dependent, most of us engaged in unprotected sex. It's difficult when you're high to insist that your partner wear a condom. Many of us also engaged in a wide variety of sexual activities—including anal intercourse—with a wide variety of partners—including chemically dependent men. Now we have to review those activities and face the likelihood that we might be infected.

It is very easy to be in denial about the possibility of getting AIDS. The media has latched upon the first group of AIDS victims—gay men—and labeled AIDS a gay disease. But we know that viruses do not discriminate. The HIV virus strikes women as well as men, heterosexuals as well as homosexuals. And those who have been chemically dependent or had unprotected sex with those who were chemically dependent are at greater risk for having contracted the infection.

If you think that you might be HIV positive, you will have to decide whether to take the test for HIV antibodies. To increase the accuracy of the test, it is generally recommended that you wait six months after your last sexual experience in which you exchanged bodily fluids and after you shared needles with someone before you take the test. For some people it takes six months or more after the initial infection for the body to produce antibodies. If you take the test sooner than six months after your last opportunity for infection, the results may not be accurate. During the six months you are waiting to take the test, do not share needles with anyone and do not exchange bodily fluids during sex. You can avoid the exchange of bodily fluids by using condoms and vaginal foam.

In the mid-1980s, AIDS support groups recommended that people not take the HIV antibody test because of issues of confidentiality and discrimination. However, in the late 1980s they reversed that recommendation. Now major AIDS groups are urging people who think that they may be HIV positive to get tested. For the first time, there are medical treatments available for HIV-positive people that can prolong their lives. In particular, the drug AZT (azidothymidine) has been found to increase the lives of HIV-positive patients significantly. At first AZT was only prescribed for patients who had survived one attack of pneumocystis pneumonia, but now AZT is being prescribed before pneumonia sets in.

There are a number of reasons you might decide to get tested. As just mentioned, you may want to know whether you're HIV positive so that you can manage your life and health with that knowledge in mind. If you are HIV positive, careful monitoring of your health with a knowledgeable physician can greatly increase the quality of your life. In addition, you may be in an absolutely monogamous relationship and hope that if you and your partner are negative, you can dispense with using condoms and vaginal foam. And if you find that you're positive, you will need to be even more careful in regard to the exchange of bodily fluids. You may also feel responsible for informing your past sexual partners of your HIV status if it's positive, so that they can be tested also. Last, your HIV status may affect your decisions about pregnancy.

All of these are good reasons for getting tested. However, they do not address the emotional issues that you will have to face if you find that you're HIV positive. It is extremely important that you receive both pretest and posttest counseling. Most states require that public health clinics provide both. If you go to your personal physician, though, it is very unlikely that you will get any counseling. Physicians are notoriously poor at addressing women's emotional concerns when dealing with physical health issues.

In many states, it is not against the law to discriminate against people who are HIV positive. And even when it is, insurance companies, employers, and landlords still discriminate. It's crucial that you carefully consider whether you desire anonymous or confidential testing.

Anonymous testing occurs in most public health clinics in large cities. Each person who wishes to be tested is given a number, then counseled about AIDS, how it is transmitted, and what is known about it. Your name and address are never known by the clinic or the counselor. After pretest counseling, you are given the opportunity to choose whether you want to be tested in light of your new knowledge. If you choose to be tested, a technician draws a small amount of blood, which is labeled with your number. In a few weeks you are required to come back to the clinic in order to receive the results in person. Your appointment and visit are arranged by your number, and your test results are presented to you by a trained counselor.

If you test positive, the counselor is prepared to help you cope with the information. The counselor can provide you with the names and numbers of support groups for HIV-positive women, with social work resources that can help you meet your needs, and with names of physicians who are knowledgeable about managing the health of HIV-positive patients.

Although the HIV antibody screening is quite reliable, it is not 100 percent accurate. Both "false positives" and "false negatives" have been known to occur. In order to increase the effectiveness of screening, the following procedure is used. First the blood is subjected to the ELISA test. If the test is negative, no more testing is done. If the ELISA is positive, it's repeated. If it's positive again, then the Western Blot test is performed. The Western Blot test is more expensive and has a much lower rate of false positives. Only when the Western Blot test confirms the positive reading is the blood assumed to be HIV positive. After all three tests give the same readings, the result is highly accurate. However, since only one negative reading is required for an assessment of HIV negative, the percentage of false negatives is higher. Some clinics suggest that if you question a false negative you return in six months for a repeat test.

If you go to a private physician for testing, you will not receive pre- and posttest counseling, nor will your testing be anonymous. You can request that your test remain confidential, however. That means that the physician is ethically bound not to disclose your HIV-positive status. Unfortunately, if the test information is placed in your medical records, it can be acquired by insurance companies, who can drop your insurance or refuse to insure you. To avoid this possibility, ask that the test request and the results be torn up and thrown away and that no notation of the test be placed in your medical records. Do not submit the bill for testing to your insurance company, because some companies drop the insurance of anyone who gets tested regardless of the results.

If Your Test Is Positive

If your test is positive, you will need a lot of emotional support to deal with the grief, anger, loss, and guilt that you will probably experience. It is vital that you get into a support group for HIV-positive women as quickly as possible. Because AIDS has been seen as a gay male disease, there aren't as many support groups for women as are needed. Women tend to become isolated, afraid to tell anyone about their HIV-positive status, and increasingly worried about their health and the future of their children. If you live in a small or medium-sized town, the tendency to become isolated may be even more pronounced. At the end of this appendix, there is a list of resources for women who are HIV positive. Call them immediately and get referrals and help. Some hot lines provide twenty-four-hour support and help.

A positive HIV antibody test does not mean that you have AIDS, nor does it tell you when or if you will get the opportunistic infections that characterize AIDS. Very few statistics have been kept on the progress from HIV infection to early symptoms of AIDS to full-blown AIDS in women. The information that we have at this time indicates that 20 to 50 percent of women who are HIV positive will develop full-blown AIDS within five years. After women are diagnosed as having AIDS, their average life expectancy is less than two years, radically less than that of homosexual white men, who now survive an average of four years. Part of the reason for women's shorter life expectancy seems to be that we are not diagnosed as having AIDS until the disease has progressed quite dramatically. Because physicians think of AIDs patients as men, they often follow up every other possible diagnosis before they start treating a woman for AIDS.

If you are HIV positive, there are many decisions that you will want to make while you're still healthy. You will have to decide who you are going to tell—including your present and former sexual partners as well as your children, family, and close friends. You may be involved in your partner's decision about getting tested. You will have to decide whether to get your children tested. You will need to decide whether to be sexual and what risks to take. You will want to decide about the custody of your children in the event of illness and about a living will for medical care should you become incapacitated or incompetent, as well as a will for the distribution of your property and possessions. You may have to decide whether to continue a pregnancy or whether to get pregnant.

All of these decisions will involve emotional strain and stress. Again, I cannot emphasize enough how important it is to get counseling and be part of an HIV-positive support group. A support group exclusively for HIV-positive women will be most effective for you, as many of the issues you will have to face will not be dealt with by men. But if the only group in town is one of gay males, the support you will get from others who are going through similar struggles will be more valuable than not attending a group at all. If there is a counselor in town who has experience working with HIV-positive patients, arrange to see him or her.

Anything that decreases stress in your life will help your immune system to remain healthy. HIV-positive people have benefited from meditation, yoga, regular exercise, and AIDS prevention and education work. It is especially important to boost your physical health as much as possible. Anything that stresses your immune system will make it more likely that you will become vulnerable to infections. Eating a healthy diet, getting plenty of rest, exercising regularly, cutting out cigarettes and coffee, getting flu shots, and avoiding live vaccines are all helpful. If you work outside the home, continuing in your job and being productive can help.

The emotional toll of facing a disease that is as stigmatized as AIDS, that has no known cure, and whose course is unpredictable is very great. Unfortunately, women are required to face their infection without the extensive support systems that have been developed in the gay male communities. The shame that HIV-positive women feel has prevented them from organizing in their own behalf, and much work needs to be done to provide the social support that women deserve.

Poor women, as in all health care arenas, have a more difficult time than middle-class women. They usually become sicker before they receive any health care at all. When they do receive care, it is of poorer quality. AZT, which costs about $10,000 a year, is generally not available to women without insurance, on welfare, or on disability. Public hospitals that care for poor women with AIDS are notoriously overcrowded and understaffed. Many health-care workers, including physicians, blame women who contracted AIDS through sharing needles or having unprotected sex with a drug-using man for their condition.

In this country, AIDS strikes African-American and Latina women in greater proportion than white women because of IV drug use among men in those communities, as well as less acceptance of the use of condoms. It is especially important that we take responsibility for getting AIDS prevention and education messages to those communities in a cultural form that can be heard.

The Symptoms of AIDS

Women often develop the opportunistic infections that characterize AIDS without even knowing that they were HIV positive. In fact, the National Women's Health Network thinks that many more women are dying from AIDS than reported because physicians aren't alerted to looking for AIDS in women. Thus, the great increase in death from respiratory infections among women may be attributable to undiagnosed cases of various pneumonias associated with AIDS. Chris Norwood has pointed out that pneumonia and influenza deaths among women aged fifteen to forty-four have jumped phenomenally between 1981 and 1986; 154 percent in New York City, 267 percent in Maryland, 225 percent in Washington, DC, 133 percent in Connecticut, and 38 percent in New Jersey.

It seems that the course of AIDS in women is different than that in men. Women contract Karposi's Sarcoma less often than men and respiratory infections more often. In addition, women often develop an HIV-related cervicitis that is a precursor to cervical cancer. The most common early symptoms of AIDS in women include a persistent rash, fever, fatigue, flulike symptoms, swollen lymph nodes, and weight loss. The most common opportunistic infections in women include pneumocystis pneumonia; candidiasis in the esophagus, bronchial tubes, or lungs; herpes simplex lesions; and mycrobacterial infections that lead to pneumonia and other respiratory infections.

Because the early symptoms of AIDS are similar to symptoms of other conditions that women are especially prone to—pelvic inflammatory disease, emotional depression, menstrual problems, and anemia—it is important that you seek out and get early medical care for health problems.

Often, women who have been chemically dependent are so scared that they may be HIV positive that they do not get medical attention for physical problems as they come up. Instead, they live in both fear and denial: denial that their health problems may be serious and fear of going to a doctor because of what they may learn. Living in both fear and denial is extremely stressful and doesn't allow for the possibility of getting help.

As we learned from our experiences being chemically dependent, denial does not serve us well—if we aren't HIV positive, it keeps us from resolving the physical problems we do have; if we are HIV positive, it keeps us from getting medical help to manage our illness and from getting emotional support from those who would be available for us.

Denying that we might be vulnerable to HIV infection keeps us from the benefits of increased medical knowledge and treatments, from the opportunity to work through our loss and grief with our friends and family, and from the ability to make choices about our lives. At present

HIV infection is life threatening; therefore, it's important that as women who may have engaged in high-risk behaviors we learn all we can about the disease and acknowledge our vulnerability.

AIDS Resources for Women

AIDS Project
Southern Christian Leadership Conference
334 Auburn Ave., N.E.
Atlanta, GA 30303
(404) 522-1420
Brochure: AIDS and the Black Community

AWARE—Association for Women's AIDS Research and Education
Ward 84, San Francisco General Hospital
995 Potrero Ave.
San Francisco, CA 94110
(415) 476-4091

D.C. Women's Council on AIDS (and Sister Care)
825-1 8th St. S.E.
Washington, DC 20003
(202) 544-8255

Fenway Community Health Center
16 Haviland St.
Boston, MA 02115
(617) 267-7573
Brochure: AIDS and Safer Sex for Women

Gay Men's Health Crisis
Box 274, 132 West 24th St.
New York, NY 10011
(212) 807-6655 or 7035 or 7517
Brochure: Women Need to Know about AIDS

Haitian Coalition
50 Court St.
Brooklyn, NY 11210
(718) 855-0972

HERO
101 West Read St.
Baltimore, MD 21201

Brochure about prenatal transmission: You Don't Have to Be White
or Gay to Get AIDS

Hispanic AIDS Forum
853 Broadway, Suite 2007
New York, NY 10003
(212) 870-1902 or 1864

Brochures: La comunidad y SIDA; Informaciones medicas sobre SIDA

Lesbian Counseling Services
6 Hamilton Pl.
Boston, MA 02108
(617) 542-5188

Minority Task Force on AIDS
New York City Council of Churches
475 Riverside Dr., Room 456
New York, NY 10115
(212) 749-1214

National AIDS Network
1012 14th St., N.W.
Washington, DC 20005
(202) 347-1317, 293-2437

Brochure: Hints for the Newly Diagnosed

Network Publications
P.O. Box 1830
Santa Cruz, CA 95061-1830

Brochure: What Women Should Know about AIDS

People with AIDS Coalition
263A West 19th St.
New York, NY 10011
(212) 627-1810

Newsletter: PWA Coalition Newsline

Women and AIDS Counseling Group
Stuyvesant Polyclinic
137 Second Ave.
New York, NY 10003
(212) 674-0220

Women at Risk Group
AIDS Action Committee
661 Boylston St.
Boston, MA 02116
(617) 437-6200, ext. 216

Women's AIDS Project
8235 Santa Monica Blvd., Suite 201
West Hollywood, CA 90046
(213) 650-1508
Brochure: Women Address AIDS

Women's Program
San Francisco AIDS Foundation
P.O. Box 6182
San Francisco, CA 94101-6182 or
333 Valencia St., 4th Floor
San Francisco, CA 94103
(415) 864-4376 or 864-5855

Brochures: Lesbians and AIDS; Women and AIDS Clinical Resource Guide; Straight Talk About Sex and AIDS

Appendix C

Helpful Books

Adolescence

Changing Bodies, Changing Lives: A Book for Teens on Sex and Relationships, by Ruth Bell. Revised edition. 1988. New York: Random House. $14.95.

No Is Not Enough: Helping Teenagers Avoid Sexual Assault, by Caren Adams, Jennifer Fay, and Jan Loreen-Martin. 1984. San Luis Obispo, CA: Impact Publishers (P.O. Box 1094, San Luis Obispo, CA 93406). $7.95.

Straight from the Heart: How to Talk with Your Teenagers About Love and Sex, by Carol Cassell. 1987. New York: Simon & Schuster. $6.95.

The Teenage Survival Book, by Sol Gordon. Revised edition. 1981. New York: Book Time (130 - 5th Ave., New York, NY 10011). $14.95.

Why Am I So Miserable if These Are the Best Years of My Life? by Andrea B. Eagan. 1979. New York: Morrow. $2.95.

Adult Children of Alcoholics

A Time To Heal: The Road to Recovery for Adult Children of Alcoholics, by Timmen L. Cermak. 1988. Los Angeles: Jeremy P. Tarcher. $15.95.

Aching for Love: The Sexual Drama of the Adult Child, by Mary Ann Klausner and Bobbie Hasselbring. 1990. San Francisco: HarperSanFrancisco. $10.95.

It Will Never Happen to Me, by Claudia Black. 1987. New York: Ballantine. $3.95.

Perfect Daughters: Adult Daughters of Alcoholics, by Robert J. Ackerman. 1989. Deerfield Beach, FL: Health Communications (3201 S.W. 15th St., Deerfield Beach, FL 33442). $8.95.

Aging

Love and Sex after Sixty, by Robert Butler. 1988. New York: Harper & Row. $16.95.

Love, Sex and Aging: A Consumer's Union Report, by Edward M. Brecher. 1984. Boston: Little, Brown and Company. $12.95.

Menopause, Naturally, by Sadja Greenwood. Revised edition. 1989. Volcano, CA: Volcano Press (P.O. Box 270, Volcano, CA 95689). $11.95.

Midlife Love Life, by Robert Butler and Myra Lewis. 1988. New York: Harper & Row. $6.95.

My Parents Never Had Sex: Myths and Facts About Sexual Aging, by Doris Hammond. 1987. Buffalo, NY: Prometheus Books (700 East Amherst, Buffalo, NY 14215). $9.95.

Ourselves, Growing Older: Women Aging with Knowledge and Power, by Paula B. Doress and Diana L. Siegal. 1987. New York: Simon & Schuster. $15.95.

The Starr-Weiner Report on Sex and Sexuality in the Mature Years, by Bernard D. Starr and Marcella B. Weiner. 1981. New York: McGraw-Hill. $5.95.

The Alcoholic Family

Another Chance: Hope and Health for the Alcoholic Family, by Sharon Wegscheider. 1982. Palo Alto, CA: Science and Behavior Books. $14.95.

Assertiveness

The Assertive Woman, by Stanlee Phelps and Nancy Austin. 1975. San Luis Obispo, CA: Impact Publishers (P.O. Box 1094, San Luis Obispo, CA 93406). $10.95.

The New Assertive Woman, by L. Z. Bloom, K. Coburn, and J. Perlman. 1975. New York: Dell. $4.95.

Self-Assertion for Women, by Pamela E. Butler. 1976. San Francisco: Harper & Row. $9.95.

Battering and Physical Abuse

Battered Wives, by Del Martin. Revised edition. 1981. New York: Pocket Books. $4.95.

The Battered Woman, by Lenore E. Walker. 1979. New York: Harper & Row. $8.95.

Chain Chain Change: For Black Women Dealing with Physical and Emotional Abuse, by Evelyn C. White. 1985. Seattle: Seal Press (P.O. Box 13, Seattle, WA 98111). $4.95.

Getting Free: A Handbook for Women in Abusive Relationships, by Ginny NiCarthy. Second edition, expanded. 1986. Seattle: Seal Press (P.O. Box 13, Seattle, WA 98111). $10.95.

Mejor sola que mal acompañada: Para la mujer golpeada, by Myrna M. Zambrano. 1985. Seattle: Seal Press (P.O. Box 13, Seattle, WA 98111). $7.95.

Bisexuality

The Bisexual Option, by Fred Klein. 1978. New York: Berkley Books. $4.95.

The Bisexual Spouse, edited by Ivan Hill. 1987. New York: Harper & Row. $7.95.

Two Lives to Lead: Bisexuality in Men and Women, edited by Fritz Klein and Timothy Wolf. 1985. New York: Harrington Park Press. $14.95.

View from Another Closet: Exploring Bisexuality in Women, by Janet Bode. 1977. New York: Pocket Books. $1.95.

Our Bodies

Eve's Secrets: A New Theory of Female Sexuality, by Josephine L. Sevely. 1987. New York: Random House. $17.95.

Fat Is a Feminist Issue, by Susie Orbach. 1982. New York: Berkley Books. $3.95.

The G Spot, by Alice Ladas, Beverly Whipple, and John Perry. 1982. New York: Dell. $4.50.

The New Our Bodies, Ourselves, by the Boston Women's Health Collective. 1984. New York: Simon & Schuster. $15.95.

A New View of a Woman's Body, by the Federation of Feminist Women's Health Center. 1981. New York: Simon & Schuster. $8.95.

The Obsession: The Tyranny of Slenderness, by Kim Chernin. 1981. New York: Harper & Row. $8.95.

Transforming Body Image: Learning to Love the Body You Have, by Marcia G. Hutchinson. 1985. Freedom, CA: Crossing Press (P.O. Box 1048, Freedom, CA 95019). $10.95.

Woman's Experience of Sex, by Sheila Kitzinger. 1985. New York: Penguin Books. $12.95.

Children

Children: The Challenge, by Rudolf Dreikurs and Vicki Stolz. 1987. New York: Dutton. $7.95.

Hablemos acerca del . . . s-e-x-o, by Sam Gitchel and Lorri Foster. 1985. Fresno: Planned Parenthood. $4.95.

A Kid's First Book about Sex, by Joani Blank. 1983. Burlingame, CA: Down There Press (Box 2086, Burlingame, CA 94011-2086). $5.50.

The Family Book About Sexuality, by Mary S. Calderone and Eric W. Johnson. Revised edition. 1989. New York: Harper & Row. $17.95.

Growing Up Free: Raising Your Child in the '80s, by Letty Cottin Pogrebin. 1980. New York: McGraw-Hill. $7.95.

Period, by JoAnn Gardner-Loulan, Bonnie Lopez, and Marcia Quackenbush. Revised edition. 1981. Volcano, CA: Volcano Press (P.O. Box 270, Volcano, CA 9568). $7.00.

Periodo: Libro para chicas sobre la menstruacion, by Bonnie Lopez, JoAnn Gardner-Loulan, and Marcia Quackenbush. 1986. Volcano, CA: Volcano Press (P.O. Box 270, Volcano, CA 95689). $7.00.

Raising Sexually Healthy Children, by Lynn Leight. 1988. New York: Macmillan. $17.95.

Talking With Your Child about Sex, by Mary S. Calderone and J.W. Ramey. 1982. New York: Random House. $2.95

Codependence

Beyond Codependence: And Getting Better All the Time, by Melody Beattie. 1989. San Francisco: Harper & Row. $9.95.

Codependent No More, by Melody Beattie. 1987. San Francisco: Harper & Row. $8.95.

The Dance of Anger: A Woman's Guide to Changing the Patterns of Intimate Relationships, by Harriet G. Lerner. 1985. New York: Harper & Row. $8.95.

Leaving the Enchanted Forest: The Path from Relationship Addiction to Intimacy, by Stephanie Covington and Liana Beckett. 1988. San Francisco: Harper & Row. $10.95.

Couples

American Couples, by P. Blumstein and Pepper Schwartz. 1983. New York: William Morrow. $12.95.

Challenges of the Heart, by John Welwood. 1985. Boston: Shambala. $12.95.

Do I Have to Give Up Me to be Loved by You?, by Jordan Paul and Margaret Paul. 1980. Minneapolis: CompCare. $11.95.

Getting the Love You Want, by Harville Hendrix. 1988. New York: Harper & Row. $8.95.

Journey of the Heart, by John Welwood. 1990. New York: HarperCollins. $18.95.

Intimate Partners: Patterns in Love and Marriage, by Maggie Scarf. 1987. New York: Random House. $19.95.

Erotica for Lesbians

By Word of Mouth: Lesbians Write the Erotic, edited by Lee Fleming. 1989. Charlottetown: Gynergy Books (P.O. Box 2023, Prince Edward Island, Canada, C1A 7N7). $12.95.

Dreams of the Woman Who Loved Sex, by Tee Corinne. 1987. Austin: Banned Books (P.O. Box 33280, Austin, TX 78764). $8.95.

Intricate Passions: A Collection of Erotic Short Fiction, edited by Tee Corinne. 1989. Austin: Banned Books (P.O. Box 33280, Austin, TX 78764). $8.95.

Lesbian Bedtime Stories, edited by Terry Woodrow, 1989. Willits, CA: Tough Dove Books (P.O. Box 184, Willits, CA 95490). $9.95.

Lovers: Love and Sex Stories, by Tee Corrinne. 1989. Austin: Banned Books (P.O. Box 33280, Austin, TX 78764). $7.95.

Pleasures, edited by Robbi Sommers. 1989. Tallahassee, FL: Naiad Press (P.O. Box 10543, Tallahassee, FL 32302). $8.95.

Erotica by Women

Deep Down: The New Sensual Writing by Women, edited by Laura Chester. 1988. Boston: Faber and Faber. $9.95.

Erotic Interludes: Tales Told by Women, edited by Lonnie Barbach. 1986. New York: Harper & Row. $7.95.

Herotica, edited by Susie Bright. 1988. Burlingame, CA: Down There Press (Box 2086, Burlingame, CA 94011-2086). $8.50.

Ladies' Own Erotica, by the Kensington Ladies' Erotica Society. 1984. New York: Pocket Books. $4.50.

Look Homeward, Erotica, by the Kensington Ladies' Erotica Society. 1986. Berkeley, CA: Ten Speed Press. $8.95.

Pleasures: Women Write Erotica, edited by Lonnie Barbach. 1984. New York: Harper & Row. $8.95.

Touching Fire: Erotic Writings by Women, edited by Louise Thornton and Amber Coverdale Sumrall. 1989. New York: Carroll & Graf Publishers. $18.95.

Female Socialization

In a Different Voice: Psychological Theory and Women's Development, by Carol Gilligan. 1982. Boston: Harvard University Press. $6.95.

Language of the Goddess, by Marija Gimbutas. 1989. San Francisco: Harper & Row. $24.95.

On Lies, Secrets and Silence, by Adrienne Rich. 1979. New York: W. W. Norton. $6.95.

Remaking Love: The Feminization of Sex, by Barbara Ehrenreich, Elizabeth Hess, and
Gloria Jacobs. 1986. New York: Doubleday. $8.95.

Sister Outsider: Essays and Speeches, by Audre Lorde. 1984. Freedom, CA: Crossing
Press (P.O. Box 1048, Freedom, CA 94019.) $8.95.

Too Good for Her Own Good, by Claudia Bepko and Jo Ann Krestan. 1990. New
York: HarperCollins. $17.95.

Toward a New Psychology of Women, by Jean Baker Miller. Second edition. 1986.
Boston: Beacon Press. $7.95.

The Woman's Encyclopedia of Myths and Secrets, by Barbara Walker. 1983. San
Francisco: Harper & Row. $24.95.

Friendship

Among Friends, by Letty Cottin Pogrebin. 1987. New York: McGraw-Hill. $7.95.

Between Women: Love, Envy and Competition in Women's Friendships, by Susie Orbach
and Louise Eisenbaum. 1987. New York: Penguin Books. $7.95.

Just Friends: The Role of Friendship in Our Lives, by Lillian Rubin. 1985. New York:
Harper & Row. $8.95.

Heterosexual Relationships

Intimate Strangers: Men and Women Together, by Lillian Rubin. 1983. New York:
Harper & Row. $8.95.

For Each Other: Sharing Sexual Intimacy, by Lonnie Barbach. Revised edition. 1984.
New York: New American Library. $4.95.

El lenguaje de la sexualidad para la mujer y la pareja, by Yael Fischman. 1986. Volcano,
CA: Volcano Press (P.O. Box 270, Volcano, CA 95689). $11.00.

Incest and Childhood Sexual Abuse

Allies in Healing, by Laura Davis. 1991. New York: HarperCollins.

The Best Kept Secret: Sexual Abuse of Children, by Florence Rush, 1980. New York:
McGraw-Hill. $5.95.

Conspiracy of Silence: The Trauma of Incest, by Sandra Butler. 1978. New York:
Bantam. $4.50. Updated edition from Volcano Press, P.O. Box 270,
Volcano, CA 95689. $11.95.

The Courage to Heal: A Guide for Women Survivors of Child Sexual Abuse, by Ellen Bass
and Laura Davis. 1988. New York: Harper & Row. $14.95.

Incest and Sexuality: A Guide to Understanding and Healing, by Wendy Maltz and
Beverly Holman. 1987. Lexington, MA: Lexington Books. $9.95.

Secret Survivors: Uncovering Incest and Its Afteraffects in Women, by Sue Blume. 1990. New York: Ballantine. $4.95.

The Sexual Healing Journey, by Wendy Maltz. 1991. New York: HarperCollins. $19.95.

Lesbian Relationships

Another Mother Tongue, by Judy Grahn. 1984. Boston: Beacon Press. $10.95.

The Lesbian Community, by Deborah G. Wolf. 1979. Berkeley: University of California Press. $9.95.

Lesbian Couples, by G. Dorsey Green and D. Merilee Clunis. 1988. Seattle: Seal Press (P.O. Box 13, Seattle, WA 98111). $10.95.

Lesbian/Woman, by Del Martin and Phyllis Lyon. 1972. New York: Bantam. $4.95.

Unbroken Ties: Lesbian Ex-Lovers, by Carol S. Becker. 1988. Boston: Alyson Publications (40 Plympton St., Boston, MA 02118). $7.95.

Lesbian Sexuality

The Lesbian Erotic Dance, by JoAnn Loulan. 1990. San Francisco: Spinsters (P.O. Box 410687, San Francisco, CA 94141). $9.95.

Lesbian Passion: Loving Ourselves and Each Other, by JoAnn Loulan. 1987. San Francisco: Spinsters/Aunt Lute (P.O. Box 410687, San Francisco, CA 94141). $10.95.

Lesbian Sex, by JoAnn Loulan. 1984. San Francisco: Spinsters/Aunt Lute (P.O. Box 410687, San Francisco, CA 94141). $10.95.

Sapphistry: The Book of Lesbian Sexuality, by Pat Califia. Third edition. 1988. Tallahassee, FL: Naiad Press (P.O. Box 10543, Tallahassee, FL 32302). $8.95.

Male Sexuality

The Hite Report on Male Sexuality, by Shere Hite. 1981. New York: Ballantine. $6.95.

The Inner Male: Overcoming Roadblocks to Intimacy, by Herb Goldberg. 1987. New York: New American Library. $4.95.

Male Sexuality, by Bernie Zilbergeld. 1978. New York: Bantam. $5.50.

Sexual Solutions: An Informative Guide, by Michael Castleman. Revised edition. 1983. New York: Simon & Schuster. $8.95.

Masturbation and Orgasm

Becoming Orgasmic: A Sexual Growth Program for Women, by Julia Heiman, Leslie LoPiccolo, and Joseph LoPiccolo. New edition. 1986. New York: Prentice-Hall. $8.95.

For Yourself: The Fulfillment of Female Sexuality, by Lonnie Barbach. 1975. New York: New American Library. $4.95.

Good Vibrations: The Complete Guide to Vibrators, by Joani Blank. Third edition. 1989. Burlingame, CA: Down There Press (Box 2086, Burlingame, CA 94011-2086). $4.50.

Sex for One: The Joy of Selfloving, by Betty Dodson. 1987. Revised edition. New York: Crown. $15.95.

Rape

Fighting Back: How to Cope with the Medical, Emotional and Legal Consequences of Rape, by Janet Bode. 1978. New York: Macmillan. $12.95.

If You Are Raped: What Every Woman Needs to Know, by Kathryn M. Johnson. 1985. Holmes Beach, FL: Johnson Learning Publications (P.O. Box 1326, Holmes Beach, FL 34218). $12.95.

The Politics of Rape: The Victim's Perspective, by Diana E. H. Russell. 1975. New York: Stein and Day. $10.00.

Rape: The Politics of Consciousness, by Susan Griffin. Third revised and updated edition. 1986. San Francisco: Harper & Row. $7.95.

Rape in Marriage, by Diana E. H. Russell. 1982. New York: Macmillan. $10.95.

Recovering from Rape, by Linda E. Ledray. 1986. New York: Henry Holt and Company. $9.95.

Romance

Swept Away: Why Women Fear Their Own Sexuality, by Carol Cassell. 1984. New York: Bantam. $5.95.

Sex Addiction

Women, Sex, and Addiction: A Search for Love and Power, by Charlotte Davis Kasl. 1990. New York: HarperCollins. $10.95.

Shame

Facing Shame: Families in Recovery, by Merle A. Fossum and Marilyn J. Mason. 1986. New York: Norton. $9.95.

Letting Go of Shame, by Ronald Potter-Efron and Patricia Potter-Efron. 1989. San Francisco: Harper & Row. $8.95.

Shame: The Power of Caring, by Gershen Kaufman. Second edition. 1985. Cambridge, MA: Shenkman Books (P.O. Box 1570, Cambridge, MA 02138). $9.95.

Spirituality and Sexuality

The Art of Sexual Ecstasy, by Margo Anand. 1989. Los Angeles: Jeremy P. Tarcher. $16.95.

Dreaming the Dark: Magic, Sex & Politics, by Starhawk. 1982. Boston: Beacon Press. $7.25.

Enlightened Sexuality: Essays on Body-Positive Spirituality, edited by Georg Feuerstein. 1989. Freedom, CA: Crossing Press (P.O. Box 1048, Freedom, CA 95019). $12.95.

Healing Love Through the Tao: Cultivating Female Sexual Energy, by Mantak Chia and Maneewan Chia. 1986. Huntington, NY: Healing Tao Books. $14.95.

The Lover Within: Opening to Energy in Sexual Practice, by Julie Henderson. 1986. Barrytown, NY: Station Hill Press. $8.95.

The Politics of Women's Spirituality, edited by Charlene Spretnak. 1982. New York: Doubleday. $12.95.

Sex and God: Some Varieties of Women's Religious Experience, edited by Linda Hurcombe. 1987. New York: Routledge. $7.95.

Touching Your Strength: The Erotic as Power and the Love of God, by Carter Hayward. 1989. San Francisco: Harper & Row. $12.95.

Women's Sexuality: Self-Reports

The Hite Report: A Nationwide Study of Female Sexuality, by Shere Hite. Revised edition. 1981. New York: Dell. $5.95.

The Redbook Report on Female Sexuality, by Carol Tavris and S. Sadd. 1977. New York: Delacourt Press. $4.95.

Shared Intimacies: Women's Sexual Experiences, by Lonnie Barbach and Linda Levine. 1980. New York: Bantam. $4.95.

Women and Love: The Hite Report, by Shere Hite. 1987. New York: St. Martin's Press. $5.95.

Women's Stories of Addiction and Recovery

A Glad Awakening, by Betty Ford and Chris Chase. 1987. New York: Jove. $4.50.

A Woman Like You, by Rachel V. 1986. San Francisco: Harper & Row. $10.95.

High and Outside, by Linnea A. Due. 1980. San Francisco: Spinsters/Aunt Lute (P.O. Box 410687, San Francisco, CA 94141). $8.95.

I'm Black and I'm Sober, by Chaney Allen. 1978. Minneapolis: CompCare. $7.95.

I'm Dancing as Fast as I Can, by Barbara Gordon. 1979. New York: Bantam Books. $4.50.

It Must Be Five O'Clock Somewhere: A True Story, by Sylvia Cary. 1986. Minneapolis: CompCare. $8.95.

The Late Great Me, by Sandra Scoppettone. 1976. New York: Bantam Books. $2.95.

Out From Under: Sober Dykes and Our Friends, edited by Jean Swallow, 1983. San Francisco: Spinsters/Aunt Lute (P.O. Box 410687, San Francisco, CA 94141). $10.95.

Turnabout: Help for a New Life, by Jean Kirkpatrick. 1978. New York: Doubleday. $8.95.

Women and Addiction

Alcoholism and Women, by Jan Bauer. 1982. Toronto: Inner City Books (Box 1271, Station Q, Toronto, Canada M4T 2P4). $12.00.

The Female Fix, by Muriel Nellis. 1980. New York: Penguin Books. $3.95.

Goodbye Hangovers, Hello Life: Self-Help for Women, by Jean Kirkpatrick. 1986. New York: Ballantine Books. $3.95.

The Invisible Alcoholics: Women and Alcohol Abuse in America, by Marian Sandmaier. 1980. New York: McGraw-Hill. $5.95.

Women & Drugs: Getting Hooked, Getting Clean, by Emanuel Peluso and Lucy Silvay Peluso. 1988. Minneapolis: CompCare. $9.95.

Women on Heroin, by Marsha Rosenbaum. 1981. New Brunswick, NJ: Rutgers University Press. $8.95.

Women Under the Influence, by Brigid McConville. 1983. New York: Schocken Books. $6.95.

Women and AIDS

Advice for Life: A Woman's Guide to AIDS Risks and Prevention, by Chris Norwood. 1987. New York: Pantheon. $5.95.

AIDS and Women: A Sourcebook, by Sarah Watstein and Robert Laurich. 1990. Phoenix, AZ: Oryx (4041 N. Central Phoenix, AZ, 85012-3397). $36.50.

Latina AIDS Action Plan and Resource Guide, by HDI Projects, 1000 16th St. N.W., Room 504, Washington, D.C., 20036. $15.00.

Making It: A Woman's Guide to Sex in the Age of AIDS, by Cindy Patton and Janis Kelly. 1987. Ithaca, NY: Firebrand Books (141 The Commons, Ithaca, NY 14850). $4.95.

Safe Encounters: How Women Can Say Yes to Pleasure and No to Unsafe Sex, by Beverly Whipple and Gina Ogden. 1989. New York: McGraw-Hill. $16.95.

Triple Jeopardy: Women and AIDS, by Judith Mariasy. 1990. Washington D.C.: Panos Institute (1717 Massachusetts Ave. N.W., Suite 301, Washington, D.C., 20036). $9.50.

Women and AIDS, by Diane Richardson. 1988. New York: Routledge. $9.95.

Mail Order Stores for Sex Information, Vibrators, and Toys

Eve's Garden, 119 West 57th St., New York, NY 10019. Send $2.00 for a catalog.

Good Vibrations, 1210 Valencia St., San Francisco, CA 94110.

Lawrence Research Group, Inc., P.O. Box 319005, San Francisco, CA 94131-9988.

Mail Order Store for Books

The Sexuality Library, 1210 Valencia St., San Francisco, CA 94117.

Appendix D

Books for Clinicians

Please see also appendix C, as many of the books listed there are also appropriate for clinicians. The following books are especially oriented toward those working with clients.

AIDS and Chemical Addiction

AIDS and Substance Abuse, edited by Larry Siegel. 1987. Vol. 7, no. 2 of *Advances in Alcohol & Substance Abuse*. $14.95.

AIDS: The Drug and Alcohol Connection, by Larry Siegel and Milan Korcok. 1989. Center City, MN: Hazelden Educational Materials (Pleasant Valley Road, P.O. Box 176, Center City, MN 55012-0176). $8.95.

Alcoholism and Addiction

The Chemical Brain: The Neurochemistry of Addictive Disorders, by Sidney Cohen. 1988. New York: Care Institute. $8.95.

Treating the Alcoholic: A Developmental Model of Recovery, by Stephanie Brown. 1985. New York: John Wiley and Sons. $37.95.

Treatment of Alcoholism and Other Addictions: A Self-Psychology Approach, by Jerome D. Levin. 1987. Northvale, NJ: Jason Aronson. $35.00.

Addiction and Women's Treatment

Alcoholic Women in Treatment, edited by E. Gorrigan. 1980. New York: Oxford University Press. $27.95.

Alcoholism Problems in Women and Children, edited by M. Greenblatt and Marc Shuckit. 1976. New York: Grune & Stratton. $63.50.

Treatment Services for Drug Dependent Women, edited by Beth Glover Reed, George M. Beschner, and Josette Mondanaro. Volumes I & II. 1982. Rockville, MD: National Institute on Drug Abuse (5600 Fishers Lane, Rockville, MD 20857). DHHS Publication No. (ADM) 82-1219.

Women Who Drink: Alcoholic Experience and Psychotherapy, edited by V. Burtle. 1977. Springfield, IL: Charles C Thomas. $35.75.

Addiction and Women's Research

Research Advances in Alcohol and Drug Problems: Alcohol and Drug Problems in Women, edited by O. J. Kalant. Vol. 5. 1980. New York: Plenum Press. $85.00.

Alcohol Problems in Women, edited by Sharon C. Wilsnack and Linda J. Beckman. 1984. New York: Guildford Press. $50.00.

Women and Alcohol Use: A Review of the Research Literature, by Paul M. Roman. 1988. Rockville, MD: National Institute on Alcohol Abuse and Alcoholism (5600 Fishers Lane, Rockville, MD 20857). DHHS Publication No. (ADM) 88-1574.

Adult Children of Alcoholics

Treating Adult Children of Alcoholics: A Developmental Perspective, by Stephanie Brown. 1988. New York: John Wiley and Sons. $37.95.

Children in Recovery, by Rosalie Jesse. 1989. New York: Norton. $24.95.

The Alcoholic Family

The Alcoholic Family, by Peter Steinglass, L. Bennett, and S. Wolin. 1987. New York: Basic Books. $27.95.

Before It's Too Late: Working With Substance Abuse in the Family, by David C. Treadway. 1989. Norton. $22.95.

The Responsibility Trap: A Blueprint for Treating the Alcoholic Family, by Claudia Bepko and Jo Ann Krestan. 1985. New York: Free Press. $26.95.

Battering and Physical Abuse

The Battered Woman Syndrome, by Lenore E. Walker. 1984. New York: Springer. $24.95.

Confronting Lesbian Battering. 1990. St. Paul: Minnesota Coalition for Battered Women (570 Asbury Street #201, St. Paul, MN 55104). $12.00.

"Overview: The Wife-Beater's Wife Reconsidered," in *The Gender Gap in Psychotherapy*, by Patricia Rieker and Elaine Hilberman Carmen. 1984. New York: Plenum Press. $45.00.

Victomology: An International Journal. Arlington, VA: Victomology (2333 N. Vernon St., Arlington, VA 22207). $85.00.

Codependence

Diagnosing and Treating Co-dependence: A Guide for Professionals, by Timmen L. Cermak. 1986. Minneapolis: Johnson Institute Books (510 First Avenue N., Minneapolis, MN 55403). $8.95.

Couples

In Search of the Mythical Mate: A Developmental Approach to Diagnosis and Treatment in Couples Therapy, by Ellyn Bader and Peter T. Pearson. 1988. New York: Brunner/Mazel. $28.95.

Family Therapy

The Family Interpreted: Feminist Theory in Clinical Practice, by Deborah Luepnitz. 1988. New York: Basic Books. $24.95.

The Gender Gap in Psychotherapy, by Patricia Rieker and Elaine Hilberman Carmen. 1984. New York: Plenum Press. $45.00.

The Invisible Web: Gender Patterns in Family Relationships, by Marianne Walters, Betty Carter, Peggy Papp, and Olga Silverstein. 1988. New York: Guilford Press. $30.00.

Women, Feminism and Family Therapy, edited by Lois Braverman. 1988. New York: Haworth Press. $34.95.

Women in Families, edited by Monica McGoldrich, Carol Anderson, and Froma Walsh. 1989. New York: Norton. $34.95.

Female Socialization

Feminism and Psychoanalytic Theory, by Nancy Chodorow. 1990. New Haven: Yale University Press. $25.00.

The Reproduction of Mothering: Psychoanalysis and the Sociology of Gender, by Nancy Chodorow. 1978. Berkeley: University of California Press. $9.95.

Women's Ways of Knowing: The Development of Self, Voice and Mind, by M. Belenky, et al. 1988. New York: Basic Books. $11.95.

Working Papers from the Stone Center. Wellesley, MA: The Stone Center (Wellesley College, Wellesley, MA 02181-8293).

Incest and Childhood Sexual Abuse

Handbook for Clinical Intervention in Child Sexual Abuse, by Suzanne Sgori. 1983. Lexington, MA: Lexington Books. $25.95.

Healing the Incest Wound: Adult Survivors in Therapy, by Christine A. Courtois. 1988. New York: Norton. $34.95.

Father-Daughter Incest, by Judith L. Herman with Lisa Hirschman. 1981. Boston: Harvard University Press. $9.95.

Rape, Incest, and Sexual Harassment, by Kathryn Quina and Nancy Carlson. 1989. New York: Praeger. $45.00.

A Jungian Perspective

Addiction to Perfection: The Still Unravished Bride, by Marian Woodman. 1982. Toronto: Inner City Books (Box 1271, Station Q, Toronto, Canada M4T 2P4). $12.00.

Androgyny, by June Singer. 1987. Boston: Sigo. $12.95.

Goddesses in Everywoman: A New Psychology of Women, by Jean Shinoda Bolen. 1984. San Francisco: Harper & Row. $10.95.

The Pregnant Virgin: A Process of Psychological Transformation, by Marian Woodman. 1985. Toronto: Inner City Books (Box 1271, Station Q, Toronto, Canada M4T 2P4). $15.00.

Myths and Mysteries of Same-Sex Love, by Christine Downing. 1989. New York: Crossroad. $22.95.

Lesbianism

Lesbian Psychologies, edited by the Boston Lesbian Psychologies Collective. 1987. Urbana: University of Illinois Press. $12.95.

Romance

Dreams of Love and Fateful Encounters: The Power of Romantic Passion, by Ethel Spector Person. 1988. Norton. $18.95.

Love and Limerance: The Experience of Being in Love, by Dorothy Tennov. 1979. New York: Scarborough House. $11.95.

Sex Therapy

Chemical Dependency and Intimacy Disorders, edited by Eli Coleman, ed. 1988. New York: Haworth Press. $18.95.

Disorders of Sexual Desire, by Helen Singer Kaplan. 1979. New York: Brunner/Mazel. $35.00.

Helping the Sexually Oppressed, by H. Gochros, J. Fischer, and J. Gochros. 1986. New York: Prentice-Hall. $44.20.

Intimate Relationships: Some Social Work Perspectives on Love, edited by W. Ricketts and H. Gochros. 1987. New York: The Haworth Press. $22.95.

The New Sex Therapy, by Helen Singer Kaplan. 1981. New York: Brunner/Mazel. $35.00.

Sexual Desire Disorders, by Sandra Leiblum and Raymond Rosen. 1988. New York: Guilford Press. $35.00.

Shame

The Many Faces of Shame, edited by Donald L. Nathanson. 1987. New York: Guilford Press. $30.00.

The Psychology of Shame: Theory and Treatment of Shame-Based Syndromes, by Gershen Kaufman. 1989. New York: Macmillan. $34.95.

Shame: The Underside of Narcissism, by Andrew Morrison. 1989. Hillsdale, NJ: Analytic Press. $30.50.

The Treatment of Shame and Guilt in Alcoholism Counseling, edited by Roland T. Potter-Efron and Patricia S. Potter-Efron. 1988. New York: Haworth Press. $14.95.

Women's Sexuality

The Nature & Evolution of Female Sexuality, by Mary Jane Sherfey. 1972. New York: Random House. $5.95.

Pleasure and Danger: Exploring Female Sexuality, edited by Carol S. Vance. 1984. New York: Routledge. $12.95.

Powers of Desire: The Politics of Sexuality, edited by Ann Snitow, Christine Stansell, and Sharon Thompson. 1983. New York: Monthly Review Press. $15.00.

Women: Sex and Sexuality, edited by Catherine R. Stimpson and Ethel Spector Person. 1980. Chicago: University of Chicago Press. $8.95.

Women's Sexuality and Addiction

The Sexual Behavior of Alcoholic Women While Drinking and During Sobriety, by Mickey Apter-Marsh. 1982. Ph.D. diss., Institute of Advanced Study of Human Sexuality, San Francisco, CA.

Sexual Experience, Dysfunction, and Abuse: A Descriptive Study of Alcoholic and Nonalcoholic Women, by Stephanie Covington. 1982. Ph.D. diss., University Microfilm: Ann Arbor, MI. .

Resources

Al-Anon Family Group Headquarters
1372 Broadway
P.O. Box 862, Midtown Station
New York, NY 10018-0862
(212) 302-7240

Alcoholics Anonymous (AA)
468 Park Avenue South
New York, NY 10016
(212) 686-1100

Incest Survivors Anonymous (ISA)
P.O. Box 5613
Long Beach, CA 90805-0613
(213) 422-1632

Narcotics Anonymous (NA)
P.O. Box 9999
Van Nuys, CA 91409
(818) 780-3951

National Association of Children of Alcoholics (NACOA)
31706 Coast Highway
South Laguna, CA 92677
(714) 499-3889

National Cocaine Abuse Hotline
(800) 262-2463

Overeaters Anonymous
4025 Spencer Street, Suite 203
Torrance, CA 90504
(213) 542-8368

Victims of Incest Can Emerge (VOICES)
Voices in Action, Inc.
P.O. Box 148309
Chicago, IL 60614
(312) 327-1500

Women for Sobriety
Box 618
Quakertown, PA 18951
(215) 536-8026

Index

AA (Alcoholics Anonymous), 60, 111, 151, 155, 212, 220
Abuse: continuum, 124–26, 165–66; and helplessness, 150–52; and intimacy problems, 202; leaving, 121, 126; and partner selection, 124–26; and sexual addiction, 110. *See also* Physical abuse; Sexual abuse
ACA (Adult Children of Alcoholics), 13
Accepting your body, 61–81
Accepting yourself, 63, 196
Acting out, 104–6, 139, 186
Addiction, 109n.; and body image, 65–70; and intimacy, 184–85; love, 215, 216; medication, 13,16, 20, 29, 59, 65–68; and morality, 33–35; and partner selection, 122–24; and power, 151; sexual, 109–11. *See also* Chemical dependence
Adolescence: lesbian, 23; second, 60
Affection, 32
Age, and desire, 55
AIDS, 245–66; avoidance practices, 251–57; defined, 247–49; resources, 264–66; symptoms, 262–63; test, 257–62; transmission of, 249–50
Al-Anon, 12–13
Alcoholics, 1, 11, 15–19, 28; and abuse, 41, 110; acting out, 104–5; and avoidance, 107; children of, 12–16, 32, 161–62, 167, 169; and depression, 53; and incest, 169–70; and intimacy, 202, 209, 210–11; intoxication and sex, 18, 19, 24, 35, 56–59, 104, 167–68, 211; and lesbianism, 22–24, 196, 210–11; and morality, 33; mothers, 159–63;

Nancy as, 154, 155; and "no-talk rule," 225; and partner selection, 122–24; and physical problems, 50, 51–52, 231–33; rape of, 164–65; and sexual addiction, 110; and sexual response cycle, 231–33, 242–43; Theresa and, 19, 20, 22, 116; and thinking self, 190
Anal intercourse, and AIDS, 249
Anger, 42, 60, 92, 100, 103, 186, 208, 210; and AIDS, 260; and depression, 53–54, as impediment to desire, 51, 56; and incest, 173–74;
Anthony, Carol K., 119
Anxiety, 16, 67, 110, 136, 186; masturbation as release for, 79, 109; about past abuse, 87, 108, 173, 179; performance, 202; 242; physical response to, 189; sex as release for, 66; about sober relationships, 22, 56–59
Arousal, 49–50, 226–27, 232–34, 235, 237, 239–41
Avoidance, 106–9
Awareness, 2–3, 34, 124–25
AZT, 258

Barbach, Lonnie, 81, 148
Barbara, distant partnership of, 127
Bass, Ellen, 205
Beckett, Liana, 12n.
Becky, pursuit by, 127–28, 136
Becoming Orgasmic (Heiman, LoPiccolo & LoPiccolo), 81
Bernice, and lesbianism, 210–11
Bertine, Eleanor, 213

14, 93–94, 165–74; feelings repressed in, 186; mothers raised in, 160–61; "no-talk rule" in, 30–31, 225; shame in, 176; thinking devalued in, 190
Dysfunctional sexuality, 14, 93–94, 101–18, 165–74

Economic support, 146, 152–56
Ecstasy, 36, 192, 222
Education, sex, 14, 32, 93, 225–26
Ejaculation: female, 148, 228; male, 230, 240–42; male premature, 240–42
Emotional component: addiction and, 122–23; AIDS-related, 258, 260, 262; of body, 188–89; of boundaries, 94–97; of desire, 48, 52–55; of intimacy, 185, 208; in same-sex attachments, 194; of sexuality, 18–19, 25, 33, 92–93, 195
Energy: lack of, 50; our essence as, 222–23
Equality, 198–200
Erection, male, 202–4, 230, 233, 239–43
Eroticism, 195
Evans, Sue, 166
Excitement, 49–50, 226–27, 230–31 237–39

Families, 88–97; boundaries in, 94–97, 108, 168, 170; checking with other members, 90–93; genogram, 128–29, 133–37; and partner selection, 121, 122; sexual unhealthiness in, 14, 93–94, 165–74. See also Children; Dysfunctional families; Parents
Fairy tales, 2, 119
Fantasies, 37–39, 127–28, 194–95
Fear: of AIDS, 263; Sarah's, 178; of sex sober, 56–59
Feelings, 5–7; 123; in body, 188–89; in intimate relationships, 206, 207, 208; knowing, 186–87. See also Emotional component
Female sexual response cycle, 225–39; figure illustrating, 230
Foam, vaginal, 252, 255
Foreplay, 208, 230, 233–34
For Yourself (Barbach), 81
Freudian drive theory, 47
Friendships, intimate, 197–200

Future, living in, 136
Genitals, 13, 38–39, 73–77, 81. See also Sexual response cycle
Genogram, 128–29, 133–37; blank, 137; figures illustrating, 134, 137; Sarah's, 134, 135–36
Gimbutas, Marija, 73–74
Grief, and desire, 54–55
Groups: and abuse, 125, 171; HIV-positive, 260–61; incest survivors', 171; and sexual identity, 212; women's, 12, 42, 98–100, 125, 212, 261. See also AA; Al-Anon; Twelve-Step programs; Women's Groups
Growing Up and Liking It, 14
G-spot, 148, 228
Guilt: and AIDS, 260; and masturbation, 75, 78, 81, 114; and mothering, 159–63; about past behavior, 98, 126, 136, 138, 151, 157–58; and sexual abuse, 51, 79, 141, 165, 170–73; sexuality influenced by, 5, 20, 30, 32, 34, 36, 59, 92, 178
Gynecological problems, and desire, 51

Healing: love as, 219; from sexual abuse, 165–74
Heiman, Julia, 81
Helplessness, learned, 148–52
Heterosexuality, 193–96, 204, 207–10, 212
Hite, Shere, 78, 147–48, 226
HIV infection, 245–66; avoidance of, 251–57; and confidentiality, 257–59; test for, 257–62. See also AIDS
Hoffman, Malvina, 85
Holman, Beverly, 173–74
Homosexuality, 35–36, 193–94. See also Lesbianism
Honesty, 43, 83, 120, 141
Hope, 9, 42–43, 145, 156, 177, 181, 212
Hypersexuality, 168

Ideal lover, 121–28, 214
Identity, sexual, 192–96, 210–11, 212. See also Heterosexuality; Homosexuality; Kinsey's Sexual Identity Scale; Men; Sex role socialization; Women
Ignorance, sexual, 5, 29–31

Dr. Stephanie Covington is a lecturer, consultant, and workshop leader in the areas of women and addiction, relationships, recovery, and sexuality. To contact Dr. Covington for speaking or consulting please write or call:

7946 Ivanhoe, Suite 201B
La Jolla, California 92037
619-454-8528